D0214642

Popular Justice
and
Community Regeneration

Popular Justice
and
Community Regeneration

Pathways of Indigenous Reform

Edited by
Kayleen M. Hazlehurst

Westport, Connecticut
London

Library of Congress Cataloging-in-Publication Data

Popular justice and community regeneration : pathways of indigenous
   reform / edited by Kayleen M. Hazlehurst.
    p. cm.
  Includes bibliographical references and index.
  ISBN 0–275–95131–6 (alk. paper)
  1. Indigenous peoples—Services for. 2. Community development.
3. Social problems. 4. Crime prevention. 5. Criminal justice,
Administration of. I. Hazlehurst, Kayleen M.
GN380.P67 1995
364.4′4—dc20   94–42815

British Library Cataloguing in Publication Data is available.

Copyright © 1995 by Kayleen M. Hazlehurst

All rights reserved. No portion of this book may be
reproduced, by any process or technique, without the
express written consent of the publisher.

Library of Congress Catalog Card Number: 94–42815
ISBN: 0–275–95131–6

First published in 1995

Praeger Publishers, 88 Post Road West, Westport, CT 06881
An imprint of Greenwood Publishing Group, Inc.

Printed in the United States of America

∞™

The paper used in this book complies with the
Permanent Paper Standard issued by the National
Information Standards Organization (Z39.48–1984).

10 9 8 7 6 5 4 3 2 1

CONTENTS

ILLUSTRATIONS

ACKNOWLEDGEMENTS

Preparation of this volume was generously supported by the Faculty of Arts, Queensland University of Technology as part of the Community and Cross-Cultural Studies Program. As editor, I wish to thank successive Deans, Professors Paul Wilson, Peter Lavery and Roger Scott, and Professor Cameron Hazlehurst, Head, School of Humanities, who have each encouraged and facilitated the completion of this work.

I particularly wish to thank Glenda Wiltshire for her tireless assistance and cheerfulness in word processing and preparing this manuscript for publication. I gratefully acknowledge the help of Sharon Petersen for her assistance in the earlier wordprocessing, Sally Whitehead for the compilation of the index, and Hilary Kent for her meticulous copy editing.

INTRODUCTION:

INDIGENOUS MODELS FOR COMMUNITY RECONSTRUCTION AND SOCIAL RECOVERY

Kayleen M. Hazlehurst

POLITICAL AND LEGAL AUTONOMY?

In September 1986 the International Working Group for Indigenous Affairs convened in Geneva to discuss ILO draft revisions of Convention 107 on Indigenous and Tribal Populations.[1] The main purpose of this meeting was to accommodate the 'shift in focus of the Convention from an integrationist perspective to one more in keeping with indigenous peoples' needs and aspirations'. Among the issues of primary concern to the indigenous participants were: the protection of social, cultural and economic aspects of indigenous self-determination; the right to humane treatment, freedom from torture and equal rights under the law; political decolonization; and an end to genocide and other violations of human rights. At this third annual meeting of the International Working Group for Indigenous Affairs it was acknowledged by the gathering that:

> constructive dialogue between indigenous populations and representatives of various governments has been established. Thus, this Working Group has become the first permanent United Nations forum devoted to the consideration of the rights, elimination of discrimination and the problems of indigenous populations (IWGIA 1987: 73-85; 94-108).

Article 8 of the new ILO 169 Convention (1989) concerning Indigenous and Tribal Peoples in independent countries specified that, in applying national laws and regulations, due regard must be given to customs and customary laws. Similarly, the draft of the *Universal Declaration on Indigenous Rights*, produced by the UN Working Group on Indigenous Rights in 1988, included the right of indigenous peoples to have their specific characteristics recognized by the political institutions and legal systems of a country.

The extent of aboriginal political autonomy, and the possible domains and shape which aboriginal legal authority might take, are still issues of continuing debate within international human rights conventions and national policy. In recent years, however, Canada, the United States, Australia, and New Zealand have seen developments in the prevention and treatment of indigenous crime which have embodied new trends towards greater self-determination. Innovations in the administration of justice alternatives, in the social reintegration of offenders and in the recovery of damaged communities have added to our global understanding of possible directions for indigenous political and legal autonomy.

This volume reports on some of the more significant experiments and reforms of the last two decades. It provides descriptions of programmes, assessment of their impact and advocacy for further change. Bringing together a diverse and dispersed group of contributors is a recognition of rapidly proliferating links and an international awareness of common interests.

The 1990s are seeing more and more indigenous people reaching out across national boundaries in a quest to find solutions to problems they know they share with brothers and sisters elsewhere. The juxtaposition of 'popular justice, and community regeneration' in our title expresses the perception implicit, if not explicit, in all of the contributions: that justice in indigenous communities is inseparable from issues of social well-being. Regenerated communities will make less call on formal justice systems. The return of indigenous justice processes to the people will itself be a catalyst for more far-reaching reform and revitalization.

WHO OWNS THE PROBLEMS?

The crucial question of 'who owns the problems of crime and social disorder' was explored by LaPrairie in a study of the James Bay Cree. In January 1990 the Grand Council of the Crees (Quebec) and the Cree Regional Authority initiated an innovative research programme in nine James Bay communities for the investigation of new approaches to justice administration. This study confirmed that decisions by the Cree would need to accommodate a complex of issues: cultural and traditional factors, as well as the constantly changing demographic and economic realities of contemporary life.

LaPrairie points out that any new justice initiatives would need to take into account that 'aboriginal communities absorb much of what occurs by way of justice problems'. In addition to the obvious social impact upon family and community life, there are a range of related problems—such as 'over-representation, access to justice, the potential for unequal treatment'—which would justify the introduction of community-grounded alternatives in the treatment of community crime and social dysfunction. Two justice issues stand out as central in this debate: 'first, a lack of information, knowledge, and understanding about the dominant criminal, family, and civil justice systems; and second, only a small proportion of crime and disorder problems find their way to formal court' (LaPrairie 1992: 418-19; see also Finkler 1985, 1988).

While communities may aspire to autonomy in justice domains, or may obtain this through legislation, the magnitude of local problems and the lack of effective informal mechanisms or training to deal with these problems often defeat these aspirations.[2] Piecemeal solutions, such as cultural sensitization and indigenization of the system, fundamentally miss the point. In the final analysis, points out LaPrairie, it is indigenous communities and groups which generate and must 'deal with the day-to-day reality of crime and disorder'. By owning the problems, more realistic formal and informal responses might be developed.

Recommendations which came from the Cree study emphasize the need for the greater exercise of local control over criminal and interpersonal problems, while 'allowing the external system to deal with serious crimes that would be too difficult for the communities to bear'. Where kinship networks were extensive and strong, alternative dispute resolution was one approach considered appropriate for dealing with most local crime problems in small communities: 'An important finding was that it is not in the legal consciousness of Cree to take people to court, particularly where disputes are interpersonal (the majority of cases). There is a desire to have some form of redress in the form of a moral rather than a legal solution' (LaPrairie 1992: 430).

The Cree study demonstrates that it will be by the recognition of their contribution to local problems that indigenous people might empower themselves in areas of crime prevention and community rehabilitation. These communities clearly wish to take a more active role in the selection and training of appropriate justice personnel and in the creation and development of new justice approaches.

INDIGENIZING THE SYSTEM?

Havemann and colleagues found that, in addition to being disproportionately imprisoned, Canadian Native people tended to receive more and shorter sentences. Similarly, in Australian findings, outcomes for offenders can be severely affected by the wide discretionary powers of the police, judicial bias, and by pre-trial and pre-sentence decision-making. In Havemann's view, cultural and social bias is reflected in assumptions about the aims, purposes and limitations of the criminal law and its processes (Havemann et al. 1985; Gale, Bailey-Harris and Wundersitz 1990). Tribal courts in the United States and Native JP schemes, fine options and courtworker programmes in Canada have worked towards reducing these trends of social and cultural disadvantage.

NORTH AMERICA

Tribal Courts

Courts of Indian Offences were first introduced in the United States well over one hundred years ago. They were replaced later by tribal courts. Courts of the Navajo Nation, for instance, were first created in 1958. Designed either to replace traditional Indian law or to adopt adversarial procedures similar to those used by the federal system, these courts did not significantly reflect Indian concerns for self-determination. It was not until the early 1980s, some thirty years later, before Navajo judges and Navajo common law principles were introduced into tribal court procedures.

In 1982 the Navajo Peacemaker Court was created. This incorporated traditional dispute resolution, family group decision-making, and other traditional approaches to justice. Today, tribal courts handle a substantial part of the trial court workload within the Navajo Nation. Their responsibility ranges from minor criminal offending to family and child welfare. In addition dealing with domestic violence, divorce and other areas of family crisis—normally the domain of the family court, the Peacemaker Court has proven effective in bringing traditional values to bear upon difficult cases of child neglect and sexual abuse. Cases which are not resolved are referred to the formal courts (Morse 1980, 1983; Zion 1992; Zion and Zion 1993).

Justice of the Peace Scheme

Canada has no tribal courts of the kind found in the United States. Since the 1970s, Native Justices of the Peace, however, have been appointed in different provinces by Band Council resolution, on request to the Minister of Indian Affairs. In Alberta, Ontario and the Yukon, for example, Native JPs have had the same or similar powers as regular JPs. Although they are usually appointed to areas with high Native populations, they perform duties in relation to both Native and non-Native peoples (Havemann et al. 1985: 76-78; Jolly 1988: 6-8; Hayes and Jolly 1988).

Native JPs offer a buffer between police and indigenous people. In respect to the discretionary powers of JPs regarding the use of more appropriate sentencing alternatives for indigenous offenders, Canadian researchers feel it is still an under-utilized mechanism. The usual disadvantages exist in Native JP schemes: that is, insufficient training, limited authority and status; lack of attractive remuneration and reluctance to serve due to conflicts of interest within the community. Programmes have also failed when they have not had the full support of communities or offenders, where workable sentencing options have not fully developed, or where there have been inadequate funding and resources for training, programme continuity and proper facilities.

There have been strong recommendations that JP programmes involve the full consultation of all participating and interested persons before development of a programme and that there be careful planning and adequate funding. Band Councils or similar community bodies should pass a resolution of support for JP programmes prior to their implementation, and all opposition should be properly explored and resolved beforehand (Havemann et al. 1985: 76-80; Prefontaine Opekokew and Tyler 1985: 19-21; LaPrairie and Craig 1985).

The question of indigenization of the justice system versus autonomy arises with Native JPs. Some Band Councils feel that Native JP courts would operate better if they were accountable directly to them. The Attorney General's Department, on the other hand, asserts that JPs must retain their independence from local politics. This debate centres on principles of assimilation of indigenous processes into the existing Euro-Canadian justice system, or the creation of indigenous parallels—legal pluralism. In Canada there has been no incorporation of indigenous law or values in substantive law, the criminal process nor in the establishment of truly indigenous courts.[3]

Fine Options: Community Work Projects

In a Canadian study in 1980 it was shown that a high proportion of prison admissions were for non-payment of fines, and that a disproportionate number of these involved Native people and the unemployed. Minor offenders can be given court orders to perform supervised community service administered by community-based agencies. Since 1983 in Manitoba for instance, amendments to the Summary Convictions Act have allowed community work projects as an alternative to fines—eliminating costly gaol sentences for those unable to pay fines.

As a result of this project community groups (including Indian Bands) throughout Manitoba now act as Community Resource Centres to administer the fine option programme. Participation in the programme is voluntary. Offenders are responsible for making the decision to either register with the programme or to pay the fine. Community Resource Centres receive a fee for each placement to help cover administrative costs. The Canadian Federal Justice Department monitors and evaluates the programme's effectiveness. But evidence suggests that despite some minor administrative problems, the programme is highly successful from both the offender's and the community's point of view.[4]

Native Courtworker Programmes

The Native Counselling Services of Alberta (NCSA), officially set up in 1970, evolved from a courtworker programme in Edmonton in the early sixties, and is now a formidable province-wide organization offering a range of justice and community programmes.

Native courtworkers help arrange legal representation for Native defendants, explain court procedure and give information about legal rights and the law. Where necessary they help to communicate with the defendant's family and arrange bail. Courtworkers brief lawyers, interview witnesses, obtain character references, and help develop sentencing options. They also act as agents to request adjournments and, when needed, they act as interpreters.

For minor offences, or if legal aid is not available, Native courtworkers will speak to the sentence on behalf of the accused in Justice of the Peace Courts and Territorial Courts. They will attend the court hearings of Native people to give moral support and advice. The work they do for these cases is readily appreciated by both the judiciary and legal profession. Initially focused upon the Criminal Courts, the NCSA has also operated a Family Courtworker Programme since 1974 and a Young Offender Courtworker Programme since 1986.

The Canadian Solicitor General's Department has given recognition to the work of Native Counselling Services of Alberta and supports and encourages its working relationship between Native people and the criminal justice system. The provincial government of Alberta actively supports these services because of their cost-effectiveness.

Many of the criticisms directed at the NCSA Native Courtworker scheme have been related to services which the programme has not been able to provide through a lack of funding or staff. For example, Native courtworkers are often not available immediately after arrest to explain to a Native person the nature of the charge, his or her legal rights, and the availability of legal aid. Other criticisms have been met through improvements in the courtworker training programme, now run with the assistance of the Faculty of Law at the University of Alberta.[5]

Contracting with Governments

Over a twenty-year period Native organizations and Canadian authorities have developed a collaborative working relationship through innovative Native programming and the privatization of Native service delivery. Through fee-for-service contractual arrangements made with government funding bodies, Native organizations administer a range of justice services, including courtworker programmes, probation and parole supervision, community corrections and juvenile offender programmes.

The Canadian Federal Department of Justice was given a mandate to establish Native courtworker programmes in each province and territory. Because of the constitutional authority of the provinces over the administration of justice, these programmes have been funded on a cost-share basis between the federal and provincial governments.

Courtworker services are now provided in Alberta, British Columbia, the Yukon, the Northwest Territories, Manitoba, Ontario, Quebec, and Labrador. Because of its size there are four separate carrier agencies in the Northwest Territories and a variety of courtwork-related services in British Columbia.[6] In the delivery of courtworker services it is the usual practice for agencies carrying these programmes to hold contracts with the Department of Justice through the provincial or territorial department.

Where there is a genuine partnership and where Native organizations are able to maintain operational independence, programmes such as this may answer some of the reservations raised by researchers regarding the value of indigenizing the criminal justice system. In indigenous terms, the objective of alternative justice programmes is to encourage aboriginal people to take some control over their own social environments, to allow them to make informed choices, and to sensitize practitioners to the issues regarding indigenous people within the criminal justice system.

RECLAIMING THE SOCIAL TERRITORY?

Multi-Service, Multi-Intervention Approach

Canadian Native workers highlight the cumulative impact of their clients' life predicaments. The cyclical consequences of poor parenting, alcoholism, offending, and imprisonment reverberate from one generation to the next. If the causes of Native over-representation in prisons are 'multiple and interactive', workers say, so must be the solutions. Solutions themselves must be cumulative, and must have a multiple impact over time.[7]

Canadian programmes have increasingly sought to restore a new balance in the lives of Native people ravaged by alcoholism and related social pathologies. Solutions, they say, must be physical, social, emotional and spiritual. This understanding has evolved over a period of growing programme diversification. It has embraced the aim of making Native people and Native communities 'whole' again. A multi-service, multi-intervention approach is urged by Canadian Native organizations. Community recovery is not seen as a single process; it should occur within an environment of positive change, which has wide implications for all aspects of community management.

Personal Sobriety and Community Detoxification

The Native-run alcohol and drug treatment centre, Poundmaker's Lodge and its associated counsellor training centre, Nechi Institute are located on the outskirts of Edmonton, Alberta. Since their beginnings in 1973 these centres have treated and trained thousands of Native people in substance abuse prevention. Poundmaker's Lodge is founded upon the principle that Native people will be most effectively counselled and rehabilitated by other Native people. Poundmaker's practitioners take an 'illness model' approach towards addiction, but they fit this approach within an understanding of the general history of social, cultural and spiritual decline which Native people experienced following colonization.

Native people identify the enforcement of residential schooling as one of the most destructive aspects of the post-colonial experience and a major influence in the degradation of Native family life. The generations of Indian people who were forcibly taken from their families and raised in these institutions have suffered severe psychological, parenting, and addiction problems later in life. It is these problems, they say, which must be directly treated.

Poundmaker's Lodge staff seek to replace maladaptive behaviours with newly taught adaptive ones through the combined techniques of individual and group counselling, spiritual and cultural awakening, traditional arts and dance, lifestyle skills and recreation. Sweat lodge rituals play an important role in the 'personal purification and spiritual strengthening of clients'.[8] Participants and staff provide a clearly defined 'sober reference group'—a community of supporters which encourages 'learning for healthy change'. Outreach programmes have also been established for adults, youth and prisoners. A growing number of Native reserves are now developing programmes of whole-community detoxification. In Canada, sobriety has become the jewel in the crown of Native re-empowerment (Hazlehurst 1994).

Support Groups

As people began to get well from addiction, the terrible issues of incest, child sexual assault and family violence came to the surface. Communities in the process of recovery had to develop strategies for dealing with the pain of the past, for facilitating forgiveness and for repairing damaged social relationships (Hazlehurst 1994: 143-45).

Support-group programmes have been the most successful means of healing the deeper historical and personal injuries of residential schooling, alcoholism, violence, and sexual assault which have so undermined Canadian Native society. But the spearhead of this healing approach, without a doubt, has been community detoxification and personal addiction treatment—a 'cause' which has now been taken up by many indigenous communities and organizations across Canada and, increasingly, in the United States and Australia.

AUSTRALIA

The Legacy of Addiction and Violence

Australian Aboriginal communities have experienced severe unemployment, alcohol addiction, ill health and widespread family violence and child abuse. Domestic fighting and inter-family feuds have led to frighteningly high levels of assault and violent death—particularly among Aboriginal women. The homicide rate on remote Aboriginal communities is ten times that for Australia as a whole. Police claim that about 90% of Aboriginal offending is alcohol-related. While they comprise only 1.5% of the total Australian population, Aboriginal people represent about 15% of the total prisoner population (Walker 1992: 69-70; Mukherjee, Neuhaus and Walker 1990: 28; Walker, Hallinan and Dagger 1992: 23, 121).

Widespread social problems in Aboriginal communities can be traced to the non-transmission of culture and the loss of self-esteem and respect for elders among the young. Inter-racial tensions are exacerbated by media reports of 'drunken rampages' on one hand, and over-zealous policing on the other. With the enforced suppression of ritual initiation and other cultural practices under missionary rule, and declining opportunities for traditional hunting, or horsemanship and stock-handling within the pastoral industry, young men are left to prove adult prowess through drinking and fighting.

David Martin, a resident anthropologist for ten years at Aurukun, northern Queensland, stressed that community disturbances usually arise over quite complex issues. One community had a massive zinc deposit at its doorstep, and was deeply divided over the proposal for a slurry pipeline running across Aboriginal trust lands, in return for jobs. Another had never resolved traditional divisions. Discrete language, marriage and ceremonial groupings, which had once occupied distinct tribal regions, had been forced to live together on one reserve since missionary days.

Poverty, unemployment, and boredom fuels these conflicts. While most major fights involve 'some oppositional groups based on region of origin', said Martin, it was the 'disaffected, alienated, angry and bitter young men' who created the tinderbox situation in remote communities (*Weekend Australian* 9-10 January 1993: 15).

The Use of Customary Processes

Between 1977 and the early 1980s the Australian Law Reform Commission undertook the delicate and complex task of examining possible avenues by which Aboriginal customary law might be formally included in the sentencing, treatment and reform of offenders. The commission proposed that legislation endorse the right of courts to seek a balance between the two laws, where this was culturally appropriate. Courts might include custodial and sentencing options that were not contrary to the general law, for example: the use of traditional processes in the settlement of disputes (Williams 1987), juvenile supervision by parents or persons *in loco parentis*, or customary sanctions such as exclusion from the land or the outstation resocialization of young offenders by elders (Law Reform Commission of Australia 1986).[9]

On the vexed question of juvenile offending, and associated problems of drinking and petrol-sniffing among Aboriginal youth, the Law Reform Commission stressed that these, in many respects, were 'social problems, beyond the power of the criminal justice system to resolve'. After exploring several Australian community justice options, the Law Reform Commission came to a conclusion that was to resound several years later in those of the Royal Commission into Aboriginal Deaths in Custody: 'Alternative sentencing options for Aboriginal communities need to be developed, taking into account local circumstances and needs, and especially in conjunction with local justice mechanisms presently in existence or established in the future' (Law Reform Commission of Australia 1986: 92).

Controlling Alcohol

The adverse effects of alcohol use and its impact upon community well-being became a central focus of evidence presented during the Royal Commission into Aboriginal Deaths in Custody Inquiry hearings between 1988 and 1990. A significant number of the ninety-nine Aboriginal people whose deaths were investigated by the commission came from communities dominated by alcohol.

In his report Commissioner Wyvill pointed out that alcohol consumption in one remote community was 'of major social, political and economic importance'. Regular drinking was the norm among the majority of the men. 'Social life is focused on the beer canteen where 12% of the community's income is spent', and possibly up to 25% when one includes expenditure on 'sly-grog'. Little money is left for food and necessities, adding to domestic friction. Binge drinking, drunken fighting and high crime rates, especially among juveniles, characterized community life. 'More than half of the injuries treated at the hospital are alcohol-related' (Johnston 1991: 313-14).

In a report to the Royal Commission, an Expert Working Group of the Alcohol and Drug Foundation concluded that, in addition to having a devastating effect upon Aboriginal family life, widespread use of alcohol was having a damaging effect upon customary social and cultural spheres, leading to the 'neglect of important ceremonies in traditional communities'. Without doubt, alcohol had become the primary cause of violence, sexual assault and community disruption in such communities (Alexander 1990: 32; Johnston 1991: 313; Hazlehurst and Hazlehurst 1989). As operators and licensees of community canteens, Aboriginal

Community Councils are in the invidious position of promoting and profiting from the addiction of their people. When they attempt to impose controls, governments are reluctant to grant them the legal authority to do so. 'Grog-runners' quickly step in to fill any gaps in alcohol supply.[10]

In several Royal Commission presentations it was stressed that it was the beverage industry (and the government through taxes, excise and customs duty) which benefited from the exploitative alcohol economy of the north. There have been few signs that the immensely wealthy and powerful liquor industry feels any compulsion to contribute towards the medical expenses, policing costs or the social repair of severely addicted individuals and their families. Aboriginal people pay directly with their welfare cheques, and indirectly through damage to property, malnutrition, lowered standards of living, poor hygiene, and the loss of social and physical well-being. Stricter legislative controls were called for during the inquiry (Johnston 1991: 315; Langton and Ah Matt 1991).

Genuine Power Sharing?

Australia has not been without its community court and para-policing experiments, although these have remained largely informal (Hazlehurst 1991). But it is doubtful whether significant or lasting improvements to the lot of indigenous Australians will be achieved without commitment to principles of self-determination at grassroots and regional levels. Administrative and practical devolution will only be successful if more imaginative and flexible methods for collaborative power sharing are developed.

A decade of state and national inquiries has created a climate of expectation for more proactive and positive responses to Aboriginal social and economic problems, and to race relations generally. But to date, community-based preventative activities still form a tiny proportion of government expenditure. For government authorities and agencies, the issue has come down to this: are they prepared to conduct business with indigenous organizations, community groups and urban collectives in a sufficiently supportive and cooperative spirit to make 'partnership' possible? Since the publication of the findings of the Royal Commission into Aboriginal Deaths in Custody (1988-1991) there has never been a time of greater receptivity in government to proposals for multi-programmed, multi-agency responses for the reduction of Aboriginal imprisonment. The problem is, still, a lack of clear direction or expertise in Australia for these developments.

Community-Grounded Solutions

An important point of consensus emerges through the proposals of various national inquiries and state working party reports on Aboriginal health and welfare. That is, that there is a need for community-grounded solutions. But the idea of locally grown preventative and interventionist programmes is still relatively new in Australia. It is a case of knowing what is needed but not knowing how to achieve it. There have been enormous difficulties in facing honestly the problems of child abuse and family violence, and the relationship between alcohol abuse, neglect and local offending. Coming to grips with intolerable situations can only occur when people begin to openly acknowledge the hurt these cause individuals, families and whole communities (Hazlehurst 1990; 1994).

When considering the social reconstructive potential of crime prevention, we quickly realise that it may well be futile to attempt to separate objectives to reduce crime from social development issues. In the absence of a 'community-base', 'community-based crime prevention' is a theory in search of reality.

The Canadian experience has shown that historical and social causes of indigenous disempowerment can be confronted directly through the introduction of empowering strategies. A promising sign in Australia is that people are now asking for training in community recovery skills. There have already been some fruitful links established between Australian Aboriginal people and North American Native organizations with the needed expertise (Hazlehurst 1994). But much remains to be done to convince policy makers to let substantial resources flow into the development of alternative justice services, crime prevention programmes and community repair rather than into the endless cycles of judicial processing and imprisonment.

NEW ZEALAND

Reintegrative Shaming

Scholars and professionals have begun to see the very powerful connection between practical change and a particular understanding of human nature. For indigenous people the most innovative programmes are those which reintroduce culturally relevant processes and a reasonable level of responsibility and control at the community level. Traditional processes frequently emphasise the personal accountability of offenders, the decision-making role of families and the solidarity of collectives.

But these understandings clearly have value for all societies. The Australian criminologist John Braithwaite (1989) built a new theory of what he calls 'reintegrative shaming', taking inspiration, in part, from a West Auckland Maori experiment which was eventually incorporated into New Zealand legislation (Hazlehurst 1985: 95-120). Braithwaite defines 'reintegrative shaming' as: 'Shaming for the purpose of *including* rather than excluding the criminal from the societal mainstream'. Communitarian societies, those with a high level of interdependency, have the greatest potential for shaming as a means of engendering conformity and socially reintegrating offenders (Braithwaite 1989: 84-104).

The New Zealand Children, Young Persons, and Their Families Act (1989) employs collective shaming and dispute settlement processes as a matter of official policy. Under this Act, Family Group Conferences provide face-to-face contact between offenders, victims and their mutual families. Here offenders witness the effect of their behaviour upon others; families are empowered to make decisions; restitution provides a means to mend the social breach and to reestablish the offender's commitment to the social group. During the conferences families formulate a plan that is acceptable to police and to victims, and thus become 'a key agency in diverting young people from formal proceedings' (Morris and Maxwell 1990: 5-6).

With its accent upon mediation, offender responsibility, redress and reconciliation, the new system moves away from the earlier welfare model, back towards a justice model with a new emphasis upon the community (Morris and Maxwell 1990: 12; Maxwell and Morris 1990; Morris and Young 1987; Maxwell 1993; Brown 1992, 1993; O'Connor 1992).[11]

RECLAIMING THE COMMUNITY

A significant question that has been raised in these North American, Australian and New Zealand models is whether it is possible to revive indigenous processes in the treatment and rehabilitation of offenders and as mechanisms of social control (Hazlehurst 1995a, 1995b).

In this book Hylton points to the failure of the Canadian social policy sector in ameliorating the 'horrific social conditions faced by aboriginal people' (3). He suggests a fundamental reexamination of the way in which social programmes for indigenous communities are designed, delivered and operated. He stresses that locally owned programmes, which allow 'varying degrees of aboriginal responsibility and control' (10), offer the most promising direction for social policy reform, on the one hand, and for the fulfilment of goals for indigenous self-determination and self-government, on the other.

The small Polynesian Island community of Tokelau provides an excellent case-study of how customary village practices can assume formal authority. In this compact study, Angelo unfolds the historical background to criminal law in Tokelau and the process by which local elders and foreign administrators from New Zealand sought to review, restructure and reform crime regulations and procedures to more strongly reflect communal priorities and traditions.

Olsen, Maxwell and Morris review the pioneering New Zealand experiment with family group conferences. This dispute resolution model took its conceptual

origin from Maori consensual systems of justice. Most notable for its high level
of success in reducing the formal court processing and punishment of young
offenders, it has attracted considerable international interest. Over a five-year
period the principles of family conferencing have been adopted by several
Australian states, but they continue to be controversial in Australian criminological
circles (Alder and Wundersitz 1994; Atkinson and Gerull 1993).

In New Zealand's increasingly multicultural setting, the objective has been to
provide a system of justice that allows different ethnic groups to call upon
customary procedures and values for the handling of a significant range of minor
offending. The New Zealand legislation, state Olsen, Maxwell and Morris,
'explicitly recognizes cultural diversity and the need for criminal justice processes
to be both culturally appropriate and culturally sensitive' (45). These authors
conclude that:

> inevitably the processes and patterns developed in small clan-based
> communities cannot be replicated in a modern, industrial, mobile and
> individualised culture. But on the other hand, as this study demonstrates, it
> is possible for the *spirit* of the community-based social systems of the past to
> adapt to modern times and to modify the individualistic and remote patterns
> that have characterised Western justice models (61).

Yazzie and Zion offer the model of the Navajo Nation Peacemaker Court as
a new way of looking at law, justice and social problems in Indian country in the
United States. In the authors' opinion, non-adversarial tribal courts represent a
genuine weapon against the 'monsters' of social disruption and social decline
which have emerged through the loss of sovereignty.[12] Yazzie and Zion reiterate
the findings of other authors throughout this book, that 'the biggest problems are
alcohol, violence within family units and harm to children' (75).

The Navajo have repeatedly asked for greater federal contribution to justice in
Indian country to assist them to deal directly with these issues. The institution,
relationships and processes of the Peacemaker Court are worthy of careful
examination, not only for the problem-solving power which they return to the
people, but because this traditional approach provides 'speedy and simple
remedies' with little public cost (80).

O'Donnell gives an account of the first Australian Aboriginal community
disputes to be settled by professional mediators in Queensland. Minor disturbances
frequently escalate into assault, injury or even death. Whole communities can be
drawn into unresolved disputes between individuals and family groups. When
alcohol is added to this, the human cost can be terrible. Between 1990 and 1992
the Community Justice Programme (CJP) expanded its services and mediation
training from its Brisbane metropolitan base to outlying regions.

That indigenous people feel a certain kinship with this process is no doubt
related to the similarities of modern dispute resolution techniques to customary

methods of collective decision-making. O'Donnell urges that while new services may be put in place, traditional techniques in dispute settlement should not be discarded.

Nielsen Adkins describes a range of Native Counselling Services of Alberta programmes designed to impact upon the Canadian criminal justice system as well as upon social problems within Native Canadian society. The mission statement of this organization, as quoted by Nielsen Adkins, is to provide 'holistic development of the Aboriginal individual, family and community by working in partnerships to provide culturally sensitive programmes and services and by promoting the fair and equitable treatment of Aboriginal people' (105). With over twenty years of experience in areas of indigenous justice service delivery, NCSA provides a unique model of what is socially and administratively possible through privatization and inter-agency collaboration.

HEALING THE HURTS

In her examination of the history of the colonial process in the United States and related contemporary issues, RedBird points to the systematic undermining of Indian social structures and the role of Indian women. To promote genuine self-determination and self-governance, she asserts, the basic institutions of Native Americans need to be re-empowered. Among those she highlights are the roles of the family and clan, the unique and shared roles of men and women, and the once good relations between them.

RedBird stresses that there is a clear connection between the destruction of the role, social values and life-ways of women and the destruction of Native American culture. 'If the erosion of sovereignty comes from disempowering women', she says, 'its renewed strength will come from re-empowering them' (135). In order to turn back the problems of domestic violence and child abuse today, governments will need to provide women's organizations with sufficient levels of funding in order for them to operate effective programmes. 'It is not enough to earmark monies to benefit women and families', she says; 'women must be the instruments of change themselves' (136).

Hoyle engages us in a study of a local justice system situated on an Ojibway reserve in Ontario. She asserts that customary and contemporary legal and conflict resolution approaches provide a rich resource for the construction of effective alternative justice systems. This author sees indigenous justice programmes as a vital part of the self-government and cultural revitalization process. In Canada, the 'pressing need to implement some form of culturally appropriate alternative to Canada's present justice system', Hoyle states, has been increasingly acknowledged by both Canada's indigenous people and by federal and provincial governments (143).

The potent metaphor of *community healing*, 'through the combined revitalization of traditional culture and the creation of new institutions', has become a central focus of the debate in Canada (145). Hoyle is concerned, however, that authentically local solutions are sought. She warns against the propensity to adopt ready-made indigenous models for legal autonomy when '"home grown", community-based options may be equally effective and may in addition contribute in a significant way to community development' (155).

The resurgence of traditional cultural practices in addressing crime and justice issues in Canadian indigenous communities occurs, say Griffiths and Belleau, against the 'larger political backdrop of the constitutional recognition of an inherent right to aboriginal self-government' (166). Increasingly, federal and provincial governments in Canada are taking policy initiatives to encourage the restoration of local authority through the design and delivery of justice services. Griffiths and Belleau provide rich ethnographic illustration of how alternative justice systems and the use of traditional ceremony can impact upon the deeper social ills of communities and can revitalize cultural and social life.

It has only been since Native people have come to see the community as the ideal centre for addictions treatment and prevention, Hodgson says, that the greatest advances have been made in the development of healing approaches in Canada. She explains the powerful processes of community reconstruction, by first referring us to Durkheim's classic theory of social decline. Native society is well familiar with the living experience and debilitating processes of 'anomie' (187). Native techniques for community healing are now reversing trends of normlessness and loss of social values.

Through the utilization of collective thought and action, small Indian communities, such as Alkali Lake and Tache Indian reserves, began to lead the way out of the maze of societal breakdown and community violence. Practical goals of whole-community sobriety and increased social well-being are sought through the use of extended family systems and the resuscitation of cultural and spiritual values. Such high-level aspirations, Hodgson says, are not achievable without a clear vision for change.

Having taken their lead from Canadian Native experiments, such as those discussed by Hodgson and others, Atkinson and Ober describe the setting up of the We Al-Li programme for personal and community healing in Australia. Group process is seen as a powerful tool in helping Australian Aboriginal and Torres Strait Islander people overcome 'family and community pain and trauma resulting from colonial domination and power abuse' (201).

As in Canada, the removal of Aboriginal children and their placement in institutions or foster homes shattered family structures and social values. Experiences of colonialism and paternalism are revisited through patterns of self-oppression, alcoholism and sexual and physical violence, and high levels of other crime. Far from being empowered, self-actualizing, self-determining people, Atkinson and Ober contend that Australian Aboriginal people have yet to recover from the grief, anger and powerlessness of dispossession.

Through a mixture of traditional ceremonies and contemporary therapies, We Al-Li seeks to give proper recognition to the past and to provide safe passage to the future through the path of healing. The objectives of the programme are cultural revival, personal and group empowerment, lifestyle counselling and the laying of new foundations for social action and social organization. It is a process, say Atkinson and Ober, which 'gives power to the community instead of giving away power to the criminal justice system' (16). 'We need to come together ... tell our stories and in dance, song, art and ceremony move into the future' (17).

From this collection, then, we could say that indigenous solutions appear to be taking a three-pronged approach:

1.   *Justice Service Delivery:* Para-professional development and programme indigenization help to introduce alternative justice and diversionary options into, and greater equality under, the formal criminal justice system. The judicial role of community forums—such as tribal courts, family conferences and conflict resolution techniques—represents a particularly strong avenue for the reinstatement of customary law and traditional processes.

2.   *Community Healing Approaches:* These embrace a range of psycho-social programmes aimed to rehabilitate individuals and whole communities. They include programmes in family life skills, alcohol detoxification treatment and training, support group programmes for victims and perpetrators of abusive behaviours and cultural and spiritual renewal programmes.

3.   *Crime Prevention Action:* Primary prevention helps to divert identified offending groups, particularly youth, away from offending by making life-involving activities more attractive than criminal ones. Popular examples include work-skills and employment training, arts, culture and dance programmes, outdoor recreation and sports, community festivals and social events—all of which enhance the social environments of communities. Healthy lifestyle activities are simply achieved and, when offered as an incentive, always impact to reduce youth offending. They also strengthen the personal qualities, relationships and leadership skills of adults, children and young people.

The cultural orientation and social reconstructive thrust of all of these programmes is possibly their greatest strength. Against the background of dispossession, deculturation and loss of dignity—endemic in the historical indigenous experience—socially reconstructive programmes quickly inspire confidence, commitment, and passion to the cause of healing in their participants. They are having important effects in the discovery of contemporary avenues for customary law applications and traditional means for social control. The strong emotions associated with personal recovery, forgiveness and family and community revitalization also appear to have, in themselves, a healing effect. But something even more powerful appears to be happening.

The fervour and international interest attracted by national and international conferences has elevated the 'Healing Our People' approach to the level of a social movement.[13] Indigenous prophecies concerning the 'coming out of night time' and the 'waking up of the elders' are related, shared, and seen to be fulfilled by these innovations in the latter twentieth century. There is excitement that indigenous people are coming into their true spiritual power. It is this movement of new-found belief which I have described elsewhere as 'a quiet revolution' (Hazlehurst 1994: 65; 139-40). Through their years of adversity and their developing skills in peacemaking and community healing, there is a growing conviction among Native people that they will eventually lead the world.

NOTES

1. The International Working Group for Indigenous Affairs (IWGIA), an all-indigenous association, was set up by the International Congress of Americanists for the purposes of monitoring United Nations developments in this area. The IWGIA meets in order to review draft recommendations on international standards for indigenous peoples by the United Nations Working Group on Indigenous Populations. In 1986 the International Labour Organization (ILO) called a meeting of experts to consider the revision of its 1957 *Convention No.107 on Indigenous and Tribal Populations*, the only international instrument specifically protecting indigenous rights. Seven countries were invited to participate at the meeting. The revised ILO 169 Convention was completed in 1989.

2. Off the reserve, it is the criminal justice system which maintains ownership over indigenous crime and deviance. Thus, over-representation of Native people tends to be highest in urban areas (LaPrairie 1992).

3. Havemann's (1985) early reservations about the JP scheme were not shared by all researchers. In his evaluation of the programme for the northwestern region of Ontario, McCallum states that there was an overall consensus that the JP programme is worthwhile and should be expanded. Although Native JPs do not enjoy a high reputation for competence among their colleagues, the majority of respondents believed that the programme goals were being achieved. According to McCallum, the programme had been successful in increasing Native peoples' sense of involvement in the justice system (McCallum 1988, 1985).

4. See Manitoba Community Services (n.d.).

5. Nielsen 1993; NCSA 1985a, 1985b, 1987, 1991, [1989]. See also Fearn and Kupfer 1981; Morse 1983, 1988; Kirby 1978; Hazlehurst 1989a, LaPrairie and Craig 1985.

6. NCSA [1993], 'The National Context' (Chapter 14), *The Native Counselling Story*.

7. Information on the Native Counselling Service of Alberta, Alkali Lake Indian Reserve, Poundmaker's Lodge, Nechi Institute and other Canadian Native

organizations was gathered by the author during two field trips in 1988 and 1990, and since then through regular correspondence. See also NCSA 1985b, 1987, 1991.

8. The Indian sweat lodge consists of a closed in, humpy-like construct, which is heated by fire to produce a sauna effect. In Indian culture the sweat lodge experience, and the prayers and rituals associated with it, represent and symbolize both physical and spiritual purification, and are actively employed in the process of healing.

9. One jurisdiction to explore this further was the Northern Territory. A report on the *Recognition of Aboriginal Customary Law* was published by the Legislative Assembly of the Northern Territory (1992).

10. The Royal Commission into Aboriginal Deaths in Custody heard evidence that the canteen at Aurukun was taking about $15,000 a week from its 250 or so regular drinkers.

11. In O'Connor's analysis, the New Zealand *Children's, Young Persons, and their Families Act* 'seeks to avoid the pitfalls of both the justice and welfare models' by preferring diversion over criminal prosecution, by emphasizing personal responsibility in offenders and by strengthening the decision-making role of the family group (O'Connor 1992: 49-52).

12. Navajo healing ceremonies involve the patient in an active battle with the elements, where nayéé 'monsters' are confronted. 'A "monster" is "that which gets in the way of successful life"' (Zion 1993: 5).

13. There have been several major conferences run by Canadian Native organizations committed to healing, such as Nechi Institute: 'Healing Our Youth' Edmonton, September 1990; 'Healing Our Spirit Worldwide', Edmonton, July 1992; 'Second Healing Our People Worldwide', Sydney, Australia, 14 November 1994.

REFERENCES

Adler, C. and Wundersitz, J. (1994) 'New Directions in Juvenile Justice Reform in Australia', in C. Adler and J. Wundersitz (eds.) *Family Conferencing and Juvenile Justice: the Way Forward or Misplaced Optimism*, Canberra: Australian Institute of Criminology.

Alexander, K. (ed.) (1990) *Aboriginal Alcohol Use and Related Problems: Report and Recommendations*, prepared by an Expert Working Group for the Royal Commission into Aboriginal Deaths in Custody, Canberra: Alcohol and Drug Foundation.

Atkinson, Lynn and Gerull, Sally-Anne (eds.) (1993) *National Conference on Juvenile Justice*, Canberra: Australian Institute of Criminology.

Braithwaite, John (1989) *Crime, Shame and Reintegration*, Cambridge: Cambridge University Press.

Brown, Michael J. A. (Judge) (1992) 'Address to the Children, Young Persons and their Families Seminar', speech, Palmerston North: Palmerston North College of Education, (unpublished 10 July).

Brown, Michael J. A. (Judge) (1993) 'Juvenile Justice in New Zealand', in L. Atkinson and S. Gerull (eds.), *National Conference on Juvenile Justice*, Canberra: Australian Institute of Criminology.

Fearn, Lorraine and Kupfer, George (1981) *A Programme Review and Evaluation Assessment of Criminal Courtworkers Native Counselling Services of Alberta*, Ottawa: Department of Justice Canada.

Finkler, Harald (1985) 'Inuit and the Criminal Justice System: Future Strategies for Socio-Legal Control and Prevention', *Etudes/Inuit/Studies* 9: 2, 141-51.

Finkler, Harald (1988) 'Community Participation in Socio-Legal Control: The Northern Context', in G. Dacks and K. Coates (eds.), *Northern Communities: The Prospects for Empowerment*, Alberta: Boreal Institute for Northern Studies.

Gale, Fay, Bailey-Harris, Rebecca and Wundersitz, Joy (1990) *Aboriginal Youth and the Criminal Justice System: The Injustice of Justice?* Cambridge: Cambridge University Press.

Havemann, Paul et al. (1985) *Law and Order for Canada's Indigenous People*, Regina: University of Regina.

Hayes, F. C. and Jolly, Stan (1988) *Ontario Native Justice of the Peace Programme: A Descriptive Outline*, Ottawa: Ministry of the Attorney General.

Hazlehurst, Kayleen M. (1985) 'Community Care/Community Responsibility: Community Participation in Criminal Justice Administration in New Zealand', in K. M. Hazlehurst (ed.), *Justice Programmes for Aboriginal and Other Indigenous Communities*, Canberra: Australian Institute of Criminology.

Hazlehurst, Kayleen M. (1990) *Crime Prevention for Aboriginal Communities*, Crime Prevention Series, Canberra: Australian Institute of Criminology.

Hazlehurst, Kayleen M. (1991) 'Australian Aboriginal Experiences of Community Justice', in R. Kuppé (ed.), *Law and Anthropology,* International Yearbook for Legal Anthropology, Law Faculty, Vienna: University of Vienna, 6: 45-65.

Hazlehurst, Kayleen M. (1994) *'A Healing Place': Indigenous Visions for Personal Empowerment and Community Recovery*, Rockhampton: Central Queensland University Press.

Hazlehurst, Kayleen M. (ed.) (1995a) *Legal Pluralism and the Colonial Legacy: Indigenous Experiences of Justice in Canada, Australia and New Zealand*, Aldershot: Avebury.

Hazlehurst, Kayleen M. (ed.) (1995b) *Perceptions of Justice: Issues in Indigenous and Community Empowerment*, Aldershot: Avebury.

Hazlehurst, Kayleen M. and Hazlehurst, Cameron (1989) 'Race and the Australian Conscience: Investigating Aboriginal Deaths in Custody', *New Community: A Journal of Research and Policy on Ethnic Relations*, Warwick 16: 1, October, 35-48.

IWGIA (1987) *IWGIA Yearbook 1986: Indigenous Peoples and Human Rights* (Andrew Gray, compiler) Copenhagen: International Working Group for Indigenous Affairs.

Johnston, Elliott (Commissioner) (1991) *Royal Commission into Aboriginal Deaths in Custody, National Report: Vol 5,* Canberra: Australian Government Publishing Service.

Jolly, Stan (1988) *Progress Report on Programmes and Initiatives for Native People in Ontario*, Ottawa: Ministry of the Attorney General.

Kirby, Justice Michael (1988) 'Domestic Application of International Human Rights Standards', *Australian Foreign Affairs Record*, 59: 5, May, 186-88.

Kirby, W. J. C. (1978) *Alberta Board of Review Provincial Courts*, Report 4, Item 18, Alberta.

Langton, Marcia and Ah Matt, Leslie (1991) '"Too Much Sorry Business": The Report of the Aboriginal Issues Unit of the Northern Territory', in *Royal Commission into Aboriginal Deaths in Custody, National Report: Vol. 5,* Canberra: Australian Government Publishing Service, Appendix D (1), 275-512.

LaPrairie, Carol (1992) 'Who Owns the Problem? Crime and Disorder in James Bay Cree Communities', *Canadian Journal of Criminology*, 34: 3/4, 417-34.

LaPrairie, Carol and Craig, Barbara (1985) *Native Criminal Justice Research and Programmes: Inventory Update*, Ottawa: Solicitor General Canada.

Law Reform Commission of Australia (1986) *The Recognition of Aboriginal Customary Laws, Summary Report, No. 31*, Canberra: Australian Government Publishing Service.

Legislative Assembly of the Northern Territory (1992) *Recognition of Aboriginal Customary Law*, Discussion Paper No. 4, Darwin: Sessional Committee on Constitutional Development, Legislative Assembly of the Northern Territory.

Manitoba Community Services (n.d.) 'The Fine Option Programme', in *The Corrections Community No 3*, Manitoba: Manitoba Community Services.

Maxwell, Gabrielle M. (1993) 'Family Decision-making in Youth Justice: The New Zealand Model', in L. Atkinson and S. Gerull (eds.), *National Conference on Juvenile Justice*, Canberra: Australian Institute of Criminology.

Maxwell, Gabrielle M. and Morris, Allison (1990) 'A Statistical Overview of Juvenile Offending before and since the Children, Young Persons and Their Families Act, 1989', Wellington: Institute of Criminology.

McCallum, Tom (1988) *Evaluation Report: The Ontario Native Justice of the Peace Programme in the Northwestern Region*, Ottawa: Ministry of the Attorney General.

Morris, Allison and Maxwell, Gabrielle (1990) *Juvenile Justice in New Zealand: A New Paradigm*, Wellington/Cambridge: Institute of Criminology.

Morris, Allison and Young, Warren (1987) *Juvenile Justice in New Zealand: Policy and Practice*, Wellington: Institute of Criminology.

Morse, Brad (1983) 'Lessons from Canada?' *Aboriginal Legal Bulletin* 7: 4, 4-6.

Morse, Bradford (1980) *Indian Tribal Courts in United States: A Model for Canada?* Saskatoon: University of Saskatchewan.

Morse, Bradford and Lock, Linda (1988) *Perceptions of Native Offenders of the Criminal Justice System*, Ottawa: University of Ottawa.

Mukherjee, S. K., Neuhaus, D. and Walker, J. (1990) *Crime and Justice in Australia*, Canberra: Australian Institute of Criminology.

NCSA (1985a) *Family Life Improvement Programme: Final Report*, Edmonton, Alberta: Native Counselling Services of Alberta, July.

NCSA (1985b) *Native Counselling Services of Alberta: Annual Report 1984-85*, Edmonton, Alberta: Native Counselling Services of Alberta.

NCSA (1987) *Native Counselling Services of Alberta: Annual Report 1986-87*, Edmonton, Alberta: Native Counselling Services of Alberta.

NCSA (1989) *The Native Counselling Story*, Edmonton: Native Counselling Services of Alberta, unpublished.

NCSA (1991) *Native Counselling Services of Alberta: Annual Report 1990-91*, Edmonton, Alberta: Native Counselling Services of Alberta.

Nielsen, Marianne O. (1993) *Surviving In-Between: A Case Study of a Canadian Aboriginal-Operated Criminal Justice Organization*, PhD. Thesis, Edmonton: Department of Sociology, University of Alberta.

O'Connor, Ian (1992) *Youth, Crime and Justice in Queensland: An Information and Issues Paper*, Brisbane: Criminal Justice Commission Queensland.

Prefontaine, D. C., Opekokew, D. and Tyler, K. (1985) 'Reflecting Indian Concerns and Values in the Justice System', Joint Canada/Saskatchewan: FSIN Justice Studies.

Walker, J. (1992) 'Prison Sentences in Australia: Estimates of the Characteristics of Offenders Sentenced to Prison in 1987-88', in P. R. Wilson (ed.), *Issues in Crime, Morality and Justice*, Canberra: Australian Institute of Criminology.

Walker, J., Hallinan, J. and Dagger, D. (1992) *Australian Prisoners 1991: National Prison Census 30 June 1991*, Canberra: Australian Institute of Criminology.

Williams, Nancy M. (1987) *Two Laws: Managing Disputes in a Contemporary Aboriginal Community*, Canberra: Australian Institute of Aboriginal Studies.

Zion, Elsie B. (1993) '"I Am Now Well by It": The Navajo Healing Way', *Hembra*, September, 5.

Zion, J. W. (1992) 'North American Indian Perspectives on Human Rights', in A. A. An-na'im (ed.), *Human Rights in Cross-Cultural Perspectives*, Philadelphia: University of Pennsylvania Press, 191-220.

Zion, J. W. and Zion, E. B. (1993) 'Hazho' Sokee'—Stay Together Nicely: Domestic Violence under Navajo Common Law', *Arizona State Law Journal*, 25: 2, 407-26.

Popular Justice
and
Community Regeneration

1 RECLAIMING THE COMMUNITY

SOCIAL POLICY AND CANADA'S ABORIGINAL PEOPLE: THE NEED FOR FUNDAMENTAL REFORMS

John H. Hylton

This chapter focuses on what is commonly referred to as the 'social policy sector' in Canada. The approaches that have been used to provide social programmes to Canada's aboriginal people are described and the failure of these approaches in ameliorating the horrific social conditions faced by aboriginal people in Canada is documented. The chapter suggests that there is a need for a fundamental rethinking of the way in which social programmes are developed and delivered. In particular, examples of programmes that have been 'owned' by aboriginal people themselves are provided, and it is suggested that providing the opportunity for aboriginal people to develop and deliver their own programmes represents the most promising direction for aboriginal policy in Canada.

INTRODUCTION

The Canadian social policy sector encompasses a wide array of human service programmes—health, justice, education and social service programmes to name a few—that are intended to ameliorate social problems such as poverty, unemployment, family disintegration, child abuse, suicide, crime, juvenile delinquency, substance abuse, illiteracy, inadequate child care and poor housing.

Social programmes are particularly important for aboriginal people in Canada for a number of reasons:

1. Aboriginal people in Canada are disproportionately affected by the problems that social programmes are intended to address.
2. Social programmes have a dramatic impact on the quality of life of aboriginal people in Canada.
3. In delivering social programmes, the state exercises broad powers that frequently interfere with the most fundamental rights and freedoms of aboriginal people.

4. Social programmes are very costly to deliver. The 'social envelope' represents the largest single group of expenditures in the federal budget. At the provincial level, social spending typically makes up about two-thirds of government expenditures.

5. Both aboriginal and non-aboriginal Canadians are unhappy and frustrated with the current approach to the delivery of social programmes.

6. For aboriginal people, their involvement in designing and delivering social programmes goes to the heart of their concept of 'self-government'.

7. There is substantial evidence that more effective and efficient options are available for the delivery of social programmes.

It is beyond the scope of this chapter to provide a comprehensive review of the research literature pertaining to social issues affecting Canadian aboriginal people, since such a review would likely occupy several volumes.[1] Rather, the objective of this chapter is to provide a broad overview of the current state of the research literature and to make some observations about the types of approaches to aboriginal social problems that have and have not worked in Canada. While some references have been provided, they are by no means comprehensive. Instead, they are intended to illustrate the types of research studies that have been undertaken in Canada.

SOCIAL PROBLEMS, SOCIAL POLICY AND ABORIGINAL PEOPLE IN CANADA

Over the past several decades, there have been literally thousands of studies conducted in Canada to answer questions about aboriginal people and a wide array of social problems and social policy issues. Some questions have been posed so frequently that a considerable body of literature is now available. Some of the more common types of research questions and the results they have produced are described as follows:

1. What is the incidence of social problems among aboriginal people? How does the incidence rate compare to that for the non-aboriginal population? These types of question are among the most common in the literature. They have inspired numerous studies. These studies typically set out to document the extent of social problems among aboriginal people. Results may be expressed in quantitative or qualitative terms. Quantitative studies often focus on incidence rates and then compare these rates to the corresponding rates for non-aboriginals. These analyses often become quite complex. They may take into consideration a wide array of social, economic, geographic, cultural, historical and other variables in an attempt to uncover correlates and causes (Havemann, Foster, Couse and Matonovitch 1985).

Qualitative studies, on the other hand, usually focus on the subjective experience of aboriginal persons and communities as they struggle to overcome their problems and find a place in Canadian society (Ponting and Gibbins 1980; Ryan 1978; Nagler 1973; Krotz 1980; Cardinal 1969; Dosman 1972; Frideres 1974). There has been particular interest in documenting the unhappy life of aboriginal people when they migrate from aboriginal communities to Canadian urban centres.

On the basis of these studies, we now know that aboriginal Canadians disproportionately experience virtually every type of social problem. Furthermore, because of replications of similar studies, we are often able to make statements about the extent of the disproportion. We also know a good deal about the social, demographic and economic correlates of social problems.

From these studies, it can be said with a good deal of certainty that, relative to non-aboriginal Canadians, aboriginal people commit more crimes and delinquencies, experience more mental and physical health problems, experience more family problems and disproportionately abuse alcohol and drugs. Furthermore, we know that aboriginal people have a shorter life expectancy, higher rates of infant mortality and higher rates of suicide. We also know that aboriginal people have lower incomes, less formal education, higher rates of welfare dependency and higher rates of unemployment. We know that aboriginal people are disproportionately poor and experience all the problems associated with poverty—poor nutrition, poor housing, inadequate child care and the like. Regrettably, these types of studies often end up 'blaming the victim'.

2. What are the participation rates of aboriginal people in various social programmes? How do the participation rates differ from the corresponding non-aboriginal rates? While similar to the earlier questions, answers to these questions are usually based on an analysis of caseload information collected by social agencies and government social programmes. These studies typically disaggregate the caseload statistics to show the number of aboriginal and non-aboriginal clients who have received a type of service. Often these statistics are compared to the composition of the general population in order to calculate participation rates. These rates are then often used to determine the extent to which aboriginal people are over-represented in various social programmes.

A considerable body of knowledge now exists that describes comparative participation rates for aboriginal people in a wide variety of programme areas. These studies consistently show that, relative to the non-aboriginal population, aboriginal people are over-represented in adult correctional programmes, hospitals, mental health care facilities, alcohol and drug abuse programmes, programmes for young offenders, family service programmes, income security programmes, social housing programmes, programmes for the unemployed, programmes for neglected and abused children and family violence programmes (e.g., Hawthorn 1966; Hull 1987; Canada, Department of Indian Affairs 1989). About the only instance where over-representation does not seem to occur is when aboriginal people do not have access to the particular programme being studied.

As with the earlier studies, these analyses often do not discuss the historical antecedents that have lead to disproportionate participation rates. Therefore, they may inadvertently 'blame the victim'.

3.   What are the social, demographic and other characteristics of those aboriginal people who experience social problems, or who find themselves on the caseloads of social agencies? As alluded to earlier, there are a multitude of studies that have addressed this question. Usually analyses are undertaken as a part of larger studies that have also examined incidence or participation rates. While it is difficult to generalize about the results, these studies have tended to show that the social problems experienced by aboriginal people have an early onset and are commonly experienced and deeply rooted in aboriginal families and communities. These studies also show that a multitude of closely related problems are experienced simultaneously.

An example may best serve to illustrate the types of findings that have been reported. The adult aboriginal offender is often found to have a history of mental health, physical health, substance abuse and criminal justice problems. He is frequently the product of a broken home, may have been abused and is likely to have been a young offender. His parents, siblings and extended family may all have experienced similar problems. He and his family are often poor, and his community is typically impoverished. He is usually lacking in formal education and training and does not have any significant employment experience. He has sometimes abused his spouse and children. He is invariably dependent on social assistance and social housing, and has participated in a wide variety of other social programmes (Hylton 1981a).

4.   Why do aboriginal people disproportionately experience social problems? Why are aboriginal people disproportionately represented on the caseloads of social agencies? These questions have also been the subject of social research. The research literature indicates, however, that there are two common but distinct approaches to answering these questions. In the first approach, questions are raised in quantitative studies that analyze incidence and/or participation rates. The researchers collect information about the background of those experiencing problems (social, economic, demographic and other information) and attempt to determine the factors that are correlated with incidence or programme participation. When correlations do exist, researchers will then often make assumptions about the temporal sequence of events so that they can make statements about causation.[2]

These studies typically conclude that social problems are the result of unemployment, poverty, substance abuse or a lack of economic opportunity. Recommendations focus on providing aboriginal people with opportunities to participate more fully in the social and economic life of Canadian society (Havemann et al. 1985).

The second approach to answering these questions is very different from the first. It typically does not involve a quantitative approach. Rather, it involves a historical analysis of the social, economic and political relations between aboriginal people and dominant society, usually as represented by its governments. This type of analysis is often undertaken by aboriginal leaders and supporters of aboriginal self-determination.

These analyses typically focus on the disenfranchisement of aboriginal people and on successive attempts by governments to extinguish aboriginal culture and traditions. Importance is accorded to the paternalism of Canadian governments and to the dependency and lack of self-sufficiency that this has created in aboriginal communities (Getty and Lussier 1983; Barron 1984; Pettipas 1988; Cole and Chaikin 1990; Carter 1990).

These analyses typically conclude that the abrogation of aboriginal culture and traditions has brought about the social and economic disintegration of aboriginal communities. The social problems now evident in these communities, it is argued, are the direct result of a long historical process. Recommendations usually focus on restoring aboriginal culture and traditions, abolishing the paternalistic relationship between aboriginal people and governments of the dominant society and restoring aboriginal self-determination.

5. How effective are existing social programmes in ameliorating the social problems experienced by aboriginal people? Programme evaluation studies have been carried out to determine the effectiveness of many social programmes in ameliorating social problems experienced by aboriginal people. While there are some studies that have examined how the introduction of a programme has affected an entire community, usually the methodology involves following a sample of clients to see whether or not their participation in a given programme has produced a desired outcome.

As will be discussed in greater detail later in this chapter, there are encouraging signs that programmes for aboriginal people, which are designed and delivered by aboriginal people, are more effective in attaining their objectives than are programmes designed and delivered by non-aboriginal people. The literature indicates that the latter type of programme usually meets with very limited success. While some exceptions can be found, social programmes designed and delivered by non-aboriginals are generally much less effective in achieving their intended outcome with aboriginal people than they are in achieving their intended outcome with non-aboriginal people. For example, relative to the non-aboriginal population:

• Adult correctional programmes are not as effective in rehabilitating or deterring aboriginal offenders and aboriginal offenders have higher recidivism rates

(Hamilton and Sinclair 1991).

• The same holds true for young offenders (Hamilton and Sinclair 1991).

• Family service programmes are not as effective in preventing the breakdown of aboriginal families; foster care and adoption placements more often fail (Johnson 1983; Kimmelman 1985).

• Employment training programmes are not as effective in leading to employment (Canada, Department of Indian Affairs 1989).

• Substance abuse programmes are not as effective in leading to sobriety (Hylton 1990; Brody 1971).

• Income security programmes are not as effective in ensuring that the basic sustenance needs of aboriginal families are met (Canada, Department of Indian Affairs 1989).

• Social housing programmes are not as effective in improving housing conditions (Canada, Department of Indian Affairs 1989).

• Educational programmes are not as effective in providing an adequate level of formal education (Barman, Hebert and McCaskill 1986).

• Health programmes are not as effective in improving health status (Canada, Department of Indian Affairs 1989).

The literature also provides information about the reasons for the general inability of non-aboriginal programmes to meet the needs of aboriginal people (e.g., Hamilton and Sinclair 1991). The following factors have frequently been identified:

• Because programmes have not been designed with the needs of aboriginal people in mind, they frequently provide services that are not relevant or, alternatively, fail to provide services that are needed.

• Policies, procedures and expectations associated with non-aboriginal programmes often fail to take into account the unique language, culture, traditions and current life situation of aboriginal clients.

• Because non-aboriginal programmes typically employ non-aboriginal staff, there is often a knowledge gap, and a corresponding lack of trust, between the non-aboriginal service providers and the aboriginal clients.

• Because aboriginal communities have had limited or no involvement in designing and delivering the programmes, there is typically limited community ownership or support. In some cases, for example, when the circuit court or the child protection worker comes to town, the community may feel that it has been invaded by a foreign authority.

• Because non-aboriginal programmes are seldom 'resident' in aboriginal communities, aboriginal people usually have limited access to them. In addition, there is typically a high turnover rate among non-aboriginal, non-resident staff. Therefore, services are not consistently or sensitively provided and there is usually an absence of meaningful follow-up.

In light of these realities, it is not difficult to understand why non-aboriginal service providers have so often become frustrated that their programmes are not more effective.

6.   *What is the subjective experience of aboriginal people who are served by non-aboriginal social programmes?*   As alluded to earlier, studies have documented the unhappy experiences of aboriginal clients who have been served by non-aboriginal social programmes (Hobbs-Birnie 1990; Ryan 1978; Krotz 1980). Results indicate that aboriginal people feel poorly and insensitively treated by non-aboriginal personnel who have limited understanding and sympathy for their predicament. Inappropriate expectations, inadequate communication, fear and mistrust seem to characterize relations.

It is significant that aboriginal people seldom choose to receive services from non-aboriginal social programmes. Rather, they do so out of necessity or because the state has compelled their participation. When aboriginal people have a choice between being served by an aboriginal or a non-aboriginal agency, the data indicate they almost always elect the aboriginal agency.

7.   *What are the attitudes of Canadians, social agency personnel and others towards aboriginal people?*   There has been a good deal of public opinion and public attitude research conducted in Canada to determine how Canadians view aboriginal people (Canada, Department of Indian Affairs 1980; Cooke 1984; Gibbins and Ponting 1978; Hylton 1981b). Studies have also examined the attitudes of programme personnel (corrections officers, social workers, the police) towards aboriginal people.

Generally, these studies have found that the wider Canadian community has very limited appreciation of the current circumstances of aboriginal people. In fact, studies have often revealed a variety of negative attitudes and racial stereotypes. There is some evidence, however, that as a result of protracted constitutional discussions, more and more Canadians are becoming sympathetic to the aspirations of aboriginal people (see the March 16, 1992, issue of *Maclean's* magazine). Results of studies involving agency personnel have been a cause for particular concern. These studies show that personnel, particularly those involved in the exercise of social control functions (welfare workers, child welfare workers, police, corrections officers, for example) often harbour negative and racially stereotypical views (Hylton 1980).

THE NEED FOR REFORM

The many social problems experienced by aboriginal people and the ineffectiveness of non-aboriginal social programmes in addressing these problems are now widely recognized in Canada. Recommendations for the reform of social programmes for aboriginal people has generally been of two types. First, measures have been adopted to attempt to improve the effectiveness of non-aboriginal programmes in meeting the needs of aboriginal people. Second, parallel aboriginal programmes have been developed specifically for aboriginal people. These programmes have involved varying degrees of aboriginal responsibility and control.

In this section, some illustrations are provided of the types of reforms that have been carried out. The effectiveness of these reforms is discussed; however, it is pointed out that there are unanswered questions about many of these initiatives.

Attempts to Sensitize Non-Aboriginal Programmes to the Needs of Aboriginal People

Attempts to sensitize non-aboriginal programmes to the needs of aboriginal people have taken many forms, but there have been a few common types of initiatives. Fortunately, a large body of evaluative research exists, and therefore conclusions can be drawn about the effectiveness of many of these initiatives.

One common measure that has been undertaken to sensitize non-aboriginal programmes to the needs of aboriginal people has involved the adoption of affirmative action hiring policies. Virtually all agencies serving aboriginal people now claim that they make a special effort to recruit aboriginal staff. Most affirmative action programmes entail the design and implementation of specialized recruitment programmes. These may involve recruiting at educational institutions with high aboriginal enrollment, advertizing in aboriginal publications, employing the assistance of aboriginal leaders in identifying suitable applicants and using specialized recruitment firms. These and other methods have been employed to recruit aboriginal welfare workers, family services staff, corrections staff, police officers and many others.

Affirmative action programmes appear to have met with very limited success. Employers claim that they are truly committed to increasing the numbers of aboriginal staff but, with few exceptions, their efforts have been largely ineffectual. Even after these programmes have been in place for some time, there are typically very few aboriginal staff employed in non-aboriginal social programmes. Employers have been hard-pressed to provide any evidence that these programmes really work (Hamilton and Sinclair 1991).

A number of reasons for the failure of affirmative action programmes have been identified (Hamilton and Sinclair 1991). During economic downturns, such as have been experienced in Canada over the past number of years, employers claim that there are few vacancies and, consequently, few opportunities to recruit aboriginal staff. Employers also say that aboriginal applicants often fail to meet the requirements for those positions that do become available. While there is certainly ample evidence that aboriginal people have limited opportunities to obtain the formal education and work experience that may be required for some positions, there are, it appears, much deeper problems.

Studies have shown that position requirements are sometimes unreasonable for aboriginal applicants. On other occasions, the requirements are irrelevant to the performance of the duties of the position. The insistence on these arbitrary requirements may amount to a form of systemic discrimination.[3]

Many aboriginal people have been discriminated against, and they are reluctant to subject themselves to further discrimination. For this reason, they may feel uncomfortable working in an environment where they are in the minority. They may be reluctant to apply to a non-aboriginal agency, especially when, as is usually the case, the recruitment process is presided over by non-aboriginal people.

Potential aboriginal applicants often question the appropriateness of the programmes and policies of the agencies that may be trying to recruit them. They may have had unhappy personal experiences. They may also have seen the effects of inappropriate policies and programmes on their communities. These concerns are particularly apparent when the potential employer exercises a social control function (e.g., policing). In these instances, potential applicants may also fear their family or community will be critical of them for becoming a part of 'the system'. Evidence indicates that these fears are justified (VanDyke and Jamont 1980).

Aboriginal people who do join non-aboriginal agencies often find it an unhappy and frustrating experience. There are many reports that they feel an absence of support for the personal and professional challenges they face. Sometimes they are even the object of discrimination in the workplace. For these and other reasons, there is evidence that aboriginal employees in non-aboriginal agencies are often unhappy with their jobs and, as a consequence, there is a greater turnover of aboriginal staff (VanDyke and Jamont 1980).

In recognition of some of the problems of affirmative action programmes, some reforms have attempted to establish specialized aboriginal units, staffed by aboriginal employees, within larger non-aboriginal programmes and agencies. Perhaps the best known example of this approach is the Indian Special Constable programme established by the R.C.M.P. Similar programmes have also been established for probation officers, corrections officers, welfare workers, substance abuse counsellors, health care providers and others. On the whole, these types of reforms seem to have been somewhat more successful than affirmative action programmes in attracting and retaining staff and in delivering quality services to aboriginal people. These initiatives have, however, encountered many of the same problems as affirmative action programmes, although not always to the same degree.

Another common approach to sensitizing non-aboriginal programmes has focused on promoting greater awareness among non-aboriginal staff about the needs and circumstances of their aboriginal clients. These initiatives have usually involved programmes of cross-cultural awareness as well as related training and education programmes. Such programmes have been widely adopted in non-aboriginal agencies that have a large aboriginal caseload. The available evidence indicates that the effectiveness of these initiatives seems to depend heavily on the programme design and the abilities of the resource persons. Results are by no means uniformly positive and, in fact, some programmes have had the opposite of the intended effect (Stephens 1983).

Other reforms have taken the form of allowing aboriginal input to decision making in non-aboriginal programmes. Elders are consulted about the sentencing of offenders. The Band Council is consulted about the apprehension of a child. Committees are established to provide community input into the work of non-aboriginal agencies.

These reforms often result in improved relations between aboriginal communities and those responsible for the delivery of non-aboriginal social programmes. In addition, there is some evidence that the effectiveness of some programmes improves because aboriginal input leads to better decisions and greater community acceptance of decisions. Yet the improvements in programme effectiveness that are brought about as a result of these types of initiatives are often far less than dramatic. Moreover, many opportunities for aboriginal input rely on informal arrangements that depend on the interests and goodwill of individual officials. Because they seldom become institutionalized, these types of arrangements usually remain in effect only for a limited time.[4]

Some reforms have involved the introduction of traditional aboriginal practices into non-aboriginal programmes. Correctional institutions, for example, sometimes permit sweat lodges, sweet grass ceremonies and the attendance of elders and spiritual leaders. The evidence suggests, however, that officials often are not fully committed to these programmes. They are often not accorded the same importance as programmes for non-aboriginal offenders and they may be cancelled or modified to comply with security and other programme requirements.[5]

There have been remarkably few efforts reported in the literature to modify significantly the social programmes or policies of the dominant society to better meet the needs of aboriginal people. Rather, the programmes and policies developed by non-aboriginal authorities are usually taken as a given. They are typically viewed by the dominant system as the best possible approach for both aboriginal and non-aboriginal clients. Various reform efforts, such as those described above, are then instituted to assist aboriginal people to fit in, accept or adjust to the non-aboriginal system.[6]

On the whole, while some exceptions do exist, the types of reform efforts described in this section have met with limited success. While some improvements in effectiveness and acceptance have been brought about, on the whole, the gains have been modest. Furthermore, even with these types of reforms, non-aboriginal programmes do not generally achieve the level of effectiveness or acceptance that these same programmes enjoy in non-aboriginal communities.

The Creation of Parallel Social Programmes Specifically for Aboriginal People

The failure of non-aboriginal social programmes to meet effectively the needs and aspirations of aboriginal people has led to a good deal of interest in establishing parallel programmes that are run by and for aboriginal people. There are now numerous examples of parallel aboriginal social programmes in Canada. They include, for example, programmes in child and family services; justice services, including policing, corrections and court services; alcohol and drug abuse programmes; recreation and community development programmes; health care services, including hospitals; educational programming, including secondary and post-secondary educational institutions; child care and day care services; and many others (Horn and Griffiths 1989).

While much more needs to be known about the effectiveness and potential of parallel aboriginal social programmes, some evaluative studies have been encouraging. While it is dangerous to generalize, some common findings are beginning to emerge from these studies (Morse 1980; Hurd and Hurd 1986; Hudson and Taylor-Henley 1987; Coopers and Lybrand 1986; Social Policy Research Associates 1983). It appears that aboriginal programmes are more successful than corresponding non-aboriginal programmes in:

• incorporating principles, beliefs and traditions that are a part of aboriginal culture;

• attracting and retaining aboriginal staff;

• involving the aboriginal community in the design and delivery of programmes;

• fostering greater acceptance by the individual client and the aboriginal community;

• creating economic benefits for aboriginal communities;

• extending services that were previously unavailable through the non-aboriginal programme;

• drawing attention to social issues in aboriginal communities and generating interest, involvement and support for social programmes in aboriginal communities;

• providing levels of service that approach or equal levels of service available to non-aboriginal communities;

• reducing the need for the intervention of the state in the lives of aboriginal people and communities; and

• providing services at a cost that is no more, and is sometimes less, than the cost of corresponding non-aboriginal programmes.

It is important to note that a substantial body of historical research now exists on traditional aboriginal approaches in dealing with many social issues and social problems (McDonnell 1991, 1992; Coyle 1986; Clark 1990; Morse 1983; Hylton et al. 1985). There has been a strong interest among aboriginal people in adapting this knowledge about what has worked in the past to present-day circumstances. As a result, many parallel social programmes that have been developed by aboriginal people have incorporated unique approaches to the problems that aboriginal people face today. There are many examples.

Aboriginal justice programmes, unlike the justice programmes of the dominant society, have tended to accord much less importance to a formalized process of adjudication. In addition, unlike Canadian justice services, they have not been preoccupied with the punishment of offenders. Rather, these aboriginal programmes have emphasized the traditional practice of restoring peace and harmony in the community. There is no schedule of penalties for different offences and, in many instances, no formal adjudication process. What is important in the aboriginal approach is that the offender, the victim and the community feel that a transgression has been dealt with appropriately and that any divisiveness in the community is healed.

In aboriginal communities, children were not viewed as possessions of their parents. Child care was a community responsibility and the extended family and the community as a whole had important roles to play in teaching and safeguarding children. Whereas the dominant non-aboriginal society has tended to view children as the primary responsibility of their parents, and have removed children from their parents in cases deemed to involve neglect or abuse, aboriginal child welfare programmes often avoid apprehensions by enlisting the support of the extended family and the community.

Health care practices of the dominant society have emphasized the treatment of physical disorders by health care experts. In aboriginal approaches, health is a holistic concept that goes beyond physical health to involve spiritual and psychological dimensions. Whereas modern medicine has only recently recognized that many disorders have an underlying cause that is not physical, this has been an important principle of aboriginal approaches to health and well-being for centuries.[7]

Despite the many positive accomplishments of parallel aboriginal social programmes, the literature (Singer and Moyer 1981; Hurd and Hurd 1986; Hudson and Taylor-Henley 1987; Coopers and Lybrand 1986; Bryant et al. 1978) also suggests there are a number of common problems:

• Financial resources provided to these programmes are typically inadequate when compared with the resources made available to corresponding non-aboriginal programmes.

• The future of these programmes is often in doubt. Budgets are subject to review as the programmes are often viewed by funders as 'experimental' in nature.

• An absence of resources forces many agencies to focus all their energies on crisis management. Prevention and community development activities are not properly recognized or funded.

• Programmes frequently have to operate without a proper infrastructure of personnel and programme policies and procedures. Funders seldom recognize the importance of developing this infrastructure.

• Relationships between aboriginal programmes and the dominant non-aboriginal programmes are often characterized by uncertainty about respective roles and responsibilities.

• Typically, aboriginal programmes are confined to a particular geographic area. It is often uncertain how members of the aboriginal community who are outside the geographic boundaries of the programme ought to be served by aboriginal and non-aboriginal agencies. This is a particular problem, for example, with off-reserve Indians.

Clearly the findings to date point to the positive potential of social programmes operated by and for aboriginal people. Yet if this approach is to move beyond isolated 'experimental' programmes so that it can be accepted as the usual and proper approach to service delivery, much more groundwork will need to be done. In particular, the following questions need to be addressed:

1. What does a comprehensive review and analysis of the Canadian experience with parallel aboriginal social programmes tell us about what works and what does not work from the standpoint of aboriginal people and government funding agencies?

2. What can we learn from other countries which have adopted parallel programmes for their aboriginal people?

3. What is the range of funding and jurisdictional options for instituting parallel programmes, and what are the advantages and disadvantages of each from the standpoint of aboriginal people and Canadians generally? Is there a preferred approach or are there a number of preferred approaches that depend on cultural, linguistic, geographic or other factors?

4. What changes in law, policy, funding and in organizational and jurisdictional structures are necessary in order to move ahead with the preferred approaches to parallel aboriginal programmes? How can the needed changes be brought about?

In short, we need to know what works, for whom, and in what circumstances. We need a plan of direction.

CONCLUSION

On April 23, 1991, in an address to a First Nations Congress in Victoria,

British Columbia, the Prime Minister of Canada announced that the government would establish a Royal Commission on Aboriginal Peoples. The Prime Minister said that the commission was part of the government's new Native Agenda and that it would 'examine the economic, social and cultural situation of aboriginal people of the country'.

The establishment of a Royal Commission was, to some significant degree, a response to the failed Meech Lake Accord—an agreement among some Canadian provinces and the federal government to reform Canada's constitution. During the Meech round of constitutional discussions, national attention and sympathy was focused on the frustrations of Canada's aboriginal people. When Elijah Harper, an aboriginal member of the provincial assembly in the province of Manitoba, withheld the unanimous consent that was required to consider the Meech bill, it symbolized for the country that major social, economic and constitutional issues could not be addressed effectively without the full participation of aboriginal people.

The formation of a Royal Commission on Aboriginal Peoples presents an important opportunity to improve the quality of life for aboriginal people in Canada, to address systematically the complex issues relating to aboriginal self-determination, and to heal the divisions that now exist between Canadians and Canada's first peoples. While the commission is not likely to complete its work for several years, it is essential for the future of all Canadians that this opportunity not be missed.

There is no need to document further the social problems faced by aboriginal people in Canada. Nor is there a need to document further the failure of non-aboriginal social programmes to respond effectively to the social needs of aboriginal people. While existing research should be reviewed, and some selected findings updated, further reiteration of existing problems should not be a priority.

There are exciting examples in Canada and elsewhere of how efficiency and effectiveness of social programmes for aboriginal people can be improved through greater aboriginal involvement and control of these programmes. Moreover, because this type of approach is seen by aboriginal people as an essential ingredient of aboriginal self-determination and self-government, it will be important for this type of approach to guide future initiatives in Canada. Canada could be a model for other jurisdictions. At the moment, however, it is caught in traditional approaches to the delivery of service that not only are ineffective, but continue to cast aboriginal people in the role of 'client'. This must change.[8]

NOTES

1. For example, a bibliography without annotations prepared by Horn and Griffiths (1989) runs some 275 pages and the subject matter is limited to criminal justice issues affecting aboriginal peoples.

2. In fact, these types of analyses are typically cross-sectional analyses that examine relationships among variables. Often, the data are collected and describe conditions as they existed at one point in time. Therefore, the data usually do not permit definitive 'chicken and egg' statements about causation.

3. For example, in recruiting for the Indian Special Constable programme, the R.C.M.P. found that stringent selection criteria related to formal education and criminal record effectively excluded many suitable aboriginal applicants. After careful review, it was recognized that each case had to be judged on its own merits without candidates being automatically excluded from consideration. Many other examples of this form of systemic discrimination continue to exist, however.

4. The Manitoba Aboriginal Justice Inquiry, for example, documented a number of cases where reforms had been instituted because of the goodwill of individual officials in the justice system. In one case, for example, a judge had decided to hold court on a reserve and he invited the input of the community in sentencing decisions. This practice, however, was later discontinued (Hamilton and Sinclair 1991).

5. Hamilton and Sinclair (1991), for example, found that elders and spiritual leaders were discouraged from attending aboriginal inmates in correctional facilities because they and their religious articles were not accorded proper respect by the staff in correctional institutions. Meanwhile, non-aboriginal religious leaders and religious articles received preferential treatment.

6. Perhaps one of the best examples of this approach was the Indian Residential School. Traditional Indian education was undermined; Indian children were removed from their communities; they were required to learn the customs and traditions of the dominant society; and they were punished for practising their language or culture. This concept was based on a belief that Indian culture and language was inferior and that Indians should assimilate to the 'better' ways of the dominant society (Haig-Brown 1988). Similar assumptions exist today, and they find their way into non-aboriginal social programmes.

7. The Canadian Mental Health Association, for example, estimates that as many as 50% of visits to family doctors may be for mental health problems.

8. A revised version of this chapter was originally prepared for the Royal Commission on Aboriginal Peoples, whose establishment was announced on 23 April, 1991.

REFERENCES

Barman, Jean., Hebert, Yvonne, and McCaskill, Don (eds) (1986) *Indian Education in Canada*, Vancouver: University of British Columbia Press.

Barron, Laurie (1984) 'A Summary of Canadian Indian Policy in the Canadian West', *Native Studies Review* 1: 28-29.

Brody, Hugh (1971) *Indians on Skid Row*, Ottawa: Information Canada.

Bryant, V. M. et al. (1978) *Evaluation of the Indian Special Constable Program (Option 3b)*, Ottawa: Department of Indian Affairs and Northern Development.

Canada, Department of Indian Affairs (1989) *Highlights of Aboriginal Conditions, 1981-2001*, Ottawa: Department of Indian Affairs.

Canada, Department of Indian Affairs (1980) *An Overview of Some Recent Research on Attitudes in Canada towards Indian People*, Ottawa: Department of Indian Affairs and Northern Development.

Cardinal, Harold (1969) *The Unjust Society: The Tragedy of Canada's Indians*, Edmonton: Hurtig.

Carter, Sarah (1990) *Lost Harvest: Prairie Indian Reserve Farmers and Government Policy*, Montreal and Kingston: Queen's-McGill University Press.

Clark, Scott (1990) *Aboriginal Customary Law: Literature Review*, Winnipeg: Aboriginal Justice Inquiry.

Cole, Douglas and Chaikin, Ira (1990) *An Iron Hand upon the People: The Law against the Potlatch on the Northwest Coast*, Vancouver: Douglas Nad McIntyre.

Cooke, Katie (1984) *Images of Indians held by Non-Indians: A Review of the Current Canadian Research*, Ottawa: Department of Indian Affairs and Northern Development.

Coopers and Lybrand Consulting Group (1986) *An Assessment of Services Delivered under the Canada-Manitoba Northern Indian Child Welfare Agreement*, Winnipeg: Coopers and Lybrand.

Coyle, Michael (1986) 'Traditional Indian Justice in Ontario: A Role for the Present', *Osgoode Hall Law Journal* 24: 605-633.

Dosman, Edgar J. (1972) *Indians: The Urban Dilemma*, Toronto: McClelland and Stewart.

Frideres, J. S. (1974) *Canada's Indians: Contemporary Conflicts*, Ontario: Prentice-Hall.

Getty, A. L., and Lussier, A. S. (eds) (1983) *As Long as the Sun Shines and the River Flows: A Reader in Canadian Native Studies*, Vancouver: Nakota Institute and University of British Columbia Press.

Gibbins, Roger and Ponting, Rick J. (1978) *Canadian Opinions and Attitudes towards Indians and Indian Issues: Findings of a National Study*, Ottawa: Department of Indian Affairs and Northern Development.

Government of Canada (1985) 'Customary Law', *In Reflecting Indian Concerns and Values in the Justice System*, Ottawa: Department of Justice, 1-18.

Haig-Brown, Celia (1988) *Resistance and Renewal: Surviving the Indian Residential School*, Vancouver: Tillacum Library.

Hamilton, A. C. and Sinclair, C. M. (1991) *Report of the Aboriginal Justice Inquiry of Manitoba*, Winnipeg: Government of Manitoba.

Havemann, Paul., Foster, Lori., Couse, Keith and Matonovitch, Rae (1985) *Law and Order for Canada's Indigenous People: A Review of Recent Research Literature Relating to the Operation of the Criminal Justice System and*

Canada's Indigenous People, Regina: Prairie Justice Research Consortium.

Hawthorn, H. B. (ed.) (1966) *A Survey of Contemporary Indians of Canada: Economic, Political, Educational Needs and Policies*, Ottawa: Department of Indian Affairs and Northern Development.

Hobbs-Birnie, Lisa (1990) *A Rock and a Hard Place: Inside Canada's Parole Board*, Toronto: McMillan.

Horn, Charles and Griffiths, Curt T. (1989) *Native North Americans: Crime, Conflict and Criminal Justice*, 4th ed., Burnaby, B.C: The Northern Justice Society.

Hudson, Peter and Taylor-Henley, Sharon (1987) *Agreement and Disagreement: An Evaluation of the Canada-Manitoba Northern Indian Child Welfare Agreement*, Winnipeg: University of Manitoba.

Hull, Jeremy (1987) *An Overview of Registered Indian Conditions in Manitoba*, Ottawa: Department of Indian and Northern Affairs.

Hurd, Carroll P. and Hurd, Jeanne M. (1986) *Evaluation: Implementation of the Canada-Manitoba-Brotherhood of Indian Nations Child Welfare Agreement*, Edmonton: McKay-Hurd Associates.

Hylton, John H. (1980) 'Public Attitudes towards Crime and the Police in a Prairie City', *Canadian Police College Journal* 14: 243-76.

Hylton, John H. (1981a) *Reintegrating the Offender: Assessing the Impact of Community Corrections*, Washington, D.C.: University Press Of America.

Hylton, John H. (1981b) 'Some Attitudes towards Natives in a Prairie City', *Canadian Journal Of Criminology* 23: 357-63.

Hylton, John H. et al. (1985) 'Customary Law', in Hylton et al., *Reflecting Indian Concerns and Values in the Justice System*, Ottawa: Department of Justice.

Hylton, John H. et al. (1990) *Alcoholism Treatment for Impaired Drivers*, Queenstown: Edwin Mellen.

Johnson, Patrick (1983) *Native Children and the Child Welfare System*, Toronto: Lorimer.

Kimmelman, Edwin C. (1985) *No Quiet Place: Review Committee on Indian and Métis Adoptions and Placements*, Winnipeg: Manitoba Department of Community Services.

Krotz, Larry (1980) *Urban Indians: The Strangers in Canada's Cities*, Edmonton: Hurtig.

McDonnell, Roger (1991) *Justice for the Cree: Customary Law*, Quebec: Grand Council of the Cree.

McDonnell, Roger (1992) *Justice for the Cree: Customary Beliefs and Practices*, Quebec: Grand Council of the Cree.

Morse, Bradford W. (1980) *Indian Tribal Courts in the United States: A Model for Canada?* Saskatoon: Native Law Centre.

Morse, Bradford W. (1983) 'Indigenous Law and State Legal Systems: Conflict and Compatibility', in Harald W. Finkler (ed.) *Proceedings of the Symposium on Folk Law and Legal Pluralism*, Ottawa: Department of Indian Affairs and

Northern Development, 381-402.

Nagler, Mark (1973) *Indians in the City*, Ottawa: Canadian Research Centre for Anthropology.

Pettipas, K. A. (1988) 'Serving the Ties that Bind: The Canadian Indian Act and the Repression of Indigenous Religious Systems in the Prairie Region, 1896-1951', Winnipeg: University of Manitoba Ph.D. dissertation.

Ponting, J. Rick and Gibbons, Roger (1980) *Out of Irrelevance: A Socio-Political Introduction to Indian Affairs in Canada*, Toronto: Butterworths.

Ryan, Joan (1978) *Wall of Words: The Betrayal of the Urban Indian*, Toronto: Peter Martin.

Singer, Charles and Moyer, Sharon (1981) *The Dakota-Ojibway Tribal Council Police Program: An Evaluation*, Ottawa: Solicitor General of Canada.

Social Policy Research Associates (1983) *National Evaluation Overview of Indian Policing*, Ottawa: Department of Indian and Northern Affairs.

Stephens, E. B. (1983) *Contributions towards Cross-Cultural Education by the Royal Canadian Mounted Police*, Saskatoon: University of Saskatchewan.

VanDyke, Edward and Jamont, K. C. (1980) *Through Indian Eyes: Perspectives of Indian Constables on the 3b Program in 'F' Division*, Regina: Royal Canadian Mounted Police.

Whitehead, Paul C., Hylton, John and Markosky, Robert (1990) *Alcoholism Treatment for Impaired Drivers*, Queenstown: Edwin Mellen.

2

MAKING THE CRIMINAL LAW YOUR OWN:
THE TOKELAU ENDEAVOUR

A. H. Angelo

INTRODUCTION

Tokelau is a small Polynesian atoll community situated almost due north of Western Samoa and lying just south of the equator.[1] Even in Pacific terms Tokelau is tiny. It consists of three atolls each separated from the other by a stretch of high sea and has a population of about 1,700 people distributed more or less equally between the three atolls. The first European contact with Tokelau was in the eighteenth century, and there was continuing contact with the outside world in the latter part of the nineteenth century.

Little is known of the traditions of Tokelau, but it is known that the communities were drastically reduced in numbers in the 1860s and that the mission influence was and is very strong. What is now regarded as Tokelauan custom is likely, in a number of areas, particularly those of interpersonal relations and public order, to have been substantially influenced by European ways, and in those respects at least the custom of the twentieth century may not predate nineteenth-century European contact.

Tokelau is small and has been strongly influenced by Christianity. It is also remote from main centres of international activity and main transport routes. The consequence is that Tokelau custom, whatever its origins and the influences it reflects, has continued in the daily life of Tokelauans in a way that custom has not been able to do in a number of other Pacific communities.

In practical terms, the customary practices of the villages as enforced by the elders are the rules that govern social behaviour in Tokelau. From an outside legalistic point of view, these customs may not have the force of law and in some cases may even be illegal. To date, this has not caused any problems for the Tokelau communities or individuals in them. The social coherence and community respect for the customary institutions remains high and, in the absence of foreign advisers or administrators, the elders govern their communities.

A feature of the social order is the respect given to the elders individually and as a group in council. This respect is complemented by a strong sense of community decision-making on a collegial and consensus basis.

The natural resources of the islands are coconut palm and the produce of the sea. Until recently the community economy has been a subsistence one and aspects of that pattern of life are still dominant. The main ethic has therefore been concern for community harmony and sharing of resources on an egalitarian basis. In such an environment a person is a member of a community rather than an individual.

In the early twentieth century Tokelau inherited a Common Law criminal law system. That system has gone through a number of changes. In the early days it was much more closely attuned to the needs of the community than at present. Tokelau is concerned now to 'bring the criminal law home', in the sense that the community wishes to come to terms with the imported English system and to adapt it to respond to the community's needs and aspirations.

The primary thrust for an interest in law in Tokelau has come from the involvement of the United Nations Special Committee on Decolonization (the Committee of 24).[2] Tokelau is being prepared for its act of self-determination and in the context of that has reviewed the law relating to crimes and criminal procedure for the community.

The purpose of this chapter is to describe the historical background of criminal law in Tokelau, the process by which the criminal law was reviewed and the product of the review process.

HISTORICAL BACKGROUND

Until the establishment of the protectorate it may be assumed that there was no impact of European legal systems on the daily lives of people in Tokelau.[3] In 1874 the Western Pacific High Commission had been established with its base in Suva, and in the Western Pacific Order in Council, 1877 (and its successor the Pacific Order in Council, 1893), the High Commission established a system of rules for the maintenance of order in the Western Pacific area. That system of rules related almost exclusively to British subjects and to British ships. The Orders in Council established the constitution for the Western Pacific High Commission and elaborate codes governing civil and criminal matters. Both orders provided systems of criminal law which were essentially those of England for the time being. It was, however, an adapted criminal procedure which counted among its particular features an inquisitorial process, an assessor system and the possibility of reconciliation and settlement even in criminal matters. This system was one well suited to the circumstances of the Pacific at the time.[4]

As each British colony in the Pacific was established, there was a local constitutional arrangement made for the colony, but in broad measure the Western Pacific High Commission systems continued to operate. The High Commission promulgated a number of regulations in the late nineteenth century, which extended to Tokelau.[5] They concerned arms[6] and alcohol[7] and were broadly promulgated in the context of the protectorate system. Later, in the twentieth century, the laws of the protectorate began to address the behaviour of local inhabitants,[8] and in the case of Tokelau this was fully taken over when Tokelau was integrated into the Gilbert and Ellice Islands Colony in 1916.[9]

An early document providing for local criminal process was the Native Laws of the Union Group 1912.[10] This document was promulgated in both Samoan and English and in brief form established a constitution for the village of each island and set up a Magistrate and a Vaipuli (Faipule) in each island who were 'responsible for the good order of the island'. It was the task of the Magistrate and Vaipuli to appoint police as necessary on the island and also to hold court on each island on the first Wednesday of every month. That monthly meeting was to 'also receive reports, and discuss the conduct and behaviour of the people generally, and all matters relating to a proper observance of the laws, and to the welfare of the island'. The basic procedure for the holding of court, and that related to criminal process, was set out. The process established was inquisitorial, with the Magistrate in control. In a second part were set out Laws I to XXIV. These laws were almost exclusively penal in nature and prescribed the penalties for the commission of various offences.

The rules proceeded on the basis of a number of assumptions. Typical is Law number I, entitled murder. It stated: 'The punishment for taking the life of another is death'. A similar pattern was followed in respect to assault, theft and adultery. Some of the offences were locally relevant, but others were the offences that might be expected in any community. The offences of adultery and fornication, slander, or cutting down or injuring trees are all of substantial significance. The other area of adaptation to the local circumstance was shown in the law relating to fines, which provided that when a person convicted of an offence could not pay the fine in money, the Magistrate could order that it be paid in coconuts at rates prescribed in the law itself. The law also provided that only the Magistrate and Vaipuli could lawfully inflict fines on the people and further that it was an offence for any person other than the Magistrate to assume magisterial powers and hear a charge. There was also a provision for appeal from the judgment of the Magistrate and Vaipuli to the British Resident in any case where a person felt he or she had not been treated justly.

The Magistrate and Vaipuli had a legislative power and could make regulations and impose penalties for the breach of those regulations. What these native laws purported to provide was a system of native government. With the establishment of the colony, Tokelau saw the native law system formalized by the Native Laws Ordinance 1917 and the entry into force for

Tokelau of the Gilbert and Ellice Gaol and Prison Ordinance 1916 and the Gilbert and Ellice Constabulary Ordinance 1916. The main feature of the Native Laws Ordinance 1917 is the Schedule, which is in two parts. These parts echo the Native Laws of 1912. Part 1 is a constitution and Part 2 a set of laws. Under this ordinance a native Magistrate was to be appointed for each island and his role was to include 'the administration of the Native Laws and Regulations, and the supervision of the Island Police, prisoners and prisons'. It was further provided that the Magistrate should decide all matters brought before him 'according to the law'. The Native Laws Ordinance also provided for the appointment of island police in each village.

Provision was made for the Magistrate assisted by the Kaubure[11] to hold a monthly court on the first Wednesday of each month. The Magistrate could have the assistance of six Kaubure to help him inquire into a case. In every case of supposed murder, there was a requirement that the Magistrate be assisted by at least twelve Kaubure. The role of the Magistrate in all cases except murder trials was that of an inquisitor. In the absence of the native Magistrate from illness or other unavoidable cause, his duties were to be discharged by the Chief Kaubure. The District Officer, on behalf of the Resident Commissioner of the Western Pacific High Commissioner, had the power to review any sentence imposed by the Native Court. Part 2 was similar to the Native Laws of 1912, but included some new offences (e.g., sorcery) and some new provisions relating to criminal procedure.[12]

The consequence of all of this was that, at the time the Union Islands (Tokelau) were integrated into the Gilbert and Ellice Islands Colony, they had a criminal law system of a European kind. There was a system of local courts for local people and a system of external courts for British subjects. There was also a system of prisons, an armed constabulary run by the government, and a system of native police under the control of each village government. The system of local courts had the external appearance of courts in the European legal mould. It was a clear indication of the rule of law and of the principles of no crime without a law and no punishment without a law.

The operation of the system in practice, however, must have been very different from the operation of tribunals in England. The process was controlled by the Magistrate who, if recent experience of the village courts is anything to go by, would have spoken Tokelauan and have read and spoken Samoan, but would have been unlikely to have a reading or speaking knowledge of English. Certainly, the Magistrates' knowledge of English law would have been limited to the impressions they gained from the ordinances and from anything gathered from visiting British officials. The substantive content of many of the offences would therefore have been provided for by local experience and not by the English case law.

Tokelau ceased to be part of the Gilbert and Ellice Islands Colony in 1926[13] and was from then until 1949 administered by New Zealand from Western

Samoa.[14]   This was a period of no legislative activity in terms of the criminal law and criminal process.

The Tokelau Act 1948 of New Zealand served to integrate the three northernmost atolls of the Tokelau group into New Zealand and also provided for the continuance in force of all existing laws except where they were inconsistent with any New Zealand acts or regulations in force in Tokelau. Tokelau continued to be administered from New Zealand offices in Apia in Western Samoa.

No legal change in the criminal law area occurred until 1969, when Section 4A was added to the Tokelau Act 1948. This section provides for the law of England of 14 January 1840 to be the law of Tokelau where there is no relevant legislation.[15]   This was the first step towards an integration of the law of Tokelau and that of New Zealand in the sense of common structures and common principles. The law in New Zealand had, as its base system, the Law of England of 14 January 1840.[16] Tokelau and New Zealand therefore had a common base for their laws—that of the deemed settlement of New Zealand by British settlers. There is no evidence that this new principle was known about or had any effect in Tokelau. The main potential the new section had was to displace custom or tradition of Tokelau, if it had been maintained under Section 5. The ostensible effect of Section 4A was to have the law of England of 1840 take precedence over that custom.

The next significant step in the alignment of New Zealand and Tokelau laws was the passage of the Tokelau Amendment Act 1970 [17] which, among other things, provided for a 'New Zealand' system of courts for Tokelau. That system was based on the idea of the appointment of a Commissioner for each atoll. In the absence of the Commissioner, the Faipule of each atoll was empowered to act as Commissioner. Above that court was the High Court of Niue and the High Court of New Zealand and beyond them the New Zealand Court of Appeal and the Judicial Committee of the Privy Council. Appeal on some land matters was to the Niue Land Court. At the same time Tokelau Crimes Regulations were promulgated and they came into force in 1975.

The Tokelau Crimes Regulations 1975 were not drawn up specifically for Tokelau but were the simple transplanting of Parts V, VI and VII of the Niue Act 1966 into the Tokelau legal system. Those Parts provide a criminal code and a basic set of procedure and evidence rules. By comparison with anything Tokelau had previously had, this set of regulations was elaborate. The list of offences, though borrowed from Niue, had its origins in New Zealand law and showed close links to the criminal code of New Zealand, which in turn had been based on the drafts of Sir James Fitzjames Stephen. In 1975, therefore, for the first time, Tokelau had a criminal law that demanded legal knowledge and expertise for its proper implementation. The 1975 regulations also proceeded on the basis of a code of criminal law in that no act or omission was to be punishable unless it was proscribed by legislation. The impact of the

1975 regulations in Tokelau at the village level is difficult to assess, but ten years later (in 1985) there was no evidence that anybody knew of the change of law and one of the atolls at least was still operating under the Native Laws Ordinance of 1917.

The new crimes regulations were ineffective practically because they were not known. Legally their fate was worse. The Tokelau Crimes Regulations 1975 were timed to come into force along with the Tokelau Amendment Act 1970. That Act was duly proclaimed for 1 December 1975 and on that date the Native Laws Ordinance 1917 ceased to have effect as part of Tokelau's law and its place was taken by the new regulations.

The Tokelau Amendment Act 1970 provided for the courts of Niue to be the principal courts for Tokelau. In 1970 Niue was part of New Zealand. In 1974 Niue became a self-governing state in association with New Zealand, and New Zealand lost the power to make laws for it except in accordance with the request and consent procedure of the Niue Constitution. The process was not followed in respect of the Tokelau Amendment Act 1970, with the result that the courts of Niue did not become courts for Tokelau. With only a limited jurisdiction given to the local lay judges of Tokelau, it was legally impossible to prosecute any serious breach of Tokelau law. Initially a NZ$20 fine was the maximum penalty that a Tokelau Commissioner could impose. That was amended in 1983 to allow fines of up to NZ$150. In one incident in the 1980s where rape was alleged to have been committed, the best the Commissioner could do was to hear the case as a case of common assault (the crime of rape was beyond his jurisdiction) and on guilt established impose a fine not exceeding NZ$150.

The 1970 Amendment Act did also vest power in the New Zealand Supreme Court but only in respect of 'indictable' offences and only if the accused was 'found in' metropolitan New Zealand. The Tokelau Amendment Act 1986 was enacted specifically in the light of criminal law reform debate taking place in Tokelau in 1986 and with a view to providing a proper constitutional framework within which any new regulations could operate. That act in particular established a new court structure for Tokelau, extended the jurisdiction of the local Commissioners, and expressly recognized the range of customary penalties that would be imposed by the elders in Tokelau. The court system established was that of the court of first instance in Tokelau, with a civil and criminal jurisdiction limited both in terms of the offences that could be dealt with and in terms of the penalties that could be imposed; a court of general jurisdiction; and the High Court of New Zealand acting as a High Court for Tokelau, with appeals being sent to the New Zealand Court of Appeal. The significant changes in this matter were the removal of all references to the Niue courts (which by that time had ceased to have jurisdiction because Niue had become independent and had not requested and consented to the legislation of New Zealand, which gave its courts jurisdiction in respect of Tokelau matters).

The other feature of the legislation was that the New Zealand Court of Appeal was made the final Court of Appeal in any Tokelau matter. In terms of the penalties that could be imposed, the law specifically recognized customary penalties such as reprimand and community service.

REFORM—THE PROCESS

Tokelau was in 1962 placed on the United Nations list of non-self-governing territories to be prepared for self-determination. The Committee of 24 first sent a visiting mission to Tokelau in 1976. In its report to the United Nations, the Visiting Committee commented on the state of law for Tokelau and noted an undertaking by the New Zealand government to look into the matter. New Zealand government officers had over the years maintained records of the legislation in force in Tokelau and had in 1975 made efforts substantially to reform the Tokelau law and make it more accessible. The goal in 1975 had been, by regulations made under Section 4 of the Tokelau Act 1948, to repeal all the subordinate legislation of previous administrative eras and incorporate in a single set of regulations those rules that were still of value to the Tokelau community. At the eleventh hour that piece of legislation was not proceeded with, and the result is that many of the pre-1949 pieces of legislation of Tokelau remain in force and in desuetude.[18] When the second United Nations mission visited Tokelau in 1981, the New Zealand government made a report on the state of the law in Tokelau and signalled the establishment of the Tokelau Law Project.

The Tokelau Law Project had a number of tasks.[19] The first step of those involved in the project was to identify and consolidate the legislation applicable to Tokelau[20] and further to seek to establish the extent of its relevance or appropriateness to the Tokelau situation.[21] Those involved with the project also spent some time working on translating terms that could be used to communicate important legal ideas to the Tokelauan community. Following that, a bilingual text[22] was prepared for the local Magistrate (the Commissioner) on each island to assist with their hearing of cases in the exercise of their jurisdiction under the Tokelau Amendment Act 1970. The handbook provided a brief description of the law and system of government that applied in Tokelau, and of the position of the local Magistrate within that system of government. The rest of the handbook was devoted to a description of the offences established under the Tokelau Crimes Regulations 1975 and the proper manner of their prosecution and resolution in the local court.

At the Tokelau level, the first signs of the Tokelau Law Project endeavours were seen in July 1983, when a Law Project team arrived to have a preliminary discussion with elders about the nature of law and the role of the Tokelau Law Project. That team comprised the Official Secretary for Tokelau (a senior officer of the Ministry of Foreign Affairs of New Zealand), the senior Tokelauan translator and interpreter, and two lawyers, one from the legal division of the Ministry of Foreign Affairs in Wellington, New Zealand, and the other from the Law Faculty of the Victoria University of Wellington.[23] The three days of discussion were held in Fakaofo.

The visiting delegation presented the prepared documents, which were the collection of laws in force,[24] the draft Commissioners' Handbook, and a statement of the nature of law and how it was distinguished from custom and tradition. In turn the elders of Fakaofo presented a written statement of their understanding of what law was in their particular community. The elders of the other two islands in turn described what was, for them, law.

It was clear from that meeting that there was much lack of understanding on both sides about the nature of the other's rule system and, from the point of view of the Tokelauans, considerable disquiet both over the fact that there might be some rule system that was over and above that administered by the elders in accordance with tradition, and over what the need for that other system might be. The meeting ended with general agreement that there should be further investigation of the interrelationship of law and custom and that further information on the law for Tokelau and its operation would be provided to the elders. In turn the elders would provide further information on the operation of their customary rules within each village.

This visit was followed by many others over the next six years. All of those visits were concerned with the brief of the Law Project team, the clarification of the law for Tokelau and, in reform terms, the adaptation of it to the needs of Tokelau. It soon became clear that one of the main areas of endeavour was to be the review and reform of the laws relating to crimes and criminal procedure. That process began in 1984.

The Tokelau Amendment Act 1970 and the Tokelau Crimes Regulations 1975 had established a theoretically complete system. The goal of the reform endeavour was to revise the criminal law and put in place a system that was both adapted to the substantive needs of Tokelau and practical in terms of the resources available in Tokelau.

The reform process began with an investigation of what was happening in Tokelau in terms of the operation of criminal law. The view of what the legal offences were varied from island to island. In some cases they were simply the customary ones, and in Nukunonu the view was that the Native Laws Ordinance of 1917 remained in force. The island *perception* of the law was therefore clearly something different from the law itself.

The practice in the field of criminal law, as far as could be ascertained, was something different again. In all cases it was the Faipule, usually with the assistance of the village elders, who acted as the judge and imposed the penalty. The offences noted were all of a kind that in a metropolitan environment would be regarded as petty or lesser crimes. Adultery, fornication, rumour mongering, drunkenness, and a few cases of petty theft were found to occur and to be punished on a reasonably regular and consistent basis. The punishments imposed were typically community service and in some cases a monetary fine (ranging from a few dollars to about NZ$70 in exceptional cases). The offence which attracted the heaviest fines was adultery.

It is interesting to note that the substance of an offence, even where it was one identifiable with the law technically in force, reflected the substantive content of the Tokelau tradition. Therefore, in the case of assault, the offence was held to have been committed if there was a breaking of the skin. Equally, adultery and fornication, though distinguished, were typically referred to as the offence of 'pregnancy' because the evidence in most cases was the state of pregnancy of the woman concerned. Punishment was applied equally both to the man and the woman in an adultery or fornication situation, and in those cases where they were free to marry, that was the usual consequence of the case. There was no evidence of any difficulty in identifying the male party, though it is not impossible that in the case of promiscuity, the wrong male was sometimes registered as the father of the child.

The punishment meted out for offences was one consistent with custom rather than the law. Preference was clearly for community service and, for offenders with access to money, a fine which was paid into the village account. Also common was a public reprimand, and in the case of children, corporal punishment. The law provides frequently for imprisonment as the main punishment but, as there are no prisons in Tokelau, this was not an option used. There is, further, no indication of a need for prisons nor of any desire to have prisons. In the few cases where restraint of an offender is required, that is usually provided by the police detaining the person in their office for a few hours. The only known instances of this were in respect of males who were in an intoxicated state.

The Tokelau Amendment Act 1970 provided for the appointment of a Commissioner on each island to act as the island's judicial officer. This person was appointed by warrant of the Governor-General and held office during good behaviour or until retirement at the age of 68.[25] As of 1983, a number of officers had been warranted and the system worked reasonably well while the warranted Commissioner was also the same individual as the Faipule of the island. In two instances in the 1980s new Faipule were elected by the villagers while the warrant of the preceding Faipule remained in force. At the village level, there was the perception that the person who should be the Commissioner was the Faipule for the time being. In one case, the warranted Commissioner was boycotted and any judicial powers that were exercised were exercised by the new Faipule. In the other case, agreement was reached between the new Faipule and the Commissioner. The Commissioner continued to perform the judicial function as the need arose until he reached the retirement age of 68. At that point, by virtue of the operation of Section 9A(1) of the 1970 Amendment

Act, the Faipule became the acting Commissioner and at a community level the two offices then coincided.   Since that difficulty of differentiation between offices, no further warrants have been issued by the Governor-General for independent judicial officers in Tokelau.

The process set in place for the reform of criminal law was one of consultation and discussion with the communities of Tokelau through their Councils of Elders.   In all, there were about twenty meetings on criminal law during the period 1984-1986.   Some of those meetings were with the island councils and some with specially convened meetings of the representative elders of each of the three islands.   Almost all took place in traditional form in open-sided meeting houses (*fale fono*), with the elders seated crosslegged around the space on plaited mats.   Fresh drinking nuts were provided as the heat of the day and rigours of discussion required.

The process began with an explanation of the existing legal situation, of the reasons for the review of the existing law, and also of the opportunities that the review presented for the law and tradition to be brought into closer alignment. The elders were very interested in the project and spent a great deal of time considering the various issues that were involved.   At one of the first meetings, however, it became clear that there were a number of assumptions about law and its operation which could not be made in the Tokelau circumstance.   The elders therefore requested that they be advised on the law as it stood and its relationship to what they were doing before they proceeded to consider a revised law.   Accordingly, meetings were held at which each of the provisions of the Tokelau Crimes Regulations 1975 was discussed and practical examples were given of its operation.   Much reform work was in fact done during those discussions because it was clear that some of the offences were not known, were not needed, or would not be applied in Tokelau.   It also became clear in the discussion of some of the provisions that there were other similar offences which Tokelau would regard as warranting penal sanction which were not included.   The result was the preparation of a new list of offences for Tokelau.

The next step in the process was to work through that new list, with the citation of practical examples, to ensure that indeed these were the offences, the actions or omissions, that the community wished to punish and that their content was understood.   Inevitably the list included a number of activities which were not then known in Tokelau but which the elders, after explanation, believed appropriate to include in the interests of the community.   There was, for instance, no evidence of murders or prostitution in the community.   The elders, however, voted in favour of retention of the crimes of murder and manslaughter and also that of prostitution.   Prostitution required a considerable amount of discussion because many of the elders did not understand the nature of the offence.   For most, the only link within their experience was with the Old Testament biblical story involving Rahab.[26]   The clear feeling was that if the practice occurred in Tokelau they would wish to punish those involved.

All the discussions proceeded on the basis of a bilingual commentary. The material was introduced in English and then translated into Tokelauan. The discussion of the material was all in Tokelauan. Following the compilation of the list of offences, a draft Crimes Regulations was drawn up and approved. At the same time, the elders were invited to comment on the questions of penalty and jurisdiction. Those decisions had to be taken in the context of the Tokelau Amendment Act 1970.

The Tokelau Amendment Act 1970 was repealed by the Tokelau Amendment Act 1986. It put in place a suitable framework for the Tokelau criminal law and was informed by the discussions in Tokelau but otherwise was of no great concern to the reform process in Tokelau, primarily because there is very little activity that would be qualified as criminal in Tokelau and further because the penalties imposed are, in terms of the jurisdictional thresholds, very small.

The elders made three decisions in the context of the draft regulations: they decided on the inclusion of a particular matter as an offence for Tokelau; they decided on the maximum penalties that might be imposed for that offence; they decided which judge or court should have the authority to hear the case.

For almost all offences, the decision was that the penalty should not exceed a NZ$150 fine or three months' imprisonment, which meant that jurisdiction would be with the island Commissioner. In a few cases (mostly those that the elders regarded as very serious and with which they had little practical experience), they chose jurisdiction in the alternative either by a Commissioner or in the High Court. For these offences, the possible penalty was up to a $1000 fine or one year's imprisonment. Even in those cases, if the matter was prosecuted before a Commissioner, the maximum penalty that could be imposed would be a $150 fine or three months' imprisonment. In only three cases did the elders choose not to have the option of the exercise of jurisdiction locally. These were murder, manslaughter, and treason—matters of which they had a clear understanding, but of which they had no practical experience. Their clearly expressed view on these three offences was that if such a serious matter occurred, then they would prefer not to be involved with the trial of it,[27] while the clear pattern in respect of all other matters, particularly where the offender was a Tokelauan, was that they were community matters and should be dealt with by the community within the community. In the case of homicide and treason, the elders were clearly of the view that this was something the community was not well equipped to deal with and would wish therefore to remove itself from involvement.

The communities have little idea of the nature or role of the international covenants relating to human rights. Part of the reason for this is simply lack of information and lack of knowledge. Another aspect is the conceptual difference about the nature of human relations between what is expounded in the various international covenants and what is the traditional way of life in Tokelau. The tradition of Tokelau is communalistic, not individualistic. The tradition has many examples of individualism as a cause of danger, not only to the person concerned but to the community at large. Individualism in the egocentric, egotistical sense is therefore not a social trait that exists or is encouraged. The thought that an individual may have rights that could be sustained over and against the community or the will of the elders is not readily comprehended by the communities and, if comprehended, not easily accepted by most. The communities in fact must, until very recent times, have been very close to the communist ideal in that everyone was expected to give and did give according to their ability and everybody received equally according to their need. The subsistence living conditions and the absence of any significant items of personal property of an enduring nature reinforced the communal ethic.

The reform discussions had nevertheless to take place within the general context of the international covenants because many are binding in Tokelau.[28] Within the criminal law area, the most significant impact is from Article 14 of the International Covenant on Civil and Political Rights. In criminal matters this covenant gives an accused certain rights which effectively require the operation of a court system, the administration of laws in the Western tradition and the availability of access to legal advice. The covenant also requires an appeal system.

Because of Tokelau tradition, the operation of an appeal system gave rise to considerable debate and considerable difficulty. First, it was not generally acceptable that a local matter should be dealt with outside the community. Acceptance of this cultural constraint effectively precluded the use of an external non-Tokelauan judge. It also became clear in the discussions that Tokelau practice excluded the use of judges from islands other than the island from which the judgment was being appealed. It was in the end agreed that for the great bulk of cases, an internal appeal body would be established on each island to fulfil the requirements of the covenant and that in those few more serious cases not covered by that system, the appeal would be to the High Court of New Zealand acting as a court for Tokelau.

The question of legal advice did not prove to be any problem at the island level. At the level of the New Zealand Parliament, however, there was some difficulty in the formulation of the 1986 Amendment Act. It was originally proposed that counsel be referred to in Section 7(4); there was a presumption that counsel would be present. At a late stage, the reference to counsel was made parenthetically in recognition of the Tokelau realities—at present there is no evidence of interest on the part of anybody (offenders, police or lay judges) to use lawyers, and there are no lawyers in Tokelau, nor are there any legally trained Tokelauans. If there was a demand by an accused for access to legal advice, that would have to be provided from outside Tokelau and it would be provided at the expense of the Tokelau government. Most trials in which a lawyer might be involved would have to be done by translation from start to finish.

The question of who can practise law in Tokelau was also a matter of some discussion. The Western Pacific Order in Council provided that the High Commissioner for the Western Pacific could admit fit persons to practise in the Court as barristers and solicitors and could make rules for admitting such people to practise. It may still, technically speaking, have some relevance to Tokelau. Also, there is provision in the Tokelau Crimes Regulations 1975 in respect of the right to be defended.[29] The decision of the elders in respect of the practice of law in Tokelau was incorporated into the draft regulations.

THE DRAFT CRIMES PROCEDURE AND EVIDENCE REGULATIONS

The full catalogue of offences identified by the elders is set out in the Appendix to this chapter.[30] The offences of most relevance to the communities on a daily basis are adultery and fornication, unmarried persons living together, animal trespass, spreading of rumours, fighting in public, noise, throwing of stones, invasion of privacy, intoxicating liquor, tobacco, drunkenness, and school attendance. Many of these are not covered by existing laws.

Of particular interest is the provision about school attendance. In colonial times, there was a requirement for parents to send their children to school.[31] That provision was abrogated with the repeal of the ordinance in 1975. There was then technically, from 1975, no legislation at all relating to schooling. The practice in Tokelau, however, was clear. Whether this was influenced by the 1917 ordinance or not is unknown, but the villages require all children to go to school until the age of 16. That provision was therefore incorporated in the new draft regulations.

Several offences gave rise to special discussion. One was trespass. The reason here was not that trespass is unknown but that the nature of trespass in Tokelau varies significantly from that of the common law. In some cases, in Tokelauan custom, access to land is forbidden both by the owners and others and entry punished by the elders. That is in respect of land declared *lafu*. However, in respect of land (as distinguished from buildings), generally the offence is in what is done on the land rather than the fact of being on the land. In other words, passage across the land is not in itself a trespass. However, use of the land to create a building or to take coconuts or to damage a tree is punishable. The trespass therefore resides in the wrongful use of the land, not in presence on the land.

Witchcraft also provoked discussion. The offence of witchcraft is in the Tokelau Crimes Regulations of 1975 [32] but was not known to Tokelau and was something which conceptually proved to be very difficult to explain in Tokelau. Here again, as in the case of prostitution, references were made to biblical texts. There were several extended debates about witchcraft both in terms of its meaning and as to whether it should be retained as an offence for Tokelau. At the final debate on the matter, before which it had been broadly agreed that the offence would be retained, there was further discussion which focussed on the difficulty of distinguishing what was prohibited and what took place on a regular and acceptable basis within the community. Three examples in particular were cited. One related to the religious leaders in the community and how what they did (which in some instances seemed to resemble the legal description of witchcraft) should be distinguished from the offence. Another example was the role of the knowledgeable elders in the community who, by their understanding of the environment and lunar and other cycles, could predict the best times for fishing and other events. And third, there was the distinction to be made between a witch and those skilled persons in the community who practised traditional medicine.[33] The final vote was a unanimous one, in favour of the retention of the offence. While the reason for that decision was not expressed, it might have been able to be assumed, in a strongly committed Christian community, that the offence would be retained. Even though it was ill-understood, the motivating factor behind the decision is likely to be the same that caused the English legal system to introduce the offence of witchcraft centuries ago—probably as much an act of faith as a desire to protect the inexperienced and the gullible from exploitation.

Other provisions warranting comment are the prohibition on the use of dangerous drugs; the offences relating to public boats, the visiting vessel, and sea voyages; and the references to telephones and electricity. None of these matters are in the existing law. All but the offence relating to dangerous drugs were within the local experience. The availability of electricity and telephones is relatively recent for Tokelau, but both gave rise to local concerns in respect of damage to reticulation systems (usually by children) and interference with the reticulation systems (typically by unqualified people). The proscription on ill-prepared sea voyages is another matter within local knowledge. Since Tokelau is far from any search and rescue operation, the person who leaves Tokelau unprepared for being on the high seas is likely to cause both a good deal of distress to, and risk taking by, those left behind and, further, is likely to die if swept offshore by bad weather. The visiting vessel which brings supplies has caused troubles from those who board the vessel and commit petty thefts or make a nuisance of themselves during the loading and unloading operations. There is no report at present of dangerous drugs in Tokelau and no evidence of any use of them. The community had, however, a limited knowledge of the existence of such substances and the harm they could cause. When the question was asked whether they would think it appropriate to create an offence in respect of the import and use of such substances, the answer was clear. The answer was also clear that this was a serious matter, because the offence was one which the elders did not reserve for trial by the Commissioner alone.[34]

The offence of failure to assist was new to the law. It was an idea strongly supported by tradition and was seen by the elders to reflect the communal nature of the social environment. On the question of the effect of drunkenness on criminal liability, the view was clear too. Those who drink alcohol must take responsibility for their actions—drinking is no excuse. Drunkenness is a social problem in Tokelau from time to time, and custom has developed strong rules about it.[35] Given the absence of prisons and also the lack of cash and the preference for community service as a punishment, the elders agreed to a conversion table for fines or imprisonment to periods of community service.[36]

The procedural part of the draft Crimes Regulations was equally as significant from a legal point of view as the substantive part, but in the community considerably less time was taken in the discussion and consideration of this. The community had a very clear view of how proceedings should be conducted (i.e., the way they traditionally conducted them) and wished that process as far as possible to be incorporated into the law. In the context of a draft which substantially did that, there was therefore no great room for debate. The procedural provisions (amounting to half of the total number of clauses in the regulations)[37] were nevertheless dealt with on the same basis as the substantive rules, in the sense that each rule was dealt with individually, its purpose discussed and specific examples of its operation given.

From the point of view of the existing law and common law principles generally, however, there are several significant features in the procedural part of the regulations. The first to note is that in process terms, there is considerable flexibility and one might say, from an outsider's point of view, considerable informality. The regulations do not preclude formality but do recognize the existing state of affairs, which is that if a member of the community is called to attend the Commissioner's court, he or she will attend willingly and without the necessity of constraint. There is also typically no need for any document to be issued to achieve that purpose. In a small, close-knit community whose culture is oral rather than literal, this makes sense. It also makes sense in the context of an equatorial climate, where the handling of documents is more than usually difficult. At the very least, insects, sun and humidity, and the not infrequent cyclones, take their toll on even the most carefully protected items. The community is not document oriented and as a consequence does not have the facilities for dealing with documents in the way that is taken for granted in an urban community.

Another significant feature of the process is that it is expressly inquisitorial. In legal terms there is nothing in that that warrants comment. It is, however, unusual in a common law context, and the assumption of the existing laws is of an accusatorial or adversarial system process. Tokelauan custom and tradition is very clearly of an inquisitorial nature, and the continental European approach to court process is much more suited to the Tokelau cultural environment than the common law one. Interestingly, the first common law system operative in the region under the Pacific Order in Council of 1877 had an inquisitorial process. That process was maintained and instituted at the local level through various laws and in particular through the Native Laws Ordinance 1917. For Tokelau it was only in 1975, with the repeal of that ordinance and the introduction of the Tokelau Crimes Regulations 1975, that the cultural discrepancy between community and legal expectations of the criminal process emerged. The elders also expressly claimed the retention of a cultural element (which also appeared in the Order in Council of 1877)—the emphasis on conciliation and settlement in matters, whether of a criminal or civil nature.

The debate on the criminal law proceeded within a number of parameters. One was the existence of the international covenants on human rights. Another was the principle of separation of powers. The separation of powers doctrine was readily comprehended by the elders but was something they had no practical experience with, and there was therefore considerable doubt about its applicability in the Tokelau situation. Tokelau is run by the elders on the basis of the community's ideas as they are filtered through to the elders by the head of each family who, by definition, is a member of the Council of Elders. The Council of Elders traditionally and perhaps, given the size of the communities, by necessity operated as the holder of all forms of governmental power. Even when in colonial legislation the various powers were separated, the holder of the powers was, in each case, the same: the Magistrate and Faipule could make laws, the Magistrate and Faipule could judge in the courts, and they also had executive functions. The powers were therefore separated, but the holder was typically one and the same person. The thrust of the New Zealand-based law was not only to separate the powers but also to attempt to provide for the powers to be held by different persons or bodies. The law reform discussions proceeded very well on the basis of these presumptions until at a late stage the rule of *nolle prosequi* was discussed. It was discussed because it exists in the present Tokelau Crimes Regulations 1975.[38]   There were two immediate responses from the elders to its inclusion. The first was that it was against the separation of powers, and the second was that it was not needed. The power was, on external advice, retained but would happily have been foregone by the elders.

On the civil side, there is little to remark. The process is inquisitorial and is consistent with the general expectations of a lawyer. This area of legal action was outside the experience of the elders of Tokelau. What they regarded as a court was a body concerned with the imposition of punishments—probably because there were no significant items of personal property or private wealth. There is no record of any civil claim coming before a Commissioner's court. The main item of property in Tokelau is land, and that is expressly excluded from the jurisdiction of the courts by the Tokelau Amendment Act 1967. All matters arising in connection with title to, or beneficial use of, land are governed by the customs and usages of the inhabitants of the island in question.[39]   In other words, land matters are settled by the elders in accordance with their traditional methods. The community did not regard land issues as civil litigation matters.

One feature of civil claims was clear to the elders. This was the question of claims for damages for personal injury. Such claims were unknown in Tokelau and unacceptable in cultural terms. The draft regulations therefore state that there shall be no civil action for personal injury in Tokelau. The community is, however, sensitive to the plight of those who suffer personal injury by accident and has for some years been operating a system of accident compensation under which the elders can grant lump sum payments to those who suffer personal injury by accident. Whether that system was inspired by the introduction of the accident compensation system in New Zealand in 1972 is unknown. However, it was instituted in Tokelau some years after the introduction of accident compensation in New Zealand.[40]

In all civil matters, as indeed in land matters, the Tokelau expectation is that the matter will be settled amicably out of court as a result of discussion between the parties and their families or in the Council of Elders. This attitude, too, would account for the lack of experience in bringing civil claims to the Commissioners' courts, particularly in recent years, when they might have been expected to arise as a result of the increase in the number of valuable items of personal property, such as outboard motors, television sets, radios and aluminium dinghies. Another feature of the society is, of course, that usually there can be no dispute about the ownership of such an item, simply because everyone in the village knows what belongs to whom. If there is a debate about property, it is most likely to be about a fishing knife that has been found on the beach. Then the debate is not about whose knife it was originally but whether it had been thrown away or abandoned and may therefore become the property of a new owner. Building materials, such as roofing iron, are less readily identifiable individually, but even there, experience would suggest that the community generally has a very good idea of what belongs to whom and the chances for debate about ownership are extremely limited. The wrongful use of roofing iron is more likely to be dealt with by the elders as a criminal matter or in response to an appeal for the return of the goods.

The draft regulations also deal with rules of evidence. This is necessary to the coherence of the regulations generally, given the absence of any other law relating to evidence outside of the common law principles; the existing Tokelau Crimes Regulation 1975 have a part dedicated to the rules of evidence.[41] There was a good deal of debate about the rules of evidence, but the prime concern was for understanding, and therefore the discussion was principally for the purposes of transfer of information.

CONCLUSION

In their final form as approved by the full Council of Tokelau (the General Fono), the draft Tokelau Crimes Procedure and Evidence Regulations were presented to the Administrator of Tokelau in Wellington for promulgation by the Governor-General by Order in Council under Section 4 of the Tokelau Act 1948. It was some time before the regulations got into the legislative programme in New Zealand. Though they have not yet been promulgated, their importance to the operation of the legal system and to Tokelau has been recognized.

One of the important functions of the exercise relating to the reform of the crimes, procedure and evidence rules of Tokelau was the communal involvement and the educative effect. The elders, and through them, the extended community, took a great deal of interest in learning about the law, learning about its possible adaptation to meet the circumstances of Tokelau and the role of the elders in the operation of the laws. The hope with these reform discussions, as with others in the context of the Tokelau Law Project, was that, after the approval of draft regulations which had been so thoroughly discussed and for which there was such support, all would go well for the implementation of the regulations in practice. Those who would have the responsibility for implementing them had in fact a good knowledge of their content and had been responsible for their promulgation.

With the passage of time, much of that impetus has been lost. The very nature of the role of an elder is that it can be short-lived. When the regulations are eventually promulgated, there will need to be a new and extensive round of discussions in the community to inform the new generation of elders and those responsible for the application of the regulations. In much the same way as the Tokelau Village Incorporation Regulations 1986,[42] the new Crimes, Procedure and Evidence Regulations will restore to Tokelau a system to which it had become somewhat accustomed in the colonial period and give it laws more in keeping with its environment.

NOTES

1. The following bibliography is useful for background reading on Tokelau:

Angelo, A. H. (1987) 'Tokelau—Its Legal System and Recent Legislation', *Otago Law Review,* 6: 477-98.

Angelo, A. H. (1988) 'The Common Law in New Zealand and Tokelau', *Melanesian Law Journal,* 16: 1-27.

Angelo, A. H. (1988) 'Tokelau - The Village Rules of 1988', *Queensland University of Technology Law Journal,* 4: 209-24.

Angelo, A. H., Kirifi, H. and Fong Toy A. (1989) 'Law and Tokelau', *Pacific Studies* 12: 3, 29-52.

Gordon, R. (1990) *Tokelau—A Collection of Documents and References Relating to Constitutional Development*, Apia: Tokelau Administration.

Hooper, A. (1982) *Aid and Dependency in a Small Pacific Territory*, Working Paper No 62, September, Auckland: Department of Anthropology, University of Auckland.

Report of the Administrator of Tokelau for the Year Ended 31 March 1991.

Report of the United Nations Visiting Mission to Tokelau (1986) A/AC 109/877 and Add 1.

'Tokelau', in Ntumy (ed.) (1993) *South Pacific Islands Legal Systems,* Hawaii: University of Hawaii Press, 1993.

2. The full name of the committee is the 'Special Committee on the Situation with regard to the Implementation of the Declaration on the Granting of Independence to Colonial Countries and Peoples'. The committee first sent a delegation to Tokelau in 1976. Following the report of that committee (A/31/23/Rev1, 1976) the New Zealand government began a law reform programme in the territory. Subsequent visits by the committee occurred in 1981 (report A/AC 109/680, 21 October 1981) and 1986 (report A/AC 109/877 and Add 1, 7 and 8 August 1986).

Tokelau was placed by New Zealand on the United Nation's list of dependent territories in 1962 (General Assembly Official Records, Eighteenth Session, Annexes, (addendum to agenda item 23A/5446/Rev1, 288-289).

3. Formal acceptance as a British protectorate occurred in 1889.

4. Rules relating to criminal law are found in Part IV (articles 23-55) of the Western Pacific Order in Council of 1877. Further provisions are found in the Schedule, Parts A (clauses 158-196) and B (clauses 197-237) and the Appendix to the Schedule, Part I (forms 1-33). The Orders are published in a consolidated form in Gordon R. (1990) *The Western Pacific Order in Council of 1877, The Pacific Order in Council 1893,* Wellington.

Rules relating to criminal law are also found in Part VI (articles 49-87). Further provisions are found in the Schedule, Parts A (clauses 1-7, with forms 1-3 appended) and C (clauses 83-113, with forms 1-23 and a scale of fees appended).

5. Tokelau was then known as the 'Union Islands'.

6. The Arms Regulation 1884, no 1 (*Fiji Royal Gazette 1884*: 87).

The Arms Regulation 1893, no 1 (*Fiji Royal Gazette 1893:* 76).

The Arms Regulation Amendment Regulation 1893, no 3 (*Fiji Royal Gazette 1893*: 320).

The aim of each of these regulations was to prohibit the supply of arms and ammunition to local native inhabitants. The Arms Regulation Amendment Regulation 1893 remains in force in Tokelau.

7. The Liquor Regulation 1888, no 4 (*Fiji Royal Gazette 1888:* 439 and

Fiji Royal Gazette 1889: 11), and the Liquor Regulation 1893, no 4 (*Fiji Royal Gazette 1893*: 323). These regulations prohibited the supply of intoxicating liquor to the local native inhabitants. The latter regulation, which repealed the earlier, is now no longer in force in Tokelau.

8. e.g., Native Contracts Regulation 1896; Small Islands Native Lands Regulation 1896; Wireless Telegraphy Regulation 1907.

9. The Gilbert and Ellice Islands Order in Council 1915 (*Statutory Rules and Orders and Statutory Instruments Revised to December 31, 1948*, Volume IX: 655) established the colony of the Gilbert and Ellice Islands and annexed it to Britain (clause 4). The Order in Council Annexing the Union Islands to the Gilbert and Ellice Islands Colony 1916, no 167 (*Statutory Rules and Orders and Statutory Instruments Revised to December 31, 1948*, Volume IX: 661) provided for the inclusion of Tokelau in the colony (clause I). It also meant that Tokelau was from that date subject to the laws of the colony.

10. Published by authority in Suva, Fiji, in 1914.

11. *Kaubure* is a Gilbertese word (in fact a loan word in Gilbertese) meaning 'chief' or 'member of the village council'. The Native Laws Ordinance was published in English, Samoan and Gilbertese. The word eventually taken over into Tokelauan for this official was the Samoan *Faipule*.

12. For example, it was provided that 'the punishment for any crime not provided for in the above laws should be based on the English laws, and any sentence imposed must receive the confirmation of the Resident Commissioner'—Part II, Law number 27.

13. The Union Islands (No 1) Order in Council 1925 passed administration of Tokelau from Tokelau to New Zealand. Under clause I of this document Tokelau was excluded from the Gilbert and Ellice Islands Colony.

14. The Union Islands (No 2) Order in Council 1925 formally transferred administration of Tokelau to New Zealand. Under clause I the Governor-General of Tokelau became the Governor of Tokelau, and under clause II could make laws for the 'peace, order and good government' of the islands. Under clause IV all laws in force when the order took effect were stated to remain in force.

15. Section 4A reads:

4A. Law of England as in 1840 to be in force in Tokelau—The law of England as existing on the 14th day of January in the year 1840 (being the year in which the Colony of New Zealand was established) shall be in force in Tokelau, save so far as inconsistent with this Act or inapplicable to the circumstances of Tokelau:

Provided that no Act of the Parliament of England or of Great Britain or of the United Kingdom passed before the said 14th day of January in the year 1840 shall be in force in Tokelau, unless and except so far as it is in force in New Zealand at the commencement of this section.

16. The Imperial Laws Act 1988, no 112, section 5. The act repealed its

predecessor the English Laws Act 1908, no 55 (section 2 of which was the equivalent of section 5).

17. No 41. Although the act is dated 1970, Part I (sections 2-12) dealing with civil and criminal jurisdiction did not come into force until 1 December 1975. See Tokelau Amendment Act Commencement Order 1975, Statutory Regulations 1975/261.

18. e.g. Arms Regulation Amendment Regulation 1893; Gilbert and Ellice (Consolidation) Ordinance 1917. For a full list see *Laws of Tokelau 1993* (Wellington, 1993) Vol 4: iii.

19. The published result of these endeavours was *Research and Revision of the Law of Tokelau—An Interim Report on Progress, May 1981* (Wellington: Ministry of Foreign Affairs). The volume sets out, on page 2, the early brief for the Tokelau Law Project:

1. To prepare a statement of the law presently in force in Tokelau.

2. To provide, by way of commentary or otherwise, the basis for a consolidated edition of the legislation in force in Tokelau; to indicate any legislative change by way of repeal, amendment, or addition necessary for the legislation—a) accurately to reflect the present constitutional and legal structures of Tokelau; b) to be internally consistent.

3. To report on the revision and reform of the Tokelau legislation with a view to the production of a systematic text in the nature of a revised Laws of Tokelau for the ready reference and use of those concerned with Tokelau law.

4. To investigate Tokelau custom with a view to its recognition by or incorporation in legislation where appropriate.

20. The result of this was a four-volume collection called *Tokelau Acts in Force as at 8 September 1983* (Wellington: Ministry of Foreign Affairs).

21. The findings were contained in *Research and Revision of the Law of Tokelau—Second Report, March 1984* (Wellington: Ministry of Foreign Affairs).

22. *A Handbook for the Commissioners 1984*.

23. Tony Browne, Hosea Kirifi, Frank Wong and Tony Angelo.

24. A consolidated collection of the regulations of the colonial period and those made under Section 4 of the Tokelau Act 1948.

25. Section 9.

26. Book of Joshua, ch 2.

27. One of the traditional punishments, probably the most serious of all of them, was banishment. In the case of decision of banishment, the offender or offenders were given a canoe and pushed out into the ocean and forbidden to return. This was clearly an effective way of dealing with incorrigible and disruptive elements in the community. For most, the decision of banishment would have been the equivalent of a death sentence. Allusions are still made in contemporary debate to this pattern of dealing with antisocial elements in the

community, and a mild form of the old punishment might still be exercised in practice by control of access to and egress from an island by the elders.

28. Tokelau is part of the State of New Zealand. As a result the international obligations which New Zealand signs also affect Tokelau e.g., ICCPR, ICSER, CEDAW, and optional protocols.

29. Tokelau Crimes Regulations 1975, regulation 3: 'Every person accused of any offence ... may make his full defence ... by himself, or by any barrister or solicitor of the High Court of New Zealand, or, with the prior leave of the High Court of New Zealand, by any other person'.

30. It forms the Second Schedule of the draft Crimes, Procedure and Evidence Regulations. It includes penalties and specifies which court has jurisdiction for each offence.

31. Native Laws Ordinance 1917, Part 1, regulation 13. All able-bodied children between ages 7 and 16 had to attend school.

32. It is Section 199 of the Niue Act 1966 which is in force in Tokelau by virtue of the Tokelau Crimes Regulations 1975. 'Every one is liable to imprisonment for a term not exceeding 6 months who pretends to exercise or use any kind of witchcraft, sorcery, enchantment, or conjuration, or undertakes to tell fortunes'.

33. In the case of Tokelau, traditional medicine is centred on the use of skills of a physiotherapeutic nature.

34. Perhaps not only because it was deemed especially serious but also because from their personal lack of knowledge of such offences; the assumption may also have been that the accused in such cases was likely to be someone from outside the community.

35. The problems are not only those of public order, but may also be of a domestic nature. In one village, for instance, a child died when a drunken father rolled on it in his sleep. Tokelau beer consumption is approximately one bottle of beer per person per day.

36. See Appendix to this paper. The list forms the Third Schedule of the draft *Tokelau Crimes, Procedure and Evidence Regulations*.

37. Part II, Regulations 82-161.

38. Section 283.

39. Section 20.

40. There is no express social security system operating in Tokelau. Health services and education are free and provided by the Tokelaua administration out of central funds. The accident compensation lump sum system is operated centrally by the elders; there is also an age allowance provided for the elderly out of central funds.

41. Part VII, sections 288-304.

42. New Zealand Statutory Regulations 1986/319. Debate on the role of the villages in law was begun at the same time as debate on the reform of the criminal law. This was a much shorter project in time and also produced a

much shorter draft law. The regulations give legal recognition to the existence of the villages, give the villages corporate status, and identify the customary leaders in the village as those with the various executive powers. The Tokelau Village Incorporation Regulations 1986 revested legal powers in the villages which existed in the Native Laws Ordinance 1917 but had been lost with the repeal of that ordinance in 1975.

APPENDIX

List of Offences

Murder
Manslaughter
Concealment of birth
Counselling suicide
Dangerous omission and things
Necessaries of life
Cruelty to a child
Abduction and detention of person or
  property
Detention of person or property
Bodily harm
Assault
Failure to assist
Incest
Unlawful carnal knowledge
Sexual intercourse with mental
  defectives
Indecent assault
Adultery and fornication
Unmarried persons living together
Miscarriage
Prostitution
Bigamy
Theft
Receiving
Conversion
Breach of trust
Fraud
Forgery
Counterfeit coin
Intentional fire

Obstruction of a public place
Fighting in public
Offensive behaviour
Noise
Throwing stones
Invasion of privacy
Drugs
Intoxicating liquor
Tobacco
Drunkenness
Use of explosives
Offensive weapons and disabling
  substances
Public boats
Use of vehicle and vessel
Endangering vessel
Visiting vessel
Poison
Polluting water
Unwholesome provisions
Insanitary premises
School attendance
Gaming
Witchcraft
Cruelty to animals
Telephones
Electricity
Sea voyages
Treason
Sedition
Official corruption

Careless fire   Abuse of office
Damage to property   Contempt
Animal trespass   False evidence
Trespass   Perverting justice
Indecent documents and things   Escape
False report to police   Offences against public officers
Accusation of offence   Law practice
Spreading rumour   Privileged communications

Community Service

Fine or period of imprisonment	Period of community service
$50 fine or up to 1 month's imprisonment	Not more than 1 month
From $50 and up to $100 fine, or imprisonment for more than 1 month but not more than 2 months	Not more than 2 months
From $100 to not more than $150 fine, or imprisonment for more than 2 months but not more	Not more than 3 months
Above $150 fine or 3 months imprisonment	Not more than 3 months Not more than 12 months

3

MAORI AND YOUTH JUSTICE IN NEW ZEALAND

Teresea Olsen, Gabrielle M. Maxwell and Allison Morris

INTRODUCTION

New Zealand has introduced a system of youth justice which attempts to integrate indigenous and Western justice processes. This chapter describes this system and evaluates the extent to which the system has responded to the needs and wishes of Maori, the indigenous people of New Zealand.[1] Attempts to incorporate elements of indigenous systems of justice within Western systems of justice have tended to take the form of token gestures: for instance, by allowing indigenous groups to resolve minor disputes within their own communities. The New Zealand system of youth justice, implemented in the Children, Young Persons and Their Families Act 1989, explicitly recognizes cultural diversity and the need for criminal justice processes to be both culturally appropriate and culturally sensitive. Its aim is to develop a system of justice which allows different ethnic groups to resolve matters in customary settings, to use customary procedures and to have access to culturally appropriate services. Although this approach is intended to apply equally to all cultural groups, the focus of this article is to assess the extent to which the act has succeeded in providing a justice system which is culturally appropriate and sensitive for Maori, the indigenous people of New Zealand.

Maori Indigenous Justice

A number of features differentiated strategies for dispute settlement in small-scale societies from criminal justice arrangements in modern urbanized and industrialized societies (Marshall 1985:46-47). First, the emphasis was on reaching consensus and involving the whole community; second, the desired outcome was reconciliation and a settlement acceptable to all parties rather than the isolation and punishment of the offender; third, the concern was not to apportion blame but to examine the wider reasons for the wrong (an implicit assumption was that there was often wrong on both sides); and fourth, there was less concern with whether or not there has actually been a breach of the law and more concern with the restoration of harmony.

These features were all apparent in the methods of dispute resolution which existed in New Zealand prior to colonization. The early settlers believed that the indigenous Maori people, who had arrived in New Zealand from the Polynesian Islands before the European colonization of 150 years ago, had no 'law' because they saw no written legal rules, no police, no prisons or the like; instead, they described what they saw as 'primitive and barbaric customs' (Jackson 1991). But it is clear that Maori did not live in a lawless society. There were rules by which they lived, which covered all aspects of Maori life.

Tikanga o nga hara, for example, translates broadly into the law of wrongdoing in which there were clear concepts of right and wrong. The law, however, was based on notions that responsibility was collective rather than individual and that redress was due not just to the victim but also to the victim's family. Understanding why an individual had offended was also linked to this notion of collective responsibility. The reasons were felt to lie not principally in the individual but in a lack of balance in the offender's social and family environment. The causes of this imbalance, therefore, had to be addressed in a collective way and, in particular, the imbalance between the offender and the victim's family had to be restored through mediation.

Maori had also created *runanga o nga tura*, which translates broadly into a council of law or court. These were headed by *tohunga o nga ture*, experts in law, but also contained *kaumatua* or *kuia* (elders), a representative from the offender's family and a representative from the victim's family. This group sorted out the wrongdoing and restored the balance. For example, they might have ordered the transfer of the offender's goods to the victim or work by the offender for the victim.[2]

In Maoridom, *whakamaa*, the shame felt by offenders who were confronted with the effects of their offending, led to remorse, followed by reintegration into the *whanau*, who took responsibility for any actions necessary to redress the social imbalance, towards both victims and offenders.[3] The role of *whanau* (the family group, which includes parent, children and other close kin) was also important in both Maori child-rearing and decision-making. In pre-colonial times all decisions, whatever their nature, were customarily made by the *whanau, hapu* or *iwi*[4] depending on the importance and nature of the decision. When a Maori child was born, the *whanau, hapu* and *iwi* decided what the child should become; for example, a warrior, an orator, an athlete or a singer. All were involved in contributing to the child's development and all were collectively responsible for the achievement of these goals; for example, by what they fed the child and how they taught him or her. In one tribe, the process was symbolized by the weaving of a cloak after the child was born. The cloak would be worn by the child as an adult and was made to fit the child when it was grown. How is this tradition to be understood? Perhaps literally, and certainly as a metaphor. *Whanau, hapu* and *iwi* make a measure of the future adult at his or her birth, and they weave the child's experiences so that the chosen role will be a cloak that fits the grown person. It was, therefore, customary for Maori children to live from time to time with different relatives within their *whanau, hapu* and *iwi*. Bringing up children and hence dealing with their delinquencies was a communal responsibility.

Maori Concerns about Pakeha Justice

Colonialism, however, all but destroyed indigenous systems of justice in all parts of the British Empire, and New Zealand was no exception (Jackson 1988; Pratt 1991). The relationship between the state and Maoridom, as set out in the Treaty of Waitangi and signed by the Crown and some Maori chiefs in 1840, was intended to be a partnership in which Maori sovereignty was preserved,[5] but this did not happen. The culture and values of the Maori were not allowed to exist alongside the culture and values of the colonizers. Dismantling these and the subsequent enforced assimilation to 'the British way of life' was what Pratt (1991) ironically calls the 'gift of civilization'. To be 'one people' required one set of laws, and since the colonizers had the power (first through weapons and later through increased numbers), it was their law that dominated. Indeed, taking the power of governance of Maori from *whanau, hapu* and *iwi* effectively destabilized the foundations of Maori society.

As a result, decisions affecting Maori in such areas as social welfare and criminal justice were made for Maori and with little consultation with Maori. Thus traditional Maori structures were weakened. One result of this was the institutionalization of a large number of Maori children and young people. Unfortunately, we have been unable to find any data on the ethnicity of the many thousands of children in institutions up to 1980, but it is widely believed that Maori were over-represented in terms of the national population by about three times. This removal of Maori from their family, community and culture was supposedly for 'their own good' and denied *whanau, hapu* and *iwi* the right to deal with their own.

In the early 1980s, however, Maori became vigorously engaged in the debates over changes to the legislation about the protection of children who were abused and neglected and the punishment of those who had offended. When the government published a discussion document on various options in 1984 and produced the first version of a new Children and Young Persons Bill in 1986, there was a strong call from Maori for revisions to past procedures. Maoridom asked for changes which recognized Maori culture, gave a voice to Maori *whanau, hapu* and *iwi*, and incorporated methods of responding to children's needs which returned to Maori the right to care for their own. Out of these intense debates, gradually the new system emerged, which was designed to restore power to Maori and to families in partnership with the state. The publication of *Puao-te-ata-tu* in 1986, the report of the Ministerial Advisory Committee on a Maori Perspective for the Department of Social Welfare, provided new guidelines for practice in the Department of Social Welfare with respect to Maori children and their families. There also emerged a broad recognition that the Treaty of Waitangi must be given real meaning, and that aspects of sovereignty over their people and over resources should be restored to Maori through the devolution of power and the restoration of lands and other resources. The Children and Young Persons Bill was redrafted to become the Children, Young Persons and Their Families Act 1989, embodying these goals. It recognizes Maori aspirations and, therefore, seeks to empower Maoridom, to involve Maori directly in decisions about their young people and thus to acknowledge their identity as *tangata whenua* (the people of the land).

Maori and Crime

The New Zealand population is made up of a number of different ethnic groups. Numerically, the most significant are of European origin, or 'Pakeha':[6] more than 80% of the juvenile population. Maori make up around 12% of the total New Zealand population.[7] Maori, however, are over-represented in various indices of social and economic deprivation: high infant mortality rates, low life expectancy rates, high unemployment rates and low incomes (Ministerial Advisory Committee on a Maori Perspective for the Department of Social Welfare 1986). Maori are also over-represented in the population of known offenders, including juvenile offenders (Maxwell and Morris 1991). Thus, according to recent police statistics (1988), 37% of known offenders are described as Maori; amongst the known juvenile offender population, 43% are described as Maori.[8] The new youth justice procedures recognize this over-representation of Maori among juvenile offenders.

Youth Justice in New Zealand

The objectives of the Children, Young Persons and Their Families Act 1989 include:

• promoting the well-being of children, young people and their families and family groups by providing services which are appropriate to cultural needs, accessible and provided by persons and organizations sensitive to cultural perspectives and aspirations;
• providing measures to deal with offending which strengthen the family, *whanau, hapu, iwi*, and family group[9] and measures to foster their ability to deal with offending by their children and young people;

• keeping young people in the community (and hence in contact with their culture).

Thus, the new legislation stresses the provision of services which are *culturally sensitive* and a process which is *culturally appropriate*. It emphasizes the importance of arriving at decisions that keep young people within their family, community, and culture. Hence the involvement of *whanau, hapu* and *iwi* is explicitly recognized within the new legislative framework in both discussions and decisions about appropriate solutions to juvenile offending.

The Family Group Conference (FGC) lies at the heart of the new youth justice system; it is a mechanism both for giving families power in the decision-making process and for achieving reconciliation between the victim and the offender. As in the traditional Maori model, social balance is achieved by reintegrating young people in their family and determining appropriate means of redress for victims.

However, it would be a mistake to describe the new system as the rejection of a Western criminal justice system in favour of the adoption of an indigenous method of resolution (and certainly the advocates of a Maori indigenous model would reject such a depiction). A distinction must be drawn between a system which attempts to reestablish the indigenous model of pre-European times and a system of justice which is culturally appropriate. The new New Zealand system is an attempt to establish the latter, not to replicate the former. As such, it seeks to incorporate many of the features apparent in *whanau* decision-making processes as seen in meetings on *marae* (Maori meeting places) today, but it also contains elements quite alien to indigenous models (for example, the presence of representatives of the state) and other principles which, to our mind, are equally important: the empowerment of families, offenders and victims. Although families and victims had a recognized role in the resolution of disputes in traditional Maori society, their part in the new system is not necessarily identical. Hence, in this chapter, we will discuss on the basis of our research findings,[10] not only the extent to which these goals of cultural sensitivity have been met, but we will also raise questions about whether or not it is possible for a Western criminal justice system to be married successfully with an indigenous model, especially given the context of a modern and mixed society.

THE OVER-REPRESENTATION OF MAORI AMONG YOUNG OFFENDERS

Maori are, as we mentioned earlier, over-represented in the known offender population. The pattern reported nationally was almost exactly replicated in our sample of young people coming to police attention. In 1988, 43% of young offenders were Maori and 43% of our sample were Maori, although Maori made up only 15% of the juvenile population in our sample areas.[11] The over-representation of Maori juveniles is more marked in the FGC sample than in the general police sample and is higher again in the Youth Court sample (see Table 3.1).

TABLE 3.1
Ethnicity of Sample Coming to Police Attention, Being Referred for FGC and Appearing in the Youth Court Compared to Population Figures in Percentages

Ethnicity	Population in Sample areas	Police Cases	FGC Referrals	Youth Court Appearances
	%	%	%	%
Pakeha	74	40	40	39
Maori	15	43	45	50
Pacific Island	8	16	15	11
Other	3	1	0	0

The extent of the over-representation of young Maori also varies depending on area. The proportion of Maori young people coming to police attention was higher than would be expected in three of our research areas, a fourth area was intermediate in this respect, while a relatively smaller proportion of Maori young people came to police attention in the fifth area. These differences are much greater than would be expected by chance.[12] The differences in the number of Maori appearing in the youth justice system in different areas, and their increased representation as the gravity of the consequences increased, raises questions about whether or not Maori offending patterns are different from those of other groups, whether or not Maori are treated differently from other ethnic groups by those making decisions, and whether or not Maori respond differently to their experiences of the system because of cultural differences. We were able to examinine these questions and concluded that it was only in the decision to arrest (which directly affects the proportion of Maori in the Youth Court) that ethnicity per se played a part. The decision to refer to an FGC was more easily explained by the seriousness of the offence and previous offences.

Maori and the Decision to Arrest

A greater proportion of those arrested in our sample were Maori than Pakeha: 62% compared with 28% respectively.[13] Indeed, the arrest rate for Maori was more than twice that for Pakeha: 15% compared with 7%. A multiple regression analysis[14] was undertaken to determine whether or not the prevalence of Maori in the arrest figures could be accounted for by the nature of the offences they commit. This showed that the seriousness of the offence was the most important factor, followed by the time of the offence, the age of the offender and the ethnicity of the offender. Thus relatively serious offences, committed at night by older offenders and by Maori offenders, were most likely to result in an arrest.

Overall, however, these factors did not provide a strong prediction of the decision to arrest. Together, they gave a multiple correlation of 0.45 and accounted for 20% of the variance.[15] This means that only in a relatively small proportion of cases would it have been possible to predict accurately the decision to arrest from information on seriousness, time of offence, age and ethnicity alone. Thus it is clear that there were other substantial factors influencing the decision of the officer to arrest. In some cases, previous knowledge of the offender and his or her family background are undoubtedly likely to have been a factor. From the interviews with officers, it seems clear that judgments about reoffending and the likelihood of absconding also played a part, and these judgments were being made on the basis of the behaviour of the offender and the impression created by the offender at the time of the arrest. Moreover, just as the evidence on difference across areas showed that police practice varied, it is equally possible that a similar variability may have occurred within a district. In addition, it is possible that particular sections on shift together under a single sergeant, who supervised decisions, may have developed different standards. The effect of area was tested using another statistical procedure, logistic regression, which showed that area differences were indeed important, although they were not as important as, and did not cancel out, the other variables we have already mentioned.

The fact that Maori were more likely to be arrested, and that this effect operated in addition to any effect from other factors known to the officer at the time of arrest—such as the seriousness of the offence, the age of the offender and time of offence—is an important finding with serious implications for the impartiality of front-line police officers. Thus we explored this further by examining the other factors associated with being Maori. The only differences we were able to identify were employment status and previous offence history. More of the Maori young offenders were unemployed and more of the Pakeha were at school; and, in comparison with Pakeha young offenders, more of the Maori were already known to the police. It is possible that other unmeasured factors, such as the attitude of the offender as perceived by the police officer, were also relevant and might have explained the differences in arrest rates. It is also possible that negative attitudes and expectations about one another have built up over time between the police and young Maori offenders and that these attitudes can sometimes lead to an over-reaction on both sides and, consequently, to the arrest of young Maori.

Explaining the Over-representation of Maori

While Maori were more likely to be arrested than Pakeha for offences of similar seriousness, there was no evidence in this study that, when the seriousness of the offence and the previous offence history were taken into consideration, young Maori were more likely to be referrred for an FGC than to be handled by police diversion, or that they were more likely than Pakeha to receive more severe penalties in the Youth Court compared to Pakeha. Thus greater representation did not appear to be a consequence of the behaviour of those responsible for managing the youth justice system even though front-line policing practice does play a part in the over-representation of young Maori.

Other potential reasons for the over-representation of Maori lie in the social and economic circumstances of Maori people. Recent studies by Fergusson and others (1992; 1993) found that, in a cohort of young people, more young Maori than Pakeha reported that they had engaged in criminal offending. Further analysis showed that the difference in self-reported offending could be explained by socioeconomic variables. However, the study also showed that a greater proportion of Maori than Pakeha had come into contact with the police. This could not be explained simply by socioeconomic factors.

A further possible explanation relates to area differences. The Maori researchers in the team suggested that the strength of the community and the relative number of *tangata whenua* (local Maori people) and *taurahere* (Maori from outside the local area) may be relevant. Certainly the relative proportions of *tangata whenua* and *taurahere* in each of the five areas would have been consistent with such an explanation. For example, in one area with a relatively large local population of Maori, there were fewer offenders than expected, while in another area where many Maori families had migrated from other parts of the country, the proportion of young Maori offenders was larger than expected.

FAMILY GROUP CONFERENCES AND CULTURE

There were various ways in which we could attempt to examine the cultural appropriateness and sensitivity of the Family Group Conference process: the venue of the FGC, the procedures used, the extent to which *whanau* were present, the cultural match and sensitivity of Youth Justice Coordinators (YJCs) and so on. From these indicators, it is clear that the aims of the legislation were not always achieved.

Venue. More Maori than Pakeha FGCs were held at home: 34% compared to 19%. *Marae* were rarely used; only 5% of Maori FGCs (3% of the total FGC sample) were held on *marae* during the sample period. Department of Social Welfare (DSW) premises were used for over half the Maori and two-thirds of the Pakeha FGC (54% and 68% respectively). The choice of venue was theoretically that of the family but, in practice, the convenience of professionals seems to have dictated the choice of DSW premises as the usual venue.

It is difficult to imagine that the practice of holding Family Group Conferencess on DSW premises is culturally appropriate for any ethnic group. The Maori researchers commented that for Maori families in particular, the DSW environment lacked the features that would have linked them to their own culture. Nor could DSW facilities provide the sense of the warmth and safety which families would have received on the *marae* or in their own homes. Families in effect could be disempowered by the nature of the venue. On DSW territory, the symbolic (and hence potentially the actual) power remained with the professionals. This may have discouraged the participation of families and young people in the process of deciding on the best outcome and hindered families in the process of taking responsibility for their young people. Moving the venue to the home of the family is one way of transferring power to the family, but an even more powerful transfer was seen by our Maori researchers to occur when the venue was the *marae*.

Process. This transfer of power was even stronger when it was accompanied by Maori *kaupapa* (the spirit and philosophy of Maori as reflected in both format and values). Such a transfer almost invariably seemed to have occurred in the FGCs held on *marae*. It was also observed to have occurred, although much more rarely, in FGCs held in other locations.[16] The best way to demonstrate this is through case histories.

Tamati's case

This FGC took place in the home of the young person's auntie. Although it was not held on a *marae*, formal Maori protocol was observed. This was made possible by the presence of two *kaumatua* (elders), both men of standing in the local community, and by the presence of various aunties, uncles and cousins from the young person's family. The actual chairing of the FGC was carried out by the more senior of the *kaumatua* and responsibility for this was passed over by the two coordinators present.

Although the professionals included two social workers, two coordinators and a Youth Aid officer, they did not dominate proceedings. There were eighteen family members present, and *kaupapa* Maori (Maori process and spirit) prevailed. That is, the meeting was controlled by the people rather than the professionals, whose roles became that of advisers.

Whaikorero (speeches of welcome), *waiata* (songs) and *karakia* (prayers) opened the FGC, the YJC made a short speech of acceptance of the *kaumatua* as facilitator and outlined the FGC's requirements under the Act, the Youth Aid officer read and checked the charges and then the family began to speak. First, concern was registered for the victims and why they were not present. One of the YJCs said work commitments precluded their attendance (this was a day time meeting) but that she had their concerns and suggestions on paper. She proceeded to present these. The family then discussed for a while the victim's position, reparation issues, the ability of the young person's immediate family to care for him and also the need for him to realize the consequences of his actions. At appropriate times DSW people added suggestions or information as to their particular stance and on what resources and services may be available. At all times, the professionals remained respectful and acted in a way conducive to the process taking place as the *whanau* wished.

At what may have been a turning point in the *korero* (discussion), the *kaumatua* asked the professionals to leave for a time. In a very short time after this, around twelve minutes, the family decided on a series of recommendations, which they put forward to the professionals. These were well thought out and took into consideration the wishes of the victims, the well-being of the young person, the fragility of his immediate family and the resources available within the wider *hapu*. In the light of this, both the police and the DSW agreed to the plan and undertook to convey it back to the judge at the Youth Court.

It was interesting to note that at first the young person did not agree with some of the recommendations, and so the family negotiated a compromise with him. It seems unlikely that the young person would have been so outspoken in an institutional setting. Follow-up for this case showed that this young man fulfilled all the FGC requirements.

John's case

This case took place in the home of the young person's parents. Although it was not run according to formal protocol in all details, it was a situation where all those present, including the victim, the young person and his family, operated in a Maori *hui* (meeting) type environment. That is, everyone seemed to feel supported enough to be able to speak as openly and as frankly as they wished. It was facilitated by an acting YJC who was at pains to be sensitive to the Maori environment of the family home. She actively encouraged people to speak and was respectful and tolerant to all parties.

The FGC started with a *karakia* (prayer) from the young person's uncle, after which the YJC advised the meeting of the requirements of the Act. The Youth Aid officer read and checked the charges with the young person, and then the YJC stood back to let the young person's family discuss the offence and reparation with the victim and his mother. The victim was present with both his mother and sister. The young person had his parents, two aunties and an uncle present. Crucial to the conciliatory atmosphere of the FGC was the young person's family taking responsibility for his actions and then offering sympathy and understanding to the victim. If the FGC had taken place in an institutional setting, the family may not have felt secure enough to be supportive to the victim and his family. The focus of all the discussion was reparation, accountability and development of the young person. The YJC offered to withdraw with the Youth Aid officer, but this was not seen as necessary by the family.

Whanau attendance. The new act encouraged the involvement of the *whanau* and the wider family group (including both kin and friends of the family) in responding to young people's offending. This was viewed as culturally appropriate since the young person, certainly in Maori terms, is the child not simply of the nuclear but also of the extended family and hence *whanau* (and *hapu* and *iwi*) have both rights and responsibilities with respect to the development of that child.

It is difficult to judge the adequacy of *whanau* involvement in FGCs. *Whanau*, or the extended family, were involved in only 39% of the FGC cases, but they were more frequently involved in cases involving reoffending (*whanau* or extended family were present for 42% of those cases where there was previous offending compared with 30% of those where there was no previous offending), in court-referred cases (*whanau* or extended family members attended 58% of court-referred FGCs as opposed to 34% of non-court-referred FGC cases), and in the more serious cases (only 21% of the least serious offences but 77% of the most serious offences had *whanau* or members of the extended family present). These findings match the comments of YJCs that, while they often held an FGC for minor first offences with only the immediate family present, they felt it was very important to locate the extended family when the offences were more serious and when the young person was involved in repeated offending. There was, in addition, a tendency for more extended family to be present in those cases where more than one FGC was held before a resolution was reached; the reason for an adjournment was often to enable more family to attend. *Whanau* involvement was also considerably greater in Maori cases than was the involvement of the extended family in Pakeha cases. Thus 58% of Maori cases had *whanau* present; the comparable figure for Pakeha was 20%. When *whanau* were present, they numbered from one to 39, with two being the most common number and the average being four. The largest Pakeha FGC included eighteen people, but several Maori FGC exceeded this number, with the largest being 39.

Of course, we have no way of knowing whether or not there were *whanau* or members of the extended family who could or should have been invited. But we asked both families and YJCs about whether or not the 'right' family members had been present. Generally they felt that they had been, though this was not always so. The involvement of *whanau* and the extended family (or the lack of it) was presented both positively and negatively by families.

The main reason for families wanting *whanau* or the extended family to be present was the support they offered:

I felt safe because my *whanau* were with me. I would have felt like stink if

> I had to face it on my own. My auntie explained it so I understood. It was good that she allowed me to take a role (Young person).

On the other hand, some *whanau* who were present knew little about the young person, their offences or the immediate family's situation:

> Other family members didn't know the facts but they kept butting in and moralizing. There were too many relatives who didn't know the facts (Young person).

> There were too many extended family members involved. It felt uncomfortable. It was like strangers telling you how to deal with your child (Parent).

> Ninety percent of them hadn't met him. I thought this is getting worse and worse as it goes on (Youth Aid officer).

Some families felt not only that the wrong people were present but that they took the wrong approach. The following quotes demonstrate the potential tension between the objectives of *whanau* involvement and the encouragement of parental responsibility. These quotes show that the value placed on *whanau* is not universally shared by Maori.

> My auntie shouldn't have been there. She talks too much. It should have been my mum that decides what happens (Young person).

> I'd prefer not to have had family there. They were the wrong people and I had no say in choosing them (Parent).

> He needed more people on his side; his aunt was vindictive. There was a large weight of adult numbers lined up against him. He was overpowered (Carer).

Some families also expressed shame about involving the wider family. One mother clearly felt pressured into having *whanau* present at the FGC and this must surely be counter-productive:

> I feel really resentful about it. I didn't want to involve the family and burden them and feel shame.

Whanau participation is, by itself, of course, insufficient to guarantee positive outcomes. In some cases, *whanau* were not necessarily as effective as they might have been because they were unaware of the role that was expected of them, because the management of the process was still with the Department of Social Welfare and because they had not had time to consider the options. The case histories described earlier, however, provide dramatic examples of the fact that *whanau* participation and knowledge can combine to produce effective solutions.

Cultural Match between Family and Youth Justice Coordinator

About a third (32%) of the FGC cases in our sample were coordinated by Pakeha coordinators (excluding cases facilitated by social workers) and more than two-thirds (68%) by Maori. This in effect meant that two-thirds of Maori young people had Maori coordinators and one-third had Pakeha coordinators.[17] This in itself would not matter if the YJCs were sensitive to cultural issues, but this was not always so.

We observed instances of what we believe to be breaches of protocol - for example, coordinators welcoming families as was usual when the FGC was held in DSW but inappropriate when the FGC was held in the family's own home, and not using *kaumatua* who were present to facilitate the FGC. Sometimes also YJCs developed a stylized response to cultural difference by providing a multi-lingual greeting and a prayer at all FGCs. This seemed at times to the researchers to be inappropriate, and it generally appeared to be accepted with tolerance rather than to be appreciated as meeting the specific cultural and family needs, which were more diverse than these formats allowed. It was usually seen as simply an FGC with a prayer and a few Maori words rather than a truly culturally sensitive way of doing things. Cultural appropriateness probably cannot be achieved without handing the management of the process over to those who fully understand the culture. In Maori terms, this means running the entire FGC according to the Maori *kaupapa* appropriate for that *iwi*, as exemplified by the two case studies presented earlier in this section.

MAORI VIEWS ON PROCESS

Some Maori saw the FGC process in Pakeha rather than Maori terms but felt that this was not necessarily bad:

It seemed to be done in a Pakeha way ... we expect the Pakeha system ... we like it as it is.

It was a Pakeha scene ... it's OK.

Other respondents felt differently and more negatively about the process remaining in Pakeha hands:

It was Pakeha *kaupapa* (procedure) ... if done in a Maori way, it would take longer; it would involve understanding everyone present and their roles.

It gives power to the *whanau*, but the ultimate power is still in Pakeha hands.

For these young people and their families, a different process would have been preferable: the presence of *whanau*, the opportunity to explore wider issues and the fact that they were able to have the FGC in their own home or on a *marae* were seen by some Maori as part of what it meant to do things their *own* way.

The setting is important—at home is good; it gives us back some power.

It was great. The boys felt shame. We had a *kaumatua* there, there was a *powhiri* (Maori welcoming ritual), *karakia* (prayer), and *kai* (food). All could speak.

He [the offender] hadn't known Maori culture and now he will.

I don't understand Maori too well but it was good for my family that we had prayers, etc. I know they were praying for me.

Only a few Maori explicitly disassociated themselves from attempts to create a Maori process:

I don't like this Maorified way of doing things—waste of time ... don't need all those relatives there.

Too much shit about the Maori way ... waste of time deep down.

THE CULTURAL APPROPRIATENESS AND SENSITIVITY OF FGCS

The Family Group Conference is an attempt to give a prominent place to process, and, at times, FGCs can and do transcend tokenism and embody a Maori *kaupapa*: they can involve the *whanau*, *hapu* and *iwi*, can be managed according to traditional protocol and can redress the social imbalance between victims, offenders and social groups. For those families who did manage the process in accordance with their own customs, the experience was very positive.

Overall, however, our assessment from observation and interviews is that this did not often occur. In the view of the Maori researchers, most of the FGCs they attended were instances in which the interpretation of the act or neglect of the intent of the act resulted in culturally inappropriate processes taking place. They felt that families had not been able to be strengthened because, often, the processes were not culturally appropriate and the objective of making available services and facilities which were appropriate to the needs, values and beliefs of Maori families had not been attained. As Maori researchers, they saw this situation arising from ignorance of the act, a dearth of resources and mismanagement rather than from any inherent faults in the legislation itself.

However, it is also our view, and that of many of the Maori participants, that there is at least the *potential* for FGCs to be more able to cope with cultural diversity than other types of tribunals. This is best summed up in the words of the Maori researchers involved in the project:

> We feel that the Act for the most part is an excellent piece of legislation which promises exciting possibilities for the future. When the processes outlined in the Act were observed, Maori families were indeed empowered and able to take an active part in decisions concerning their young people. It is not difficult to see the beneficial influences that the Act may eventually exert on wider Maori, Polynesian and Pakeha society. Maori society could gain immensely from legislation that acknowledges and strengthens the *hapu* and tribal structures and their place in decisions regarding the wellbeing of young people and [from legislation] that provides them with an opportunity to contribute to any reparation and to support those offended against. The same scenario would apply to Pacific Island peoples. Pakeha society would also benefit from a process which acknowledges the family and gives redress to victims.

CULTURE IN CONFLICT

Real difficulties can arise, however, when offenders are of one ethnic group and victims are of another. Pakeha victims on occasion claimed not only that they felt intimidated by the presence of a large number of *whanau* but also that they resented discussions in Maori and felt alienated in a Maori environment. And in at least one case in the research the family would clearly have preferred to hold the FGC on their *marae* but did not do so out of deference to and concern for the victim. In some cases, the dilemma over whether to use a setting that best meets the needs of the young person and their family or one that will be more comfortable for the victim can be resolved by negotiation between the family and the victim. In others, it might be preferable for the process to have two distinct stages. In one case we observed, the YJC effectively acted as a go-between to negotiate an agreed settlement between the family and the victims, who did not wish to meet one another. But while it may be possible to devise practical measures which aim to resolve such tensions, a wider theoretical issue remains unresolved. Certain processes which empower one group—for example, the family—may disempower another—for example, the victim.

MAORI IN THE YOUTH COURT

Although Maori were over-represented in the Youth Courts because of their higher arrest rate, there appeared to be no differences in the way the court handled Maori and Pakeha young people in our sample: neither the court process nor court outcomes were discernibly different. Questions can be raised, however, about the quality of the process and its impact on young people, who might have different values and expectations as a consequence of their different cultural background and experience. The comments of the young offenders in our sample who appeared in the Youth Courts showed not only that they recognized that the court was part of an alien world, but that it was a world seen by Maori young people and their families as: *pretty much a Pakeha scene.*

To most Maori, 'a Pakeha scene' was what they expected and accepted from the court, although there were certainly no suggestions from anyone that the court was biassed in its decisions. Comments which contrasted the approach of the court with the approach of the FGC emphasized not only the features we discussed earlier but also the fact that the FGC was more of 'a Maori way' of doing things:

> The court was more strict. At the FGC you are with your *whanau* (Young person).

> *Whanau* had more say at the FGC because it was done in the Maori way (Mother).

> Things were not done in a Maori way—there was no support in court (Parent).

> The court was frightening—it wasn't done in a Maori way (Young person).

The Youth Court in particular found it difficult to accommodate Maori process and etiquette. The courtroom rituals that are most likely to have an impact will be those that are meaningful in terms of the cultural background of the offender. Thus, for Maori families, a court process which blends Maori and Western traditions would seem not only consistent with the objectives of the act but also more likely to be effective in reinforcing the message of the court than a traditional Western approach. This is especially true given the existence of a Maori protocol, widely understood within Maoridom, for dealing with disputes and involving the expression of remorse, issues of reparation and decisions that settle disputes. This protocol includes the participation in the proceedings of the principal parties to the dispute.

But again, our view, and that of many of the Maori and Pacific Island participants, was that the court process (and hence spirit and outcomes) remained

Pakeha and unresponsive to cultural differences. Some of the courts we observed did respond to the desire to change procedures—for example, by allowing *whanau* to be present to offer prayers and to make submissions on behalf of their young people. When this happened, there was considerable satisfaction with the process. But the courts were not always responsive, and when *whanau* were not heard or listened to, the process drew considerable criticism. One particular point to note is that only one lay advocate[18] was appointed during the whole of the research period in the Youth Courts we observed, and only nine lay advocates were appointed throughout the whole of New Zealand during 1991.[19]

CONCLUSION

The Children, Young Persons and Their Families Act 1989 attempted to create a youth justice system which was culturally appropriate and sensitive. To be effective, this required an environment in which the introduction of different processes, different types of spirit and underlying philosophies and different outcomes from those traditionally available in criminal justice contexts was made possible. That this has not yet fully occurred speaks to the power of traditional systems to resist reform (as demonstrated by some front-line police officers, some social welfare profesionals and some of the judiciary). And it speaks to the power of resources. The failure to fund adequately *iwi* and cultural authorities as envisaged under the act has meant that the new system cannot fulfill its true potential. Much of what was intended has remained rhetoric.

A further question is whether or not an indigenous process is possible within a modern society. The answer is, in our view, that inevitably the processes and patterns developed in small clan-based communities cannot be replicated in a modern, industrial, mobile and individualized culture. But on the other hand, as this study demonstrates, it is possible for the *spirit* of the community-based social systems of the past to adapt to modern times and to modify the individualistic and remote patterns that have characterized Western justice models. The development of the New Zealand system shows that it is possible to use an indigenous model as a basis for radical change. Further, capturing the essence of an indigenous model has the potential to protect young people against alienation and to nurture self-esteem for Maori and Pakeha alike. In our study, we noted the ease with which Maori were able to make the Family Group Conference system their own when they were given the power to do so. Thus the model *can* validate the values of an indigenous group and transfer power to them *providing there is the will to do so*. It can moderate the anger and rage of victims by providing reparation and can contribute to the healing process. It can provide for the social reintegration of the young person within the wider group. It can help bind communities into a cohesive supportive structure in which families can exercise their responsibilities effectively. But this depends on the dominant culture giving up power, validating alternate processes and resourcing the groups who are the repositories of traditional indigenous values and knowledge. While the transfer of power is dependent on the will of those within the state system, the effectiveness of the process will remain vulnerable. Greater effective transfer of both power and resources to indigenous communities—in Maori terms, the guarantee of *tiro rangatira* status (the right of governance of one's own people) within the terms of the Treaty of Waitangi—is necessary to secure the preservation of Maori value systems within modern society.[20]

NOTES

1. Many Maori words are both plural and singular, such as marae, meaning one or several meeting places. In New Zealand this has gained increasing usage. 'Maori', therefore, is used to refer to both an individual and a people; 'the needs of Maori' is used today instead of 'needs of the Maori'.

2. These penalties were not always mild. The concept of *'utu'* (revenge/compensation) meant that, in some instances, reparation resulted in the confiscation of all the possessions of the offender's family and even the taking of slaves or life.

3. Very similar theoretical ideas are advanced now by Braithwaite (1988), who uses the term 'reintegrative shaming'. Braithwaite distinguishes non-integrative shaming, which is associated with traditional court procedures and their resultant stigmatization of the offender (encapsulated in Garfinkel's [1956] notion of status degradation), and reintegrative shaming, which seeks to combine shaming with reconciliation between the offender and the victim and reaffirmation of the offender's status in the community rather than his or her exclusion from, or rejection by, the community. Reparation (actual or symbolic) may affect reintegration (actual or symbolic). Braithwaite argues that the process is more likely to be effective when it involves *relatives, friends or a personally relevant collectivity* (1988: 69).

4. The nearest literal translation of these Maori words is *'whanau'* = extended family, *'hapu'* = clan and *'iwi'* = tribe. But the words carry additional meaning relating to the way Maori society functions and the role these basic kinship units play in social organisation.

5. There has, however, been considerable debate over the exact meaning of some of the critical words in the treaty.

6. Pakeha refers to anyone of European origin.

7. Pacific Island Polynesians, who have immigrated more recently than the Maori, make up 4% of the New Zealand population. It is estimated that by the year 2020, one in four of the population will be of Polynesian descent, including both New Zealand Maori and other Pacific Island Polynesian (Interdepartmental Committee on Population Policy Guidelines 1990).

8. There are problems with the identification of ethnicity, particularly for Maori. The police usually include as Maori all those who appear to be Maori or have a Maori name, while population data based on the census describe as Maori persons of half or more Maori blood or those who identify as Maori. The police categories, therefore, are likely to include a larger number than would be identified as Maori in the usual population statistics. Even statistics on New Zealanders of Maori descent are unlikely to be as inclusive as police identifications, as the former depend on self-identification as Maori. On the other hand, it could also be argued that police identification could fail to acknowledge Maori with a European name and appearance.

9. The use of the term 'family group' in the act is intended to signify the appropriateness of including family friends and supporters as well as kin.

10. During 1990-91, we were part of a team undertaking research on the new youth justice system. The research examined in five areas of New Zealand what happened to the young people, including young Maori, who became involved with the police (approximately 700 young people), took part in Family Group Conferences (FGCs) (approximately 200 young people) and appeared in the Youth Court (70 young people). Wherever possible, researchers attended the FGCs and the Youth Court hearings and interviewed the participants. See Maxwell and Morris (1993) for more detail. At all stages, the process has been informed by the participation of Maori advisers, and Maori researchers collected much of the data and commented upon them. Throughout, their comments have been used to guide analysis and interpretation. The authors of this chapter are two Pakeha and one Maori.

11. The proportion of Pacific Island young people in the police sample was about double what would be expected on the basis of population figures.

12. Chi-squared $=20$, df$=4$, p$<.001$.

13. The comparable percentages of each group in the non-arrest sample were 38% (Maori) and 45% (Pakeha).

14. The stepwise multiple regression used here tries out each of the individual factors included in the analysis in turn as a predictor and then sorts out those which, in order and uninfluenced by the other factors, are the best predictors.

15. A correlation describes the amount of association between two factors. A correlation of 1.00 indicates complete agreement between two factors, while a correlation of 0 indicates no association whatsoever. In this case the multiple correlation of .45 is only a moderate correlation and accounts for 20% of the variance. This means that it would be possible to predict police officers' decisions accurately in only about 20% of the cases from knowing the seriousness of the offence, whether or not it occurred at night and the age and ethnicity of the offender.

16. It is difficult to know how often this happened in total, but the Maori researchers estimated that perhaps only 10% of Maori FGCs were in accord with Maori *kaupapa* (spirit and customary process).

17. On the other hand, less than a quarter (21%) of Pakeha offenders had a Pakeha coordinator and more than three-quarters (79%) had a Maori coordinator.

18. In part, this came about because of the inadequate pay rates arranged for lay advocates, but in part it must also reflect a lack of appreciation by the court of the extent to which such appointments are important and useful.

19. Unpublished Justice Department statistics.

20. The authors wish to acknowledge the assistance of the Department of Social Welfare (now the Social Policy Agency), which commissioned the research; the support of all those in the Department of Social Welfare (now the Children and Young Persons Service); the New Zealand Police and the Youth Court; the help of other members of the research team and the cooperation of young offenders, their families and the victims, who gave us their views on the processes they experienced.

REFERENCES

Braithwaite, J. (1988) *Crime, Shame and Reintegration*, Cambridge: Cambridge University Press.

Fergusson, D. M., Horwood, L. J., and Lynskey, M. T. (1992) 'Ethnicity and Bias in Police Contact Statistics', unpublished manuscript.

Fergusson, D. M., Horwood, L. J., and Lynskey, M. T. (1993) 'Ethnicity, Social Background and Young Offending: A 14 year Longitudinal Study', *Australian and New Zealand Journal of Criminology 26*, 155-170.

Garfinkel, H. (1956) 'Conditions of Successful Degradation Ceremonies', *American Journal of Sociology*, 61: 420.

Interdepartmental Committee on Population Policy Guidelines (1990) *The Human Face of New Zealand: A Context for Population Policy into the Twenty-first Century*, Wellington: Department of Statistics.

Jackson, M. (1988) *The Maori and the Criminal Justice System, Part II*, Wellington: Department of Justice.

Jackson, M. (1991) 'Criminal Justice for Maori', unpublished lecture to students, Wellington: Institute of Criminology, Victoria University of Wellington.

Marshall, T. (1985) *Alternatives to Criminal Courts*, Aldershot: Gower.

Maxwell, G. M. and Morris, A. (1991) 'Juvenile Crime and the Children, Young Persons and Their Families Act 1989', in G. Maxwell (ed.), *An Appraisal of the First Year of the Children, Young Persons and Their Families Act 1989*, Wellington: Office of the Commissioner for Children.

Maxwell, G. M. and Morris, A. (1993) *Families, Victims and Culture: Youth Justice in New Zealand*, Social Policy Agency and Institute of Criminology, Wellington: Victoria University of Wellington.

Ministerial Advisory Committee on a Maori Perspective for the Department of Social Welfare (1986) *Puao-te-ata-tu: (Daybreak). The Report of the*

Ministerial Advisory Committee on a Maori Perspective for the Department of Social Welfare, Wellington: Department of Social Welfare.

New Zealand Police (1988) *Digest of Statistics*, Wellington: New Zealand Police.

Pratt, John (1991) 'Citizenship, Colonisation and Criminal Justice', *International Journal of the Sociology of Law*, 19: 293.

4

'SLAY THE MONSTERS': PEACEMAKER COURT AND VIOLENCE CONTROL PLANS FOR THE NAVAJO NATION

Robert Yazzie and James W. Zion

INTRODUCTION

Once again, crime and violence are national priorities. The cries in response to reported violence[1] are 'Tougher laws!' 'Increased penalties!' and 'More police!' Violence is not a new issue, and '[i]n some 100 years of national sovereignty, Americans have been preoccupied repeatedly with trying to understand and control one form of violence or another'.[2]

Violence is a Navajo Nation issue as well. In October of 1993, the Navajo Nation Council, galvanized by reports of gang vandalism and family violence, resolved to make gang violence and family disruption a legislative priority. Should the council's upcoming debates focus on more laws, more penalties, more police and more gaols? Too often, policy makers and legislators limit their debates to legal procedures, what to do with individual offenders and talk of 'rights'. That is, 'microjustice' (Nader 1980), where planners ask what to do with people rather than address causes and systemic problems. Policy makers become so preoccupied with what to do with individual offenders that they fail to address larger problems. They sometimes forget to look at causes, trends and the big picture.

This policy study seeks to view law, justice and social problems in a new way to respond to violence and social disruption. It attempts to do 'macrojustice' to address the nature and causes of violence in the Navajo Nation. Courts must anticipate new conditions or emerging events and adjust their operations to meet them.[3]

Macrojustice is a particularly appropriate approach for the courts of the Navajo Nation. The first Indian courts in the United States—Courts of Indian Offences—were created on 10 April 1883 (Hagan 1966: 109). The historical record shows that they were specifically designed to destroy traditional Indian law and replace it with a new system which allowed the United States government to take control.[4]

The Navajo Nation experience anticipated courts for Indian nations. When Navajos were confined in a concentration camp at Bosque Redondo, New Mexico, the army experimented with a court model. A board of army officers held a meeting on 26 April 1865 to adopt a plan to divide Navajos into twelve villages and establish a 'superior court' composed of the 'principal chief' of each village.[5] Navajos returned to their homeland in 1868, and the Navajo Nation received its Navajo Court of Indian Offences in 1892 (Aberle 1982: 34,36). It introduced adjudication to Navajos, with the notion of a judge who is personally disinterested and reacts to an event rather than guides action (Ladd 1957: 71). That concept of 'legal justice' is alien to Navajos, because the 'function of what might be called a judge is not to make awards on the basis of desert, but rather to conciliate the parties in controversy and restore social harmony' (Ladd 1957: 71).[6] The Bureau of Indian Affairs (BIA) appointed Navajo judges to sit in judgment of others. How does adjudication work when Navajos believe in consensus? A 1942 report on 'Law and Order Conditions on the Navajo Indian Reservation' shows that the Navajo judges cannily adapted adjudication to the traditional method of discussing legal problems as a group.[7] The report found some degree of independence from federal supervision, in that both judges and litigants fully talked out disputes to solve them through consensus.

The Courts of Indian Offences were an arm of the Bureau of Indian Affairs, under the direct supervision of agency superintendents. John Collier, the Roosevelt administration commissioner of Indian affairs responsible for New Deal Indian policy, attempted to create tribal courts in a proposed Indian government statute. When Congress rejected the approach of tribal courts and a national federal court for Indian cases, Collier sought a legal opinion on the scope of the 'existing powers' language of section 16 of the Indian Reorganization Act.[8] One of those powers is the authority to administer justice (Cohen 1982: 250-52), and that is the basis for tribal courts. They are created as an exercise of inherent Indian nation sovereignty, and do not get their powers from any other source.

The Navajo Nation chose to retain its BIA-controlled court for a quarter century following the passage of the Indian Reorganization Act of 1934. A combination of events prompted the creation of the Courts of the Navajo Nation in 1958: an opinion by the Commissioner of Indian Affairs that the Navajo Nation could not appoint or supervise judges, and a move in the Arizona legislature to assert civil and criminal jurisdiction in Indian country. The Navajo Nation Council created the Courts of the Navajo Nation in a Judicial Branch thinking that if they looked like a state court, the surrounding states would see no need to assert jurisdiction over the Navajo Nation. The traditional procedures of the judges of the Navajo Court of Indian Offences went out and were replaced with procedures which are very similar to those used in the federal system.

By 1981, Navajo Nation leaders realized that Navajo Nation law had gone too far in copying non-Navajo rules. The Navajo Nation chairman, members of the Judiciary Committee of the council and others urged the courts to develop traditional approaches to justice. They demanded methods to incorporate Navajo common law into the system.[9] Navajo judges increased the use of Navajo common law principles in written decisions, and in 1982 they created the Navajo Peacemaker Court, a method of traditional dispute resolution which promotes the use of traditional legal procedures in communities.[10] Navajo judges and court staffers are articulating their thinking on the process of 'going back to the future' with Navajo common law.[11] These developments are relevant to the approach used in this policy study.

Farella points out that there are traditional approaches to violence associated with social disorder. What is the Navajo word used to describe social problems? It is *nayéé*, which means 'anything that gets in the way of a person living his life'. The literal translation is 'monster'. What are the things that 'get in the way' of life? They include depression, poverty, physical illness, worry, a bad marital relationship, and old age. 'The "monsters" are ... merely the objectification of these relatively intangible entities so as to make them manageable or exercisable' (Farella 1984: 8, 51). To slay or weaken a monster, you must know its name, ways and habits. Monsters have children, and the children of violence include despair, depression, escape with drugs or alcohol and all the other human weaknesses which cause frustration and result in acts of violence. Navajo macrojustice requires a careful examination of the monsters we are attempting to kill or at least weaken.

The process also requires a careful reexamination of institutions, relationships and approaches. Most tribal courts use the state model of adjudication and adversarial litigation. Are those procedures legitimate in the context of a given culture? Who are the actors in Indian justice systems and what is their role?[12] Adjudication and adversarial process may not be the best approach to deal with monsters. The Navajo Nation may wish to abandon or modify imported procedures following a century of experimentation with them. The 1982 report of the National Minority Advisory Council on Criminal Justice describes the effect of a century of Western justice well:

The displacement of Indian sovereignty by the encroaching Anglo-European system of laws and values has had pernicious, debilitating effects to the present. The legacy of this dispossession is graphically revealed in current criminal justice statistics. American Indians have, by far, the highest arrest rate of any ethnic group. Their arrest rate is consistently three times that of blacks and ten times that of whites. As many as 80% of Indian prisoners are incarcerated for alcohol-related offences, a rate twelve times greater than the national average. The major crime rate is 50% higher on reservations than in rural America. The violent crime rate is eight times the rural rate, murder is three times the rural rate, and assault is nine times as high. Furthermore, the percentage of unreported crime on reservations is higher than anywhere else; thus, the situation is actually worse than the statistics portray, according to a 1975 Task Force Report on Indian Matters by the Department of Justice.[13]

Are there ways to put the power to solve problems back in the hands of the people who are the victims of violence? Are there alternatives to the imposed procedures which destroyed traditional justice and created this situation? They can surely be developed through a careful reexamination of Navajo institutions, expectations and relationships.

We must also reexamine the relationship between the Navajo Nation and the United States government. Congress fails to follow through when it creates new programmes or responsibilities. One example is the Indian Civil Rights Act of 1964.[14] In addition to discounting the objections of many Indian nations, including the Navajo Nation, Congress failed to provide adequate funding for Indian nations to implement the act for more than twenty years.[15] In 1990, Congress passed the Indian Child Protection and Family Violence Protection Act.[16] It authorizes $30,000,000 per year for fiscal years 1992 to 1995 for Indian nation child protection and family violence prevention programmes.[17]

Although the act became law on 28 November 1990, the Bureau of Indian Affairs did not begin to develop the regulations required by it until 1 June 1993. While the B.I.A. asked for $1.5 million for family resource centres and $5 million for family violence prevention programmes this year, to date, programmes under the act have not been funded because the BIA has not asked for monies to implement the protection and prevention programmes.[18] Tribal self-determination programmes and funds for tribal courts are 'no longer a high priority' for the bureau.[19]

While its inaction in the face of widespread violence against women and children is inexcusable, Congress also abdicated its trust responsibility to assure justice in Indian country. The continuing reality is that until Congress honors the basic human rights of Indians and their governments, people will be hurt and die. The relationship between Indian nations and the United States needs a thorough overhaul. Official neglect is a monster.

THE NAMES OF THE MONSTERS

We will name the monsters, describe their ways and discuss weapons to use on them in the context of Navajo thought and society. We see the monsters in the workload on the trial courts of the Navajo Nation. In fiscal year 1993 (1 April 1992 to 31 March 1993), the Navajo Nation Courts received 47,979 new cases and brought forward 42,739 from the previous fiscal year.[20] An examination of the workload of the trial courts[21] shows that 51% of the docket of the district courts is criminal cases; 45.7% is traffic matters and 1.8% civil actions. In addition, 26,631 new criminal charges were filed in fiscal year 1992, and with the 19,958 cases brought forward, the total criminal caseload was 46,589 cases.

The major categories of criminal charges involved alcohol and personal violence: they were 1) offences against the public order[22] (a caseload of 17,159 charges—36.8% of them criminal); 2) driving while intoxicated (3,194—13.5%); 3) offences against persons[23] (6,243—13.4%); 4) intoxicating liquor possession or sales (5,848—12.5%) and 5) offences against the family[24] (2,659—5.7%). Property crime was comparatively low: criminal damage to property (2,027—4.2%), theft (687—2.7%), trespass and burglary (489—1%), forgery (315—less than 1%), and robbery 3 make up slightly over 8% of the criminal docket. The five major categories of crime were approximately 82% of that docket. Other violent crimes against persons were low: weapons and explosives charges (470—1%), sexual offences (i.e. sexual assaults; 214—less than 1%) and robbery 1 were comparatively few.[25] There were few drug or controlled substances cases—184 (less than 1%).

The largest category of offences, those against public order, show a need to address two problems: public intoxication and disorderly conduct. The Judicial Branch proposes to address public intoxication by decriminalizing it as an offence. The major purpose of the existing law is to prevent deaths from exposure to the cold by taking disabled people into custody.[26] Disorderly conduct is a more serious issue than it may otherwise appear. It is a catchall for less serious conduct, but it should be taken seriously. A study of Navajo drinking patterns shows that it takes place out of doors or at public gatherings, including 'stomp dances', Enemyway ceremonies and other gatherings.[27] A recent study of violence says that 'Intoxicated Navajo fight almost exclusively with family members'.[28] Disorderly conduct is an important offence because officers frequently make arrests for alcohol-related fighting. It is associated with high numbers of driving while intoxicated charges and offences against persons; it is most likely associated with offences against the family and sexual assaults. If the conclusion is correct, that most Navajo Nation crime is related to alcohol and assaults involving relatives,[29] then disorderly conduct charges should be more closely scrutinized. The same holds true for assaults.

Sexual misconduct is a more difficult problem. We do not know the extent to which offences against the public order, offences against the family and sexual offence are interrelated. Violence against women often involves the use of sexuality for punishment or control, and sexual assaults at public gatherings are reported to be common. As it is with other offences, defendants attempt to excuse their conduct by saying, 'I was drunk'.

How people behave under the influence of alcohol is determined by cultural practices and beliefs. Cultural patterns of Indian drinking have been identified.[30] However, if we tolerate drunkenness as a form of 'time out', this aggravates the problem.[31] There is an identified psychopathology known as 'crazy violence' or 'crazy drunken violence', which Navajos use to explain deviant and bizarre behaviour.[32] Violence should never be excused by explanations for behaviour which takes responsibility out of the hands of the individual. If alcohol-related crime is taken seriously, with drunkenness seen as an aggravating and not a mitigating factor, that should have an impact on defendants. While the Navajo Nation gaols are overcrowded, the court's policy toward alcohol-related crime should be that special attention will be given to it. Some non-gaoling options include use of the Navajo Peacemaker Court to address denial, mandatory restitution to victims, involvement of offender and victim families and intensive probation coupled with required treatment.

How do these patterns apply to youth crime? In F.Y. 1993, 724 delinquency cases were filed in the Navajo Nation family courts, and 248 were brought over, for a total caseload of 1,072 matters. The major categories of delinquency were public intoxication (a caseload of 157—14.6%), assault or battery (140—13%), 'other' offences (a broad range; 138—12.8%), property damage (104—12.8%), and disorderly conduct (98—9.1%). Driving while intoxicated, unlike adult crime, was only 4.3% of the delinquency docket (47 cases). Possession of liquor petitions (66) was only 6.1% of the caseload. There is some violent crime involving juveniles, as is shown by resisting arrest (36—3.3%) weapons (32—2.9%), and threatening (30—2.7%) charges. Juveniles appear to be more involved in property crime, as is shown by theft (88—8.2%), burglary (44—4.1%), and trespassing (33—3.0%) petitions. There were few charges for inhalation (of toxic substances; (16—1.4%) and possession of marijuana (11.1%). Again, the low number of filings may reflect a law enforcement problem, the use of prosecutorial discretion or other factors, and it does not necessarily mean that those problems are not present in larger numbers.

While youth crime follows a wider pattern, the same problem of alcohol-related crime and personal violence is present. There are few treatment, detention or foster care facilities for youthful offenders. Court programmes should address educating young people about their roles and behaviour because those avenues are limited. Children look to their parents and relatives for example. In some instances, parents and relatives provide liquor to the young, encouraging drunken behaviour. In others, relatives have become too dependent upon the criminal justice system to deal with their children. Delinquency procedures should include use of the Navajo Peacemaker Court to require children to confront their conduct, with relatives present to see what is happening to their children. Given the fact that at least 35% of juvenile charges involve property damage or injury to others, the Navajo Nation should consider increasing parental liability for restitution. There is a concept of a 'traditional probation officer', where parents and clan members assume responsibility for paying for the injuries caused by relatives, and watch an offender closely.[33] Parental and custodian liability for youthful offenders could be used to revive the effective role. The Peacemaker Court can be used to counsel children and relatives in a specific case, and Peacemaker Courts should be instituted in school systems as a means of teaching children their traditional Navajo responsibilities.

Children's status offences are few. Of the 378 case filed and 135 brought forward (for a caseload of 513 'child in need of supervision' - CHINs cases), 266 (51.8%) were for traffic violations, 159 (30.9%) were children 'beyond control', 87 (16.9%) were truants and there was one 'other' petition. CHINs cases are unique to our justice system, because it processes children for offences which would not be a crime if committed by an adult. While they are comparatively minor, they point to possible misconduct when a child is an adult. Children who are truant or 'beyond control' need special care, because they may be victims of adult neglect. The focus of such cases should be the family situation as a whole.

The injury done to children is reflected in the figures for dependant and neglected children. In F.Y. 1993, 428 petitions were filed and 346 were brought forward for a caseload of 774. The largest category of cases was physical abuse or neglect (427—55.1%).[34] The number of guardianship cases (119—15.3%) shows the extent to which private remedies to deal with child abuse are used and needed. Guardianship is essentially a procedure where a family member can petition the court to deal with poor parenting, neglect or abuse by appointing another person—usually a relative—to care for a child. Many tribal social service programmes and courts prefer to avoid the stigma of legally removing a child from parents and prefer the procedure of placing the children with others. Guardianship is important to grandparents and other relatives, who wish confirmation of a familial arrangement for child placement. Those relatives need a guardianship decree to receive benefits, place children in schools, provide for medical treatment, and qualify for housing, and so forth. Actions to remove children legally from parents or placements were 25% of the dependant/neglect docket. That includes termination of parental rights (53—6.8%), custody (34—4.3%) and Indian Child Welfare Act referrals (34—4.3%) (Fahey 1975: 10, 12). The family court had 21 sexual abuse cases (2.7%) and eight 'other' cases.

Here too, placement and treatment facilities are limited. Placement outside the child's home or family is a last resort, not only due to Navajo family values, but to the lack of any other placement option. One of the best approaches to child welfare in this area is requiring families to deal with their own children and to assume responsibilities toward them. The Navajo Peacemaker Court is proving to be a successful approach for dependant/neglect cases, because it unites family members to discuss their childrens' problems and assists with the placement process. Child sexual abuse (which is most likely present in many of the 1,158 'offences against the family' criminal cases) is particularly difficult to address. Some abusers attempt to justify sexual conduct with a child or with a stepchild on the ground that it was 'traditional' to have relations with a girl who had just reached puberty, or 'traditional' to have sexual relations with a wife's young sister or child from a previous relationship. Incest was one of the most horrible of crimes under Navajo common law. Peacemaking can be used to address abuser denial. In cases where proof of sexual contact is lacking, a child's family can be alerted to the possibility of abuse and develop safeguards to prevent it in the future.

The family court domestic relations caseload shows other cases which affect children. The largest category of cases (673—35.2%) was divorce, followed by name changes (271—14.1%). Other categories of cases which affect children included orders to show cause (to enforce court orders; 218—11.4%), 'other' family matters (217—11.3%), paternity (134—7%), child support (70—3.6%), and modification of prior decrees (55—2.8%). The other work of the family court included probates (159—8.3%), quiet title actions (44—2.3%), and validations of marriage (27—1.4%).[35] There were 41 Peacemaker actions in family court, which covered a wide variety of family disputes.

The domestic relations cases, as with guardianships, are important because they give individuals a private remedy for injuries done to them in a family setting. A divorce action can be an important means of private protection to prevent family violence or child abuse. A domestic relations action is an individual procedure to address abuses which social welfare officials or police may not detect or do not have the resources to address. While the Navajo Nation does not wish to encourage divorce as a matter of public policy, it is important for petitioners—particularly women—to have a means to get relief. At present, DNA-Peoples' Legal Services cannot handle divorces, except for situations involving domestic violence, due to the high demand. The Navajo Nation law of separation (for which there is no statutory provision) is unclear. Many women who want a divorce, or at least support, cannot get into court, due to their poverty and lack of access to a lawyer.[36]

Where members of the public cannot get a simple and inexpensive day in court, two things happen: women and children remain in abusive or neglectful environments, and the potential for violence increases. There should be private civil remedies to allow woman and child victims to escape a bad situation at their own choice and to lower the victimization. Adequate civil remedies also prevent violence by providing peaceful alternatives to settling disputes through personal family violence. While we do not yet have figures to show the extent to which recent domestic violence proceeding laws are working, family judges are reporting a sharp increase in filings. This shows the extent to which the Navajo Nation public wants private remedies to deal with victimization. Also, the large numbers of private actions, in comparison with filings by the Navajo Nation on behalf of children, shows that offering private remedies is a viable option to increasing social service functions.

The district court's civil actions are also relevant to the topic of violence. They are a means for the public to resolve peacefully disputes and provide compensation for injuries. While civil cases were only 1.8% of the district court's work, they are important. Contract actions were 62.9% (caseload of 953) of the docket. The usual pattern of these cases is that they are brought by lending institutions to collect loans, repossess property sold on credit, or to resolve other contractual disputes. Unemployment and a lack of income opportunities are tied to crime and violence, and offering civil remedies to businesses is tied to the Navajo Nation's business climate and the opportunities it offers. To the extent poor individuals need access to courts in civil actions to curb consumer abuses, small claims procedures are necessary.

The second highest category of civil case was torts and personal injuries (with a caseload of 133 matters; 8.8% of the civil docket). A tort action is a private remedy for an injury. In the past, Navajos filed criminal charges to deal with personal injuries, but the overburdened criminal justice system cannot deal adequately with this problem. To some extent, the burden of injuries to others should be shifted to the civil docket, except for matters which require punishment or criminal sanctions. Civil remedies are a means to prevent abuses caused by government officials; there were 59 civil rights actions (3.9% of the civil docket) and 54 prisoner relief petitions (3.6%). District courts possess the power to order specific relief to prohibit conduct or to require an action, and there were 44 such cases (2.9%). There are many kinds of civil actions, and the categories of 'other' (122—8%) and 'miscellaneous' (92—6.1%) were a significant portion of district court workload.

These are the monsters. As is shown by the figures, the biggest problems are alcohol, violence within family units and harm to children. The Navajo Nation repeatedly demands significant increases in the federal contribution to justice in Indian country but this is unlikely to come in these days of federal budget cutbacks. The Navajo Nation inherited a 'policing' model of justice from the United States, but this is breaking down. Only the most violent of crimes are prosecuted in the Courts of the Navajo Nation due to gaol overcrowding and a decree which sharply limits the numbers of prisoners the gaols can hold.

Western adjudication is a police model. It assumes that social order is maintained by using force and authority. That is the policy which underlies the formation of Indian police and courts in the nineteenth century[37] and the Navajo Nation system. Modern federal initiatives such as promoting tribal courts and recommending model codes only reinforce a model which is designed to promote federal governmental authority and assimilation. Recent legislation and proposals to increase the federal presence in Indian country are another aspect of the police model. Given the fact that most of the social problems of Indian country arise in the family, do we need to 'federalize' family conduct and subject family members to federal action?

Adjudication is another aspect of the police model. While it offers private remedies, people must seek the services of attorneys to invoke them. Licensed attorneys, whom people hire to advocate their positions, are authority figures who attain their privileged position through a tightly-regulated system of education and discipline. Most Navajos cannot afford a private attorney to seek remedies for violence or neglect of familial duties.

THE WAYS AND HABITS OF THE MONSTERS

While in theoretical and practical terms we may not have enough information on the causation of violence, we have various avenues by which to identify problems and to take coordinated action to address them.[38]

The Courts of the Navajo Nation must consider their role in this process. It is obvious that, given a lack of gaols and treatment facilities, the courts will have to increase their probation activities when dealing with adult criminal and juvenile offences. To do so, we need better understanding of the nature of problems which come before the courts.

There are many theories about alcoholism, but courts are most concerned with the dynamics of escapism within the use of alcohol. One of the biggest problems is denial. It is a difficult phenomenon. It manifests itself in criminal cases where defendants plead guilty at rates in excess of 90%. There are many reasons for this, despite the fact that Navajo Nation judges carefully counsel defendants on their rights. One is that alcohol-dependent defendants simply submit themselves to punishment, then return to their prior behaviour. That is a form of denial—denial of the individual's responsibility to care for himself. Another form of denial is the refusal to accept personal responsibility for the consequences of individual conduct by dealing with it. That is, driving-while-intoxicated defendants deny they have a drinking problem; abusers deny domestic violence or blame the victim for it; sex abusers deny the act and are adept in hiding it; parents deny responsibility for their children; children deny their responsibilities to their parents (particularly in elder abuse situations).

The usual approach to the common problem of denial is to use professionals to communicate with people who deny. The effectiveness of this approach relies upon the degree of respect people have for authority figures. It may be minimal, as with the person who is forced to speak to a probation officer, social worker or mental health professional. The circumstances may inhibit communication: judges see thousands of defendants each year; probation officers are overburdened; social workers cannot keep up with their caseloads; police do not want to be counsellors; school teachers prefer to teach. We cannot expect to receive or raise the resources to fully use a professional counselling approach to deal with denial.

One weapon or policy initiative for the Navajo Nation to address social problems is to use traditional leadership authority to address denial. The Navajo Peacemaker Court builds on the tradition of the *naat'aanii*—the Navajo civil leader. A *naat'aanii* is someone whom the community recognizes and acknowledges for a reputation of wise thinking and planning. Planning is a traditional Navajo justice concept. It assumes that people can solve their own problems if everyone affected by them talks out what happened and what can be done to address it. Plans or agreements which are produced by the talking-out process are binding, because they are reached through consensus and a group agreement about what to do. The *naat'aanii* tradition is used in the Navajo Peacemaker Court through the selection of peacemakers by chapters.[39] Peacemakers reinforce the tradition that the people who have a dispute should be the ones who decide how to resolve it. The incentive for resolution is the presence of the participants' family members. A peacemaker gets at denial through 'the lecture', which is a practical review of the problem in light of Navajo values. Family members are also effective agents to eliminate or reduce denial.

A recent Peacemaker Court case illustrates the point: a woman sued a man for paternity in a family court case, and he denied responsibility in court. When the judge referred the case to the Peacemaker Court, the parents of both children were present. They knew the relationship of the couple and turned the discussion of the question of paternity to what the parents were going to do about the future of *their* child. Given the poverty of the father, the families negotiated an agreement for him to provide firewood in lieu of cash. In another case, parents brought their children into Peacemaker Court to prevent them from committing incest. The case involved two first cousins who were committing incest in violation of both Navajo and Anglo values. The families were able to touch at least one of the couple to dispel his denial that there was anything wrong going on. The Navajo Peacemaker Court is proving to be an effective tool to reach driving-while-intoxicated (DWI) defendants. While many argue the effectiveness of mandatory minimum gaol sentences in DWI cases, we may also argue that punishment is more effective when a drunken driver must face his spouse, children, family and even victims in an intimate setting to discuss his conduct.

The Peacemaker Court seeks to return justice to the community as well as the parties to a dispute or problem. Too often, communities rely upon their police and courts to solve problems, and become dependent upon official action. When a lack of personnel or resources produces official inaction, the public loses respect for its government. Dependence upon governmental authority produces another form of victimization, and communities hide behind locked doors to avoid directly becoming victims of violence. An active participating community can have a great impact on community problems. For example, if it is correct that drunken behaviour can be curbed through the exercise of public opinion, then Navajo chapters have the means to deal with their violent or dangerous drinkers through direct action. A chapter can appoint and actively support peacemakers, and chapters have the ability to call community peacemaking meetings to return to the old Navajo procedure of discussing deviant conduct as a group.

While the Peacemaker Court was originally designed to solve most legal problems, it has been an underutilized avenue until recent days. Most of the domestic relations matters just discussed can be addressed through peacemaking. It is an appropriate place for guardianships, name changes, probates and even divorces. The problem lies with cases where the parties cannot afford the services of a peacemaker or the public experts that serve will be provided by the Navajo Nation government. The Navajo Nation must make an investment in the process.

A root cause of social disruption is the destruction of traditional family and clan arrangements. Traditional social controls in the form of the Navajo language, religion and social structure were destroyed by boarding schools, a transition to a wage economy, consumerism and modern media (i.e., radio, television films and the personal video player). Are traditional social controls still effective? They can be if communities choose to put them back in place. There are roles for families, clans and chapters to address violence, mistreatment of children and alcohol-related misconduct.

WEAPONS

This approach recognizes shortcomings in modern adjudication, the police model and institutions which take power away from individuals and groups of people. One of the major initiatives which the Navajo Nation must begin is to move justice back to the chapters and involve families in the justice process. The Navajo Nation is large. Too vast to cover with police, given limited resources. This shortcoming in policing and treatment resources mandates a change in policy. In addition, individual and community empowerment—and opportunity to speak and deal with one's own problems—is more in harmony with Navajo thinking.

There may be instances where litigants, who do not want consensual justice methods, refuse to cooperate with peacemaking or prefer action by a judge. What can the courts do to address those problems and forge other weapons to use against the monsters?

There is an ancient European tradition of access to the courts which can be revived by the Navajo method of adjudication. It comes from an ancient European belief that poor people should receive special treatment; that they should have a right to speak freely to have their grievances resolved.[40] The legal right of access comes from canon law, which had 'the concept of a dual system of procedure, one solemn and formal, the other simple and equitable. The simple procedure was available to certain types of civil cases, including those involving poor or oppressed persons and those for which an ordinary legal remedy was unavailable. It dispensed with legal counsel as well as with written pleadings and written interrogatories' (Berman 1983: 250-51). English common law recognized a similar right, expressed in the doctrine of *in forma pauperis*. Under English common law, litigants who swore they had less than a stated minimum income had fees waived, and received appointed counsel in civil cases. Under American law, fees are waived under limited circumstances[41] and there is no right to appointed counsel in a civil case. There is a due process right of access to the courts for relief. Governments cannot 'unreasonably' restrict access, and denial can be a violation of due process of the law.[42] The American legal doctrine is more restrictive than canon law or English common law, but there is a right of access to the courts to demand relief. Modern court performance standards recognize the right and require court planners to consider access to justice as a priority.[43]

There are other European precedents which address easy access to courts by people who cannot afford lawyers. In the latter Middle Ages, Europeans sought to develop procedures for judicial accommodation to ease the impact of law upon people who were at a special disadvantage in demanding justice. Three principles emerged: first, there was an obligation to provide special protection for widows, orphans, the aged, crippled or seriously ill persons, the poor 'and in general, the wretched of the earth'. Second, to ease the impact on those groups, their cases were to be handled by a summary hearing and rapid decision to avoid 'long-drawn-out and expensive forms of ordinary suits and proceedings' (Borah 1983: 11). Third, all lawyers were obligated to serve the poor and needy at reduced fees or no fees at all, or the state would provide an official to offer free legal representation (ibid: 11-12). Those ideas went to the Americas with the conquest of the New World.

The Spanish struggled for many centuries to frame their relations with Indian nations (ibid: 13).[44] There were three schools of Spanish thought about Indian law and government: first, that Indians have their own societies and that they are entitled to their own institutions and laws; second, that there is but one society (namely Spanish) and that Indians should be fully integrated into it; third, that there are two republics—Indian and Spanish (ibid: 15). Spanish law for the Americas acknowledged the first point of view by decrees which ordered Spanish bureaucrats to observe the 'usages and customs of the Indians'.[45] The Indian groups of Mexico quickly learned Spanish institutions and legal procedures, and the governors of New Spain studied how to accommodate Indian complaints and stem frustration (ibid: 28-29). On 9 April 1591, a royal order created the *Juzgado General de Indios* (General Court of Indians) for Mexico (ibid: 34, 370). It, and an accompanying letter, provided for a summary court to 'hear suits by Indians against Indians, Indians against

Spaniards; and Spaniards against Indians'. It also created an office for attorneys, to be paid from fines or levies on Indian communities, who would represent Indians without fee.

The concept of the General Court of Indian Offences was simple: it provided speedy, simple and inexpensive legal remedies for Indians and Indian groups. All a litigant needed to do was to seek out one of the staff attorneys, relate the complaint to him, and he would do the rest. After hearing a complaint, the court attorney would prepare all the necessary papers and process them through a summary legal procedure. While there is disagreement among historians regarding the motives or the effectiveness of the court, its principles can be used to modify Navajo Nation court procedures. A similar tradition in England was that of the justice of the peace. Those individuals held positions of respect, and the office was sought for the honour it gave. English justices of the peace stopped riots, informed the central government of any problems in their jurisdiction, heard the complaints of the poor and regulated ale houses (the bars of the day). They also used summary procedure, questioning people about the nature of the offence against them (Notestein 1962: 212, 216).

The Courts of the Navajo Nation should achieve the same goals: provide speedy and simple remedies for those who cannot afford a lawyer or the expense of normal legal proceedings. This would represent a shift from adversarial proceedings conducted by lawyers, to a system which would receive the public and process their cases without cost. It would require court staff members and modern equipment to prepare court papers and orders. Court staff members could brief the judge on the nature of the case and do everything necessary to provide for summary hearings.

Judges would have to modify their present usages somewhat. Rather than rely upon lawyers to question witnesses to bring out all the facts of a case, the judge would have to ask the questions. This is 'inquisitorial procedure', which goes back to canon law and is still used by some Europeans courts. The canon law doctrine was that a judge must be convinced of the judgment to be rendered by questioning parties and put himself in the position of the person before the court to ascertain what he does not know or what he wishes to hide.[46] Judges can receive case briefings from members of the court staff to become familiar with each case, then allow the parties to tell their stories. If anything is unclear, a judge can ask appropriate questions to get all the information needed for a decision.

SLAY THE MONSTERS!

The foregoing analysis uses Navajo legal thinking and modern strategic planning. In Navajo legal thinking, it is important to identify the source of problems to deal with them. Navajos do not believe in punishment for its own sake. They believe it is better to identify reasons for misconduct and deal with them. The analysis uses court statistics to identify the biggest problems in terms of offences and also the public demand for judicial services. That is strategic planning.

In the criminal area, the Navajo Nation courts must focus on the rights of victims. This is not only a modern trend in American criminal law, but a fundamental tenet of Navajo common law. It is *nalyeeh*, or a demand to be made whole for an injury. *Nalyeeh* is also a process for reconciliation of victim and offender, whereby people in ongoing family, clan, and community relationships 'talk out' their problems for resolution. The Navajo common law principle dictates a policy that the Navajo Nation courts must develop summary procedures to allow victims to demand restitution (or reparation). Where an offence involves a family member, the Navajo Peacemaker Court is the best forum to use consensual problem-solving to resotre or build proper relationships.

There are many social problems which are better addressed using civil rather than criminal remedies. In our analysis, we discovered that Navajos are using the guardianship action as a private child welfare remedy. Navajo Nation social service agencies, which are a variant on the police model and assume that professional intervention works best, are overburdened with cases and focus primarily on sexual abuse. They ignore child neglect cases, so grandmothers and aunts exercise their traditional duties toward children by seeking appointment as a guardian. Navajos have long recognized that prompt intervention is necessary to keep children out of the cycle of violence, and family members have a duty to intervene when children are placed at risk. The Navajo Nation courts previously promulgated summary domestic or family violence remedies to address family disruption, and summary procedures for child support enforcement will be implemented in the near future.

We call the plan 'Slay the Monsters!' We will get at the monsters of alcohol-related violence and dysfunctionalism in families and communities through summary remedies. As it was with the *Juzgado General de Indios*, individual Indians will be able to go to a Navajo Nation courthouse for immediate relief. In modern times, the court advocate (or 'commissioner') will use a computer rather than a quill pen to record the individual's grievance. Using standard computer forms, the commissioner will process the paperwork for restitution in a criminal case, reference to the Navajo Peacemaker Court, or summary proceedings. A commissioner will meet with the parties to discuss the documentary evidence they must present to the court and coordinate the appearance of witnesses. The commissioner will then schedule a hearing before the court and present a prepared file to a judge. The hearings will be relaxed, and the judge will question the parties. In 1991, the Navajo judges adopted the *Navajo Nation Code of Judicial Conduct*. This encourages judges to utilize

Navajo ethics regarding consensual agreements through discussion to conduct informal hearings.

This is not simply an academic essay. It is a plan for action. A draft of this essay was presented to LaNeta Plummer, Esq. of Southern Arizona Legal Aid. Ms. Plummer contacted the Navajo Nation courts to ask how funding from the National Legal Services Corporation could best serve Navajo justice needs. The text of this essay became a proposal for those funds, and the 'Slay the Monsters' Programme became reality on 1 July 1994. Using the federal funds provided, the Navajo courts will hire a planner to write plain-language computer forms and a manual which outlines summary procedures. The priority areas are child support enforcement, victim compensation in criminal cases, peacemaking, family violence intervention, guardianships, simple divorces, and other kinds of domestic relations cases. Following development of the forms and manual, the courts will hire two commissioners for each court and have them available at computers to serve the public. The funds are limited to the Window Rock and Chinle districts in the Arizona portion of the Navajo Nation, but the forms and manual will be available to the other five judicial districts, and this plan will be used to seek funding from other sources.

In 1982, the Navajo Nation courts chose to 'go back to the future' in the Navajo Peacemaker Court. The judges revived traditional Navajo justice in a modern setting. This plan also goes back for something else new. It utilizes traditional Navajo justice thinking and medieval concepts about summary justice to provide prompt and efficient remedies.

The non-Indian police model does not serve Navajos well. It does not meet their expectations. Navajos look to their judges as leaders whom people can seek out at will. As it was during the time of creation, Navajo leaders will seek out the monsters and slay or weaken them in procedures which attempt to get at the source of problems. The Navajo Peacemaker Court will be used to a greater extent, and coordinated with summary adjudication methods. The primary drive behind this policy is to generate simple justice methods which allow victims of crime and social disruption to have their problems solved in ways they understand. Police and courts took away this power. It is time to return the ability to frame the future to the hands of the people.

NOTES

1. See (1993) 'America the Violent: Crime Is Spreading and Patience Is Running Out', *Time*, 142: 8, 23 August (cover theme), 22-23.

2. National Research Council, *Understanding and Preventing Violence*, xi (1993). This study of the scientific aspects of violence reports and builds upon several twentieth century studies, including the National Advisory Commission on Civil Disorders (1967), the National Commission on the Causes and

Prevention of Violence (1968), the Commission on Obscenity and Pornography (1968) and the Scientific Advisory Committee on Television and Social Behavior (1969). Id., xii-xiii.

3. 'The trial court anticipates new conditions or emergent events and adjusts its operations as necessary'. Standard 4.5, Commission on Trial Court Performance Standards, *Trial Court Performance Standards 20* (1990).

4. The 2 December 1882 letter from the Secretary of the Interior to the Commissioner of Indian Affairs, which shows this motivation, is published in Prucha, Francis Paul (1978) *Americanizing the American Indians, 295*: 296-99. The rules for the court, as repromulgated in 1982, are at ibid: 300-305.

5. The proceedings are republished in Roessel Jr., Robert A. *Pictorial History of the Navajo from 1860 to 1910*, 22-26. The superior court had the power to impose the death penalty.

6. Ladd (1957: 71) says that Navajos view 'quasi-judicial' offices as a matter of facing choices by the people themselves—the agent—not making disinterested decisions as a judicial spectator.

7. Boyden, John S. and Miller, William E. (1942) *Report of Survey of Law and Order Conditions on the Navajo Indian Reservations*. Boyden was an Assistant United States Attorney from Salt Lake City, and Miller was a Special Agent of the Federal Bureau of Investigation from Phoenix. The report records observations and notes on the cases they watched.

8. Act of 18 June 1934, ch 576, § 16, 48 Stat. 987 (codified at 25 U.S.C. § 476(e) [1988]).

9. In 1981 James W. Zion participated in those discussions. The term 'Navajo common law' means the customs, usages, traditions and values of the Navajo people.

10. See Zion, James W. (1983) 'The Navajo Peacemaker Court: Deference to the Old and Accommodation of the New', *American Indian Law Review* 11: 89; Bluehouse, Philmer and Zion, James W. (1993) 'Hozhooji Naat'aanii: The Navajo Justice and Harmony Ceremony', *Mediation Quarterly*, 10: 4, 327.

11. See Tso, Tom (1980) 'The Process of Decision Making in Tribal Courts', *Arizona Law Review*, 31: 225, and Tso, Tom (1992) 'Moral Principles, Traditions, and Fairness in the Navajo Nation Code of Judicial Conduct', *Judicature*, 76: 1, 15. Associate Justice Raymond D. Austin of the Navajo Nation Supreme Court says that Navajos are going back to their own fundamental values, and 'Indians are going back to their own law—back to the future'. Austin, R. D. (1993) 'Freedom, Responsibility and Duty: ADR and the Navajo Peacemaker Court', *Judges' Journal*, 32: 2, 8, 48. Indian women are using this 'retraditionalization' process 'to integrate traditional and contemporary demands in a positive, culturally-consistent manner. The structure of the cultural system remains intact, but the specific jobs are modernized in accordance with social change'. See LaFromboise, Teresa D., Heyle, Anneliese M., and Ozar, Emily J. (1990) 'Changing and Diverse Roles

of Women in American Indian Cultures', *Sex Roles*, 22: 7/8, 455, 469.

12. For an excellent discussion of this approach, see Pommersheim (1988).

13. National Minority Advisory Council on Criminal Justice (1982) *The Inequality of Justice: A Report on Crime and the Administration of Justice in the Minority Community*, 131. As shocking as those statistics are, the council admits they 'are somewhat suspect' (ibid: 133). The national data bases on Native American violence is too small for 'stable estimates' and they need to be expanded. National Research Council, supra, n. 2, at 48-49, 90. A pressing priority for Navajo Nation initiatives is the need for an adequate and coordinated statistical system for all elements of the justice system.

14. Pub. L. 90-284, title II, April 11, 1968, 82 Stat. 77 (codified at 25 U.S.C. §§ 1301-1303).

15. United States Commission on Civil Rights (1991) *Indian Civil Rights Act*, 72.

16. Pub. L. 101-630; title IV, 28 November 1990 (codified at 25 U.S.C. §§ 3201-3211 [1992 supp.]).

17. 25 U.S.C. § 3210 (i), (a).

18. Singer, Geraldine (1993) 'Senate Committee on Indian Affairs Hearing on P.L. 101-630, the Indian Child Protection and Family Violence Prevention Services Act, and Other Indian Child Abuse Issues on 28 October 1993', 8-10 (Memorandum on hearing).

19. (1993) 'BIA Says Tribal Self-Determination and Tribal Court Grants Are "No Longer a High Priority"', *The Tribal Court Record* 6: 2, 9.

20. Judicial Branch of the Navajo Nation, Annual Case Activity Report, 1 April 1992 to 31 March 1993.

21. Ibid.

22. Which include public intoxication and disorderly conduct.

23. They include assault, aggravated assault (with a weapon), battery and aggravated battery.

24. Most commonly incest and child sexual abuse.

25. These figures do not show the extent of violence and criminal conduct in the Navajo Nation. They do not address issues such as policing in large rural areas or prosecutorial discretion in light of overcrowded jails. They do show the problems presented to the courts.

26. This is a serious issue, aside from the case statistics. Studies of death in New Mexico show that death from excessive cold, exposure or neglect was the second leading cause of death from unintentional injury in New Mexico and the third leading cause for Indian women. Death from exposure and excessive cold 'occurs almost exclusively among American Indians'. One study states that American Indians are 22% more likely to die from exposure, with risk factors of alcohol and remote geographic locations. See Sewell, C. Mack, Becker, Thomas M., Wiggins, Charles L., Key, Charles R. and Samet, Jonathan (1993) 'Injury Mortality', in *Racial and Ethnic Patterns of Mortality*

in New Mexico, 118, 125-126, 127-128.

27. Topper, Martin D. (1980) 'Drinking as an Expression of Status: Navajo Male Adolescents', in Jack O. Waddel and Michael W. Everett (eds.) *Drinking Behavior among Southwestern Indians*, 103: 130-34.

28. National Research Council, supra n. 2, at 198. The council does not cite a source for the statement.

29. The literature consistently shows this. See Ferguson, Francis N. (1968) 'Navajo Drinking: Some Tentative Hypotheses', *Human Organization* 27: 159; Lubben, Ralph A. (1975) 'Anglo Law and Navajo Behavior', *Kiva* 29: 1, 60; Levey, Jerrold E., Kunitz, Steven J. and Everett, Michael (1969) 'Navajo Criminal Homicide', *Southwestern Journal of Anthropology* 25: 2, 124; Jensen, Gary F. and Stauss, Joseph H. (1977) 'Crime, Delinquency and the American Indian', *Human Organization*, 36: 3, 252; and May, Philip A. (1982) 'Contemporary Crime and the American Indian: A Survey and Analysis of the Literature', *The Plains Anthropologist*, 225: 27-97.

30. National Research Council, supra n. 2, at 198-99.

31. MacAndrew, Craig and Edgerton, Robert B. *Drunken Comportment,* 83-99. These authors apply the theory of tolerance to drunken behavior to the stereotype 'Indians can't hold their liquor', and conclude that Indian drinking patterns are associated with stereotypical perceptions (ibid: 136-64).

32. Kaplan, Bert and Johnson, Dale (1964) 'The Social Meaning of Navaho Psychopathology and Psychotherapy', in Ari Kiev (ed.) *Magic, Faith and Healing: Studies in Primitive Psychiatry Today*, 203, 216-20.

33. One author asserts that the greatest category of child neglect is 'dumping' children on grandparents or leaving them alone while on drinking bouts. Physical abuse and sexual abuse is comparatively minor in relation to neglect, which is associated with parental alcohol use.

34. Most often, Indian Child Welfare Act (ICWA) cases involve children outside the territorial jurisdiction of the Navajo Nation. The grounds for ICWA cases involve the same conduct as is addressed in child abuse/neglect and termination of parental rights cases.

35. Probate, quiet title, and validation of marriage actions most often involve disputes over property, usually grazing permits and land leases. How they are handled affects the caseload figures for criminal cases, particularly assaults, and the Peacemaker Court. Navajos are very adept in selecting the legal tool which is most effective for reinforcing their position in a property dispute.

36. The Navajo Peacemaker Court had one case where a wife resorted to violence to get payments from her husband; she was driven to frustration and assault by her inability to get a court order to require maintenance. A restraining order against her in domestic violence proceedings was resolved in the Peacemaker Court, which helped the woman negotiate a maintenance agreement from her husband—what she wanted in the first place.

37. Barsh, Russell Lawrence and Henderson, J. Youngblood (1976) 'Tribal Courts, the Model Code, and the Police Idea in American Indian Policy', in Lawrence Rosen (ed.) *American Indians and the Law*, 25.

38. See the summary of recommendations of the National Research Council, supra n. 2, at 21-27. They include 1) problem-solving initiatives, 2) modifying and expanding violence measurement systems, 3) research projects, and 4) a multi-community research programme. The recommendations require a great deal of planning and coordination of existing programmes, initiatives the Navajo Nation should adopt.

39. A 'chapter' is a form of local government consisting of 110 local units of government in the Navajo Nation. Each chapter has elected officials who carry out the wishes of the community following periodic meetings of the entire community. Chapter government is much like the New England town hall form of government, which is maintained in the notion of the 'town hall meeting' in contemporary politics.

40. Leonardo Boff develops this theory for use in modern times in *St. Francis: A Model for Human Liberation*. He says that an individual can be 'poor' in the sense of not being able to participate in public affairs or speak out against felt injustices and there is hence a general obligation to support poor and oppressed peoples. Boff is a leading proponent of liberation theology and a 'preferential option for the poor' as well as Indian issues.

41. Namely a divorce filing fee, but not bankruptcy fees or fees in seeking judicial review of an administrative ruling reducing payments. Boddie v. Connecticut, 401 U.S. 371 (1971); United States v. Kras, 409 U.S. 434 (1973); and Ortwein v. Schwab, 410 U.S. 371 (1973).

42. See Antieau, Chester J. (1969) *Modern Constitutional Law* 1: 542-543. The leading modern case in point involved a North Dakota statute which required Indian nations to waive sovereign immunity as a condition for bringing a civil suit in that State's courts. Three Affiliated Tribes of Ft. Berthold Reservation v. Wold Engineering, 90 L.Ed.2d 881 (1986).

43. See Commission on Tribal Court Performance Standards, Standards 1.1 (open proceedings), 1.2 (adequate facilities), 1.3 (effective participation), 1.4 (courtesy, responsiveness and respect) and 1.5 (affordability).

44. That struggle continues up to these days, and modern Spanish republics in the Americas still attempt to frame Indian affairs policies. In Mexico, there are armed Indian uprisings as a result of ignoring Indian nation government.

45. See also Parry, J. G. (1990) *The Spanish Seaborne Empire*, 187, 190, 199, 218, 279; MacLachlan, Colin M. (1988) *Spain's Empire in the New World*, 64; Haring, C. H. (1975) *The Spanish Empire in America*, 56; and Simpson, Lesley Byrd (1982) *The Encomienda in New Spain*, 109, 153, 195.

46. Notestein (1962) 214, 218, 219, 222-23.

REFERENCES

Aberle, David F. (1982) *The Peyote Religion among the Navajo*, Chicago: University of Chicago Press.

Antieau, Chester James (1969) *Modern Constitutional Law*, Rochester, N.Y.: Lawyers Co-operative Publishing Company.

Barsh, Russell Lawrence and Henderson, J. Youngblood (1976) 'Tribal Courts, the Model Code, and the Police Idea in American Indian Policy', in Lawrence Rosen (ed.) *American Indians and the Law*.

Berman, Harold J. (1983) *Law and Revolution: The Formation of the Western Legal Tradition*, Cambridge, Mass: Harvard University Press.

Boff, Leonardo (1982) *Sao Francisco de Assis. Saint Francis: A Model for Human Liberation* [translated by John W. Diercksmeier], New York: Crossroad.

Borah, Woodrow W. (1983) *Justice by Insurance: The General Indian Court of Colonial Mexico and the Legal Aides of the Half-real*, Berkeley: University of California Press.

Cohen, Felix S. (1982) *Handbook of Federal Indian Law*, Charlottesville, Va.: Bobbs-Merrill.

Deloria, Vine and Lytle, Clifford M. (1983) *American Indians, American Justice*, Austin: University of Texas Press.

Deloria, Vine and Lytle, Clifford M. (1984) *The Nations Within: The Past and Future of American Indians' Sovereignty*, New York: Pantheon Books.

Fahey, John (1975) 'Native American Justice: The Courts of the Navajo Nation', *Judicature*, 59.

Farella, John R. (1984) *The Main Stalk*, Albuquerque: University of New Mexico Press.

Hagan, William T. (1966) *Indian Police and Judges: Experiments in Acculturation and Control*, New Haven: Yale University Press.

Haring, C. H. (1975) *The Spanish Empire in America*, New York: Oxford University Press (1st ed. 1947).

Kaplan, Bert and Johnson, Dale (1964) 'The Social Meaning of Navaho Psychopathology and Psychotherapy', in Ari Kiev (ed.) *Magic, Faith and Healing: Studies in Primitive Psychiatry Today*, Glencoe/New York: Free Press.

Ladd, John (1957) *The Structure of a Moral Code: A Philosophical Analysis of Ethical Discourse Applied to the Ethics of the Navaho Indians*, Cambridge: Harvard University Press.

MacLachlan, Colin M. (1988) *Spain's Empire in the New World: The Role of Ideas in Institutional and Social Change*, Berkeley: University of California Press.

Nader, Laura (1980) 'Old Solutions for Old Problems', in L. Nader (ed.), *No Access to Law: Alternatives to the American Judicial System*, New York:

Academic Press.

Notestein, Wallace (1962) *The English People on the Eve of Colonization, 1603-1630*, New York: Harper (1st ed. 1954).

Parry, J. G. (1990) *The Spanish Seaborne Empire: The History of Human Society*, New York: Knopf (1st ed. 1966).

Pommersheim, Frank (1988) 'The Contexual Legitimacy of Adjudication in Tribal Courts and the Role of the Tribal Bar as an Interpretive Community: An Essay', *New Mexico Law Review*, 18: 49.

Sewell, C. Mack., Becker, Thomas M., Wiggins, Charles L., Keys, Charles R. and Samet, Jonathan (1993) 'Injury Mortality', in Thomas M. Becker et al. (eds.) *Racial and Ethnic Patterns of Mortality in New Mexico*, Albuquerque: University of New Mexico.

Simpson, Lesley Byrd (1982) *The Encomienda in New Spain: The Beginning of Spanish Mexico*, Berkeley: University of California Press.

Waddell, Jack O., Everett, Michael W. and Brown, Donald N. (1980) *Drinking Behavior among Southwestern Indians: An Anthropological Perspective*, Tucson: University of Arizona Press.

Zion, J. W. and Zion, E. P. (1993) '"Hazho' Sokee"—Stay Together Nicely—Domestic Violence Under Navajo, Common Law', *Arizona State Law Journal*, 25: 2, 407-26.

5

MEDIATION WITHIN ABORIGINAL COMMUNITIES: ISSUES AND CHALLENGES

Marg O'Donnell

It is clear that Aboriginal and Islander people are searching for new ways to solve increasingly difficult disputes. The high rate of incarceration of Aboriginal and Torres Strait Islander people, the levels of alcohol consumption and related violence are a source of distress and dislocation to people both on communities and in urban and regional settings. Add to this the changes which have occurred in Queensland as a result of the Aboriginal Land Act 1991, the High Court *Mabo* decision, and the proposed new legislation relating to management and decision-making structures on Aboriginal communities. These developments will have significant impacts on communities in the next five years. In anticipation of these changes, and in acknowledgment that Western justice systems and, in some cases, traditional dispute resolution systems are not adequate to meet the challenges, there has been a recognition that there is a need for enhancement of existing conflict management and resolution strategies.

The Community Justice Programme (C.J.P.) within the Department of the Attorney-General in Queensland is attempting to provide resources, services and ideas to Aboriginal people, particularly those on D.O.G.I.T. communities, to enable them to manage their own disputes in a creative and powerful way.[1] In doing so, the C.J.P. is mindful of the need for ongoing consultation and liaison with Aboriginal and Torres Strait Islander people and communities. The preservation of functional, existing dispute resolution structures is also perceived to be of paramount importance as care is taken not to introduce yet another 'solution' which communities neither want nor find relevant.

This chapter describes briefly the operations of the Community Justice Programme, the attempts made to respond to the Aboriginal community's requests for assistance in dispute resolution, and the development of a coordinated and coherent project to provide mediation services to D.O.G.I.T. communities. In describing these processes, attention will be paid to some issues of concern which have surfaced. These issues include the neutrality of the mediator, confidentiality of the mediation process, whether mediation should be voluntary or mandatory and whether mediation should occur when violence is a current issue between disputants. Broader issues such as who should become mediators and how they will be trained will be referred to. Explicit in the discussion that follows is the belief that traditional Western processes of dispute resolution are no longer always appropriate, if they ever were, in the wider society and in particular in Aboriginal communities.

The Community Justice Programme, an initiative of the Attorney-General of Queensland, the Honourable Dean Wells, opened its doors for business in Brisbane on 1 July 1990. Its brief was to provide a dispute resolution service to the state of Queensland, first in the southeast corner, and then to extend gradually to all major provincial cities which would, in turn, service the surrounding regions.

A service is provided to the entire southeast region, from Gympie to the New South Wales border, west to Toowoomba and the Darling Downs, Cairns, Townsville and Mt. Isa. Since opening, approximately 500 mediation sessions have been held. Settlement has occurred in around 85% of these cases. The types of disputes which have presented include the traditional disputes brought to neighbourhood justice centres in Australia and overseas, that is disputes between neighbours, family members, co-workers, landlords and tenants, resident groups and local authorities. There is currently a panel of around 120 accredited mediators. These are people from all walks of life, ages and ethnic backgrounds. Twelve of these accredited mediators are of Aboriginal or Torres Strait Islander descent. All have undertaken and passed a 72-hour skills development training course.

The C.J.P. in Queensland has pioneered several innovative fields of practice in Australia. Two of these are the Crime Reparation Programme and the Police Complaints Mediation Initiative. Both of these projects will eventually have an enormous impact on the administration of justice on Aboriginal communities. The Crime Reparation Programme, currently being trialled at the Beenleigh and Holland Park Magistrates Courts, provides a voluntary opportunity, after conviction and before sentencing, for adult and juvenile offenders to come together to discuss the offence which has occurred. It also provides an opportunity for the victim and offender to participate in the determination of mutually acceptable reparation for the victim, thus personalizing the criminal justice processes for both victims and offenders.

To date, the pilot has targeted non-habitual adult offenders and repeat juvenile offenders who plead guilty to property offences, e.g., breaking and entering, vandalism or minor theft. What is said at mediation is confidential, but parties sign a waiver which enables the C.J.P. to provide a copy of the agreement reached to a Community Corrections Officer who reports to the court. The Magistrate may then choose to take the outcomes of the mediation into account in sentencing offenders. There are other points in the process of contact between the offender and the criminal justice system where mediation is being currently considered. For example, it could be used prior to charging as a diversionary option, as a sentencing option, as a condition of a parole order, or post-sentencing as part of a correctional strategy, either during probation or during a term of imprisonment in more serious crimes.

The Police Complaints Mediation Initiative is also a pilot programme which flowed from discussions and agreement between the C.J.P., the Criminal Justice Commission and the Queensland Police Service to mediate in complaints of a minor nature against police and other public officials.

DEVELOPMENT OF AN ABORIGINAL FOCUS:

In early 1990 the Aboriginal Co-ordinating Council in Cairns approached the Attorney-General seeking assistance in developing a mediation service for Aboriginal communities. Visits were made to the Aurukun and Yarrabah communities with Barbara Miller from the Aboriginal Co-ordinating Council to gauge interest. Despite support for the concept from within the C.J.P., the decision was made at that time to direct the energies of the yet to open programme to the provision of alternative dispute resolution services in the Brisbane and southeast corner.

Doomadgee Dispute

In March-April 1991 an approach was made to the C.J.P. via the office of Rob Hulls, the then Federal Member for Kennedy, for the service to contact the Doomadgee community. The people of Doomadgee were at that time experiencing a good deal of upheaval and adverse public exposure relating to the management of alcohol and the levels of violence on their community.

After seeking permission from all major groups (the women, the council, and so on) within Doomadgee, consultation with the Aboriginal Co-ordinating Council staff and attending a full Aboriginal Co-ordinating Council meeting, a team of three mediators (two white, one black) flew to Doomadgee to begin a six-day process of meetings. Meetings were held with individuals, with groups, and then with the wider Doomadgee community to help them identify their major concerns, discuss them more fully and establish priorities for the way forward. The role of the mediators was to act as a neutral, third party, willing to preserve the confidentiality of the issues and able to encourage all parties to speak fully and constructively to each other about past concerns and future options and directions.

Feedback from sections of the Doomadgee people has indicated that they achieved positive outcomes and found this process of dispute resolution empowering for themselves as a community and also as individuals. The Doomadgee people have since re-enacted some of that settlement process for a video on Aboriginal mediation which the C.J.P. produced in 1993.

Since then, Community Justice Programme mediators have been asked to assist in the settlement of disputes or the facilitation of issues in the following cases:

• August 1991: facilitation of a three-day meeting convened by the Department of Family Services and Aboriginal and Islander Affairs (Qld.) with representatives from a number of Aboriginal and Islander communities and organizations, and relevant government and community-based organizations to develop a strategy for Caring for Returned Human Remains and Burial Artefacts.[2]
• October 1991: mediation/facilitation with Palm Island community representatives to formulate a response to community problems and establish appropriate community laws.
• December 1991: mediation with members of the Aboriginal community Mt. Isa.
• March 1992: mediation on Darnley Island of a dispute between two members of the community which had been escalating over a period of years and had spread to the stage where it involved other family and community members.
• The arrangement by the Department of Environment and Heritage of a Cultural Heritage consultation with Aboriginal representatives from community organizations in South East Queensland.
• The facilitation on the community of Yarrabah conducted throughout the 1993 year by the C.J.P. over land rights claims under the provisions of the Aboriginal Land Act (1991).
• The facilitation of a series of meetings in early 1993 in a country town between the town council and representatives of Aboriginal communities, in the wake of inter-racial violence.
• Assistance provided to the Doomadgee Aboriginal community to help formulate plans for the management and consumption of alcohol on the community.

Darnley Island Dispute

In giving some idea of how the mediation process works when C.J.P. mediators visit communities, I will quote extensively from the report of Alex Ackfun, C.J.P. Project Officer:

The visit I am most familiar with is the one to Darnley Island and I'll refer to this. The dispute was essentially between two family members surrounding issues of the 'old ways' versus the 'new ways'. The content of the mediation session is confidential and cannot be discussed. The session took place over a three day period.

Prior to the visit to Darnley, we had to establish that the disputing parties were ready to attend mediation. A lot of ground work was done on this aspect in consultations with the parties and Island Community Council. The Council itself had an interest in the matter because it could see the dispute disrupting the harmony of the island and its administrative operations.

Even though the dispute at face value appeared to involve two family members, it soon became clear the decisions they made in their negotiations would affect the whole social fabric of the community. The dispute was a classic example of parties in conflict—starting out as a little matter but a lot of aggravation and concern developing between the parties, with neither able to sit down together and discuss issues concerning them.

Arriving at the Island, we took some care to visit the two parties separately and in their own homes. Here the steps of the mediation process were explained to each party and care was taken to provide identical information to both. The sequence of the mediation steps was altered in this case. Private caucus took place at the beginning and summaries of the parties' concerns were taken down by the mediators. A proposed agenda was established and confirmed with the parties.

The mediators assisted the parties to decide on the manner in which proceedings would commence, e.g. what time, where, who could attend and speak at the mediation session. Both agreed that anyone in the community could speak. Some ground rules were also established, e.g. allowing the other to speak uninterrupted so concerns could be heard, following a set number of steps in the mediation session.

This process saw the mediators walk from one party's house to the other to finalize proceedings for the next day. It was decided by the parties to hold their mediation session as a public meeting at the Council Chambers. The building of trust in the mediators and in the process was in effect taking place. And this was a conscious effort on the part of the mediators.

The session from then proceeded as a normal mediation would, with parties 'in exploration', talking about the past, but encouraged by the mediators to look at options for the future. Some care had to be taken to reaffirm the role of the C.J.P. mediators—that the parties themselves would be working out solutions and options for themselves—the mediators would assist them in doing this—no conditions were to be imposed on them by the C.J.P.

At the end of the second day, the options worked out by the parties were prepared and delivered to each of the parties in their homes. Mediators clarified and acknowledged progress made by the parties. The list of options also allowed them to discuss these with other members of their family. Here the mediators recognized other stakeholders needed to be consulted by the parties to give the process a chance of success.

On the third day the parties were encouraged to focus on the future. A restating of the role of the C.J.P. and the fact that we were not going to solve the dispute for the parties was also necessary. A number of positive items were gained from the Darnley experience. They can be reflected in any other mediation outcome if handled successfully. These positives were:

- an opportunity for parties to air concerns and be heard;
- some understanding of the other's concerns;
- the adoption of a manageable plan of action;
- the achievement of some acceptable outcomes;
- the regaining/maintaining of respect by the parties;
- an understanding of the mediation process; and
- a new way to resolve differences.

The Darnley Island mediation provided reinforcement of the rewards possible using conflict resolution processes. Similar rewards have been encountered on other communities where the C.J.P. has intervened.[3]

As well as this 'on the ground' experience, staff of the C.J.P. met with the Legislative Review Committee and prepared documentation ('Towards Self-Government', Community Justice Programme) for discussion regarding the introduction of mediation services on D.O.G.I.T. communities. Subsequently, alternative dispute resolution mechanisms were recommended for Aboriginal and Torres Strait Islander communities in the final report on the Inquiry into the Legislation Relating to the Management of Aboriginal and Torres Strait Islander Communities in Queensland by the Legislative Review Committee (Legislative Review Committee 1991).

ABORIGINAL MEDIATION INITIATIVE

As a result of this growing interest in alternative dispute resolution services within the Aboriginal community, and in order to respond at last to the approaches to the department from the Aboriginal Co-ordinating Council, special funding for the 1991-92 and 1992-93 financial years was allocated by the Attorney-General to the Alternative Dispute Resolution Division (C.J.P.). The funding was given so that a special focus could be made on the development of Aboriginal mediation initiatives, including the provision of services but emphasizing the training of Aboriginal people in mediation skills.

Project Officer Alex Ackfun was appointed to develop this process. A decision was made to target D.O.G.I.T. communities. Initially, the brief was broad and consultation was to be an inherent part of the process.

There were three guiding assumptions:

- The project needs to be developed in consultation with individual communities. It cannot be imposed. We are aware that arrangements to introduce formal alternative dispute resolution services in D.O.G.I.T. communities must reflect local perceptions of justice.

• We need to avoid undermining traditional dispute processing mechanisms, which are in place to varying extents in different communities.

• We are aware of the complexities regarding management and resolution of conflict in the communities and the need to develop a comprehensive and coherent set of interlocking strategies, of which mediation is only one, to address problems of disputation and violence (Welsh 1992).

Conflict Management on Communities

At this point it is important to acknowledge that there is a diversity of mechanisms in place throughout the communities for the maintenance of social order. These range from the handing down of correct codes of behaviour from appropriate and knowledgeable members of the community, to the traditional process of public dispute management required between rival families or clan groups. Some common issues of concern are those of violence on communities, children, physical conditions, and funding arrangements. Land disputes arising out of the Aboriginal Land Act 1991 also are expected.

Concern is often expressed regarding the term 'dispute resolution' in relation to these disputes. Conflict is regarded as an essential part of life, and there is a high tolerance of anger and aggression. Aggression had traditionally been accepted and managed in a ritualized structure which encompassed a strict set of rules and expectations. Large numbers of people became quickly involved in supporting their kin and 'blockers', who acted as referees, intervened to prevent serious harm. Skillful management of the process allowed the participants to control and enjoy the interaction. On occasion, these controls proved inadequate; however, the structure generally worked to reduce the level of conflict. The desired outcome was a return to harmony and balance within the society, rather than a win/lose resolution. One of the main reasons for violence was that it was a means of regaining the balance upset by a former injury or death.

Alcohol abuse has transferred controlled violence into uncontrolled violence on many communities and changed the nature of conflict. Alcohol-induced conflict is now a major social problem. Traditional processes often escalate the violence and people are looking for alternative means to manage disputes. There are as well, it is acknowledged, formal Aboriginal structures, such as Aboriginal Courts and Community Councils, which have played important parts in the resolution of conflict in communities, alongside the more traditional, informal processes.

The Project

Although the details of the project needed to be developed in consultation, there was a broad vision which encapsulated the advice, knowledge and experience which was already at hand. This vision entailed three key strategies.

First, the C.J.P. would continue to provide a 'visiting' expert dispute resolution service to communities when asked, when possible, and when appropriate. Provision of this service would, when feasible, rely upon the assistance of Aboriginal and Torres Strait Islander mediators, working sometimes in conjunction with white mediators and sometimes on their own. Recognition was also given to the possibility that alternative dispute resolution services would sometimes be provided through the use of an all-white mediation team.

Second, the C.J.P. would train Aboriginal and Torres Strait Islander people, both on and off communities, in dispute resolution skills so that they could effectively manage their own disputes. Third, in conjunction with existing legal, justice, policing and welfare processes, the C.J.P. would assist D.O.G.I.T. communities to establish structures and arrangements on their communities which would allow the full utilization of a range of alternative dispute resolution possibilities. For example, the establishment of victim-offender mediation processes, as piloted in Beenleigh, may require specialist interventions and assistance from C.J.P. staff to set up fully on remote communities.

The dilemma in planning such innovative services and programmes is persuading Treasury officials to fund a project broad enough in vision, which will only proceed *after* consultation with relevant key stakeholders. The challenge has been for the C.J.P. to present a draft plan of action without preempting the wishes or decisions of the Aboriginal communities.

So far into this project, the C.J.P. has produced a video on Aboriginal mediation called 'Talk About It'. This video was mostly filmed at Doomadgee, with members of that community talking about their experiences of mediation and re-enacting some mediation processes. In 1992 the first mediation skills training course was offered in Cairns. Fifteen Aboriginal and Torres Strait Islander people undertook and completed the 35-hour course. This group now forms the nucleus of a pool of Aboriginal mediators in the north. Their role will be both to assist in dispute settlement service delivery and to help train other Aboriginal people, especially those on communities, to be mediators.

CHALLENGES AND ISSUES

Alternative dispute resolution is a concept whose time has definitely come. Alternative dispute resolution services throughout Australia and overseas have mushroomed from the neighbourhood mediation services to more complex court-annexed, mandatory processes such as in the Family Court, attached to Tribunals

(A.A.T.), grievances (P.S.M.C. in Queensland), complaints (Health Rights Commission Act 1991), as part of government procedures manuals and sometimes as standard elements of contracts in business agreements.

Aboriginal people have also responded enthusiastically to a procedure which resembles more, in its origins, traditional dispute resolution processes within Aboriginal society than Western legal traditions. The emphasis on personal and group empowerment and resolution, the face-to-face confrontation of protagonists, the structured discussions, the free expression of feelings as well as facts, the ability to deal with 'substantive' as well as perceived issues of alternative dispute resolution are significantly different elements to those found within the arcane rituals and structure and mystifying language of the court experience.

Some Aboriginal people have expressed views similar to Danish criminologist Nils Christie (1977), who argues that we ought to think of conflicts as property and furthermore that we ought to guard our conflicts jealously and not allow them to be stolen from us or give them away. Christie says that in modern Western societies, conflicts have been taken away from the parties directly involved and in the process have either disappeared or become someone else's property. This is a problem, he argues, because conflicts are potentially very valuable resources for us as individuals and as communities. Nowhere is this whole process more painfully apparent than in the operation of the criminal law, where offences have become offences against the state, and others, primarily lawyers, generally speak on behalf of both victim and offender.

The Alternative Dispute Resolution Process

Central to discussions of alternative dispute resolution, in particular mediation, are the key issues of voluntary participation by the parties, the confidentiality of the process and outcome, and the neutrality of the mediators.[4]

Voluntary Attendance. Although voluntary attendance at mediation is seen by most as desirable, it is worth considering whether or not there may be some cases where parties should be required to attend. The Race Discrimination Act 1975 and Sex Discrimination Act 1984 have powers to require parties to attend conciliation conferences, and the industrial arena is another where compulsory conferences between parties are common.

It may be that mediation may be used as a compulsory pre-court diversionary option, or as a sentencing option by Aboriginal Courts in criminal matters. In civil matters people may be required by the Community Council or a respected elder to attend mediation. It has been suggested that mediation may only be considered acceptable on some communities if a respected older person 'orders' mediation for parties as the prescribed method of dispute settlement in particular cases. The alternative dispute resolution process is flexible enough to accommodate these variations. They should be considered by communities and decided according to local needs.

Confidentiality. The mediation process as practiced by the C.J.P. and most dispute resolution services is characterized by its universal commitment to the confidentiality of the process. This confidentiality is seen by many as essential and as a major incentive for people to attend in the first place.

The disadvantages of the court—the expense, time—are hugely compounded by the public exposure that court brings. The confidentiality provisions also ensure that parties cannot use what was said in mediations as a basis for future legal action or public prosecution of the other.

Aboriginal communities, it need hardly be said, do not resemble the same dispersed and private living arrangements as those found particularly in urbanized Australian society. Privatization of disputes through mediation as experienced in cities would not only be absolutely impossible on communities but also, in many cases, completely unacceptable. It is expected that disputes on communities *will* be public and polycentric, that is involve issues of shifting focus and importance and affect the wider community beyond merely two protagonists.

Families and interested parties may need to be aware of negotiations and outcomes and settlement may often require pressure from appropriate family members and the widest possible publication throughout the community.

Neutrality. The neutrality of the mediator, as with the concept of 'blind' or impartial justice, is held to be of paramount importance in effective dispute resolution practice. It is considered, however, that neutrality of mediators will be almost an impossibility within communities due to family and kinship affiliations. A respected person appears to be a more appropriate person, as these are the people who have traditionally been required to take a role in dispute management. Some disputes may involve conflict within whole communities or between communities and government or organizations such as mining companies. In these latter cases outside (neutral) mediators may be used.

As with the issues of voluntary attendance and confidentiality, neutrality is a concept which will have special and sometimes limited application in the management of disputes on Aboriginal communities. It would be expected that local rules and procedures governing these fundamental concepts would emerge on a community basis.

Domestic Violence

The question of whether mediation is appropriate between couples with a history of domestic violence is one of the significant policy debates in the field of alternative dispute resolution in Australia at the current time.

The issue is contentious and a general policy consensus has not yet been achieved.

The Community Justice Programme's position is essentially consistent with that promoted by the National Committee on Violence Against Women. Key elements of the National Committee on Violence Against Women policy include:

- an intention to exclude the majority of disputes from mediation where there has been domestic violence;
- the introduction of procedural guidelines to provide effective protection for those victims who find themselves in mediation or who make a free and informed choice to use mediation.

The guidelines adopted by the National Committee on Violence Against Women and by the Dispute Resolution Centres Council acknowledge that mediation is undesirable in many cases of domestic violence in that it may expose the victim to several kinds of unacceptable risk.[5] However, they also provide for the reality that it is not possible to screen out all couples affected by domestic violence, and for the rights of victims or survivors of domestic violence to choose a method of dispute resolution. It is apparent that the most common presenting problems in the Aboriginal community are conflicts within families and extended families, and that they are most likely to involve some degree of domestic violence. Those are the very issues we found that people want mediated.

There is widespread alarm and distress at the degree of Aboriginal family violence, and the number of women dying as a result of that violence. Many more Aboriginal women die as a result of violence than Aboriginal people die in custody. Yet they have little access to appropriate support groups or agencies, and have a negative contact with the formal justice system.

In the position paper prepared for the National Committee on Violence Against Women, Dr Hilary Astor explains that:

> many Aboriginal women who are the victims of domestic violence have strong doubts about using the protections of the formal justice system if it results in their husband, fathers and brothers being sent to jail. European women also have such doubts, but the consequences of using the formal justice system are different for Aboriginal women. However, some Aboriginal women do want and need the protections of the formal justice system but their experience of seeking to use these protections is that, in most cases, nothing is done and their complaint is not taken seriously. Other women fear that complaining will bring the intervention of the white welfare system and that they will lose their kids (Astor 1991:19-20).

It is therefore obvious that alternative dispute resolution services provided by and to Aboriginal women may well include meetings between perpetrators and victims of domestic violence. In looking at providing this service to Aboriginal women, care will need to be taken that appropriate safeguards are in place to minimize risk to the woman's safety and checks made to ensure that any arrangements or agreements entered into are not the result of fear and powerlessness on the part of the women concerned.

CONCLUSION

It is my view that Aboriginal people could benefit from exploring current developments in alternative dispute resolution. They could take from these processes what is useful and relevant for themselves and their communities, and evolve a coherent set of interlocking strategies which will address their problems of disputation and violence. While new alternative dispute resolution processes are put in place, older traditional conflict management processes must not be discredited or dismantled. It is important that new ways do not bring about the loss of face or authority of key elders. A further consideration relates to the ethos of the Community Justice Programme version of mediation, which promotes collective decision-making arising out of negotiated, community-based agreements. The challenge will be to integrate this underlying principle with more traditional top-down decision-making processes as practised in Aboriginal communities. This and other challenges outlined in this chapter are set before the Community Justice Programme and the communities. The goal of an integrated and effective dispute resolution service on communities is there for us to aim towards.

NOTES

1. D.O.G.I.T.—Deed of Grant in Trust. Land granted in trust under the Land Act 1962 for the benefit of Aboriginal inhabitants or for the purpose of an Aboriginal reserve, Queensland.

2. See ADR (1991) 'Report of a Queensland Advisory Meeting to Develop a Strategy on Caring for Returned Human Remains and Burial Artefacts'.

3. Ackfun, Alex (1992), Presentation to ADR Townsville Seminar, Brisbane: C.J.P. internal report, May.

4. The legislative base upon which the C.J.P. operates provides for these principles at Sections 4.4, 5.3 and 5.4 respectively within the Dispute Resolution Centres Act 1990.

5. ADR (1992) 'Guidelines for Mediation in Domestic Violence', Canberra: Alternative Dispute Resolution Division, Department of the Attorney-General, March.

REFERENCES

ADR (1991) 'Report of a Queensland Advisory Meeting to Develop a Strategy on Caring for Returned Human Remains and Burial Artefacts', Brisbane: Alternative Dispute Resolution Division, Department of the Attorney-General.

ADR (1992) 'Report of the National Inquiry into Racist Violence in Australia', Brisbane: Alternative Dispute Resolution Division, Department of the Attorney-General.

Astor, Hilary (1991) 'Mediation and Violence Against Women', a position paper, Canberra: National Committee on Violence Against Women.

Charles, Kevin (1991) 'The Royal Commission into Aboriginal Deaths in Custody: Report of the Working Party on Implementation of the Recommendations' (including attachments 1, 2 and 3), October.

Christie, Nils (1977) 'Conflicts as Property', *The British Journal of Criminology*, 17: 1, January.

Darnley Island Report (1992) *Community Justice Programme*, Brisbane: Alternative Dispute Resolution Division, Department of the Attorney-General.

Dispute Resolution Centres Act (1990).

Faulkes, Wendy (1991) 'Mediation for Aboriginal Communities', discussion paper no. 1. Sydney: Community Justice Centre, NSW, April.

Faulkes, Wendy (1991) 'Mediation for Aboriginal Communities', discussion paper no. 2. Sydney: Community Justice Centre, NSW, April.

Hazlehurst, Kayleen M. (1988) 'Resolving Conflict: Dispute Settlement Mechanisms for Aboriginal Communities and Neighbourhoods', *Australian Journal of Social Issues*, 23:4, November, 309-22.

Legislative Review Committee (1991) '"Towards Self Government": A Discussion Paper inquiring into Legislation Relating to the Management of Aboriginal and Torres Strait Islander Communities in Queensland', Brisbane: Community Justice Programme, Department of Attorney-General, August.

Miller, Barbara (1991a) 'Crime Prevention and Socio-Legal Reform on Aboriginal Communities in Queensland', *Aboriginal Law Bulletin*, 2: 49, 10-13.

Miller, Barbara (1991b) 'Working Together for Crime Prevention', conference paper for 'Healing Our People' Conference, Canberra: Australian Institute of Criminology, April.

Murray, Gwenn (1991) 'Mediation and Reparation within the Criminal Justice System', a discussion paper, Brisbane: Community Justice Programme, Department of the Attorney-General, August.

Nolan, Christine (1991) *Guidelines for Mediation in Domestic Violence*, Brisbane: Division of Alternative Dispute Resolution, Department of the Attorney-General.

Von Sturmer, John (1991) 'Talking with Aborigines', reprint from newsletter, *Australian Institute of Aboriginal Studies New Series* 15: March.

Welsh, Joan (1992) 'Aboriginal and Islander Mediation Initiative', project proposal, Brisbane: Division of Alternative Dispute Resolution, Department of the Attorney-General.

Williams, Nancy M. (1987) *Two Laws: Managing Disputes in a Contemporary Aboriginal Community*, Canberra: Australian Institute of Aboriginal Studies.

6

'THE STRENGTH OF COMMUNITY': THE NATIVE COUNSELLING SERVICES OF ALBERTA STORY

Amanda Nielsen Adkins

INTRODUCTION

Native Counselling Services of Alberta (NCSA) is one of the most stable, successful and reputable Native organizations in the world. The experience and expertise of NCSA has been recognized locally, nationally and internationally. NCSA's work in the field of aboriginal criminal justice has pioneered the way for individuals and communities worldwide. Today, NCSA stands as a testament to the strength and courage of Aboriginal people and a beacon of light for the visions of tomorrow.

Native Counselling Services of Alberta (NCSA) found its roots during one of the most unstable periods in Canadian history. The 1960s marked the start of a growing awareness by Native people about the social, political and economic disadvantages they endured.

The Indian Act of 1876, and the subsequent 1951 revision, empowered the Canadian government to regulate virtually every aspect of Native life. Until the early 1960s, Native acceptance of established government practices was understood by most Canadians to indicate agreement and even support. It was thus with astonishment and resentment that many non-Native Canadians greeted the genesis of the Native Canadian movement.

Dempsey (1986: 200) describes Native students of the time as 'angry young Indians' who were 'erudite, eloquent and expressive'. It was a time of anger as Native people across Canada began revolting against a desperate situation characterized by 'pervasive poverty, high rates of unemployment and reliance upon public assistance, low levels of formal education, high death rates from accidents and violence and increasing rates of family breakdown (Siggner 1979; Griffiths, Yerbury, and Weafer 1987)' as cited in Griffiths and Verdun-Jones (1989: 546).

As public pressure mounted, the government responded with a report entitled *Indians and the Law* (Canadian Corrections Association 1967), revealing that the 'number of Indian people appearing in courts in this country ... is a cause for deep concern' (ibid: 39). Estimates from 30% to 74% representation of Natives incarcerated in federal and provincial correctional institutions[1] (Schmeiser 1974) demonstrated the gravity of the problem, as Native people constituted only about 5% of Alberta's population (Statistics Canada 1971).

Since that time, of 28 major reports describing criminal justice involvement and socio-demographic conditions, most made similar recommendations (Cawsey 1991; Nielsen 1992): the situation facing Native people coming into conflict with the criminal justice system must be resolved. Barriers preventing Native people from receiving fair and equitable treatment included 'unfamiliarity with legal and government procedures, language barriers, reluctance to speak up for themselves, lack of knowledge about which agencies provide assistance, confusion about the law, and confusion about individual rights' (Native Counselling Services of Alberta 1991: 2). The Laing Report (Canadian Corrections Association 1967) concluded:

> It appears that Indians have little understanding of their legal rights, of court procedures or of resources such as legal aid ... It appears that most Indian people enter guilty pleas either because they do not really understand the concept of legal guilt and innocence, or because they are fearful of exercising their rights. Access to legal counsel is seldom possible for them. In remote areas, Indian people appear confused about the functions of the court ... (1967: 39-40).

Responding to the overwhelming need, the newly developed Canadian Native Friendship Centre[2] began hiring workers to aid Native people in the Edmonton[3] courts. Services were focused primarily on providing assistance with liquor offences. The third worker hired in 1964 was Chester Cunningham,[4] the founder and Executive Director of NCSA. He quickly pushed the boundaries of the mandate and began offering assistance to Native people charged with virtually all types of offences. Within seven years, Cunningham was unable to respond to the volume of requests coming in from all areas of the province.

In 1970, Cunningham formed the Native Courtworkers Services of Alberta under the auspices of the Métis Association of Alberta, or MAA (now known as Métis Nations of Alberta). By 1971, Cunningham broke away from the MAA and changed the name of his independent organisation to 'Native Counselling Services of Alberta' to better reflect the holistic nature of programme services.

Throughout the next 23 years, Cunningham developed and refined the organization into a province-wide, non-profit organization dedicated to the betterment of aboriginal people worldwide.

PHILOSOPHY OF NCSA

The NCSA mission statement embodies the organization's philosophy and strength of NCSA: 'Our mission is to contribute to the holistic development of the Aboriginal individual, family and community by working in partnerships to provide culturally sensitive programmes and services and by promoting the fair and equitable treatment of Aboriginal people' (Native Counselling Services of Alberta 1991).

The subsequent 'guiding principles' emphasize NCSA's commitment to community and equality. NCSA is dedicated to the accomplishment of three main objectives: to lower the Native incarceration rate, to gain fair and equitable treatment for Native people involved with the criminal justice system and to assist Native communities and individuals in developing their full potential.

NCSA's staffing practices most clearly demonstrate the philosophy of the organization. Employees are selected for their caring, enthusiasm, inter-personal skills, stability, knowledge, work experience and education—in descending order. From full-time permanent positions to volunteer or student placement programmes, NCSA believes in using the work experience as a chance for self-development. Often, work experiences with NCSA lead individuals to pursue full-time employment or advanced education.

NCSA has become a training ground for many government and private organizations. Hiring local community individuals and developing them through NCSA training and work experience has created a pool of talented and qualified people. Past staff have gone on to such professions as counsellors, lawyers, police, band managers, chiefs and executive directors, and have been seconded into all levels and areas of government. The development of many staff at NCSA and their subsequent return to their community has greatly increased the ability of the communities to heal themselves.

The strength of NCSA lies in the commitment to the community and the client. For this reason, NCSA has avoided all political or religious affiliations. The agency's seven-member Board of Directors are appointed, not elected, and represent the main geographic areas of Alberta as well as status and non-status Indians and Métis.[5] These practices have allowed NCSA to respond exclusively to the needs of its clients and to pursue the creation and development of new initiatives without restraint.

NCSA adopted the logo of a bear within a raised paw to signify its belief in the importance of Elders, cultural values and the strength of community.

CURRENT PROGRAMMES AND SERVICES

NCSA is a non-profit organization registered under the Societies Act of Alberta. NCSA's six million dollar annual budget is funded through various federal and provincial government departments and private sources. NCSA currently employs over 140 staff, of whom over 80% are of Native descent.

Twenty-five programmes and services covering all stages of the criminal justice system, including prevention, intervention and after-care, are offered by the organization. Programmes employ holistic approaches and a community spirit, starting from their development to their eventual implementation and ongoing operation. Every NCSA programme combines the experience of the agency, the expertise of the staff, the contributions of the funders and the partnership of the people.

Criminal, Family and Young Offender Courtwork

All courtwork programmes focus on ensuring fair and equitable treatment for Native people by providing information, support and assistance to all groups involved with the criminal justice system. Courtwork programmes are offered province-wide. Pre-court services focus on assisting police with their inquiries, informing clients of their rights and responsibilities, assisting clients to complete necessary forms, explaining police and legal procedures, and preparing court reports.

During court, services include explaining legal rights, options and responsibilities, court procedures and available programmes of assistance; clarifying legal terminology; translation services; providing clients with moral support; assisting clients to complete necessary forms; and speaking on behalf of the client regarding adjournment, bail, pleas and sentencing. After-court services encompass counselling, referrals to NCSA programmes or other organizations and liaising between clients, their families and communities.

Other areas of responsibility include providing legal education to the community (e.g., provincial statutes, gun control, legal/social systems), providing Native awareness training to criminal justice system personnel (e.g., Native culture, barriers to accessing services, current issues, Native rights) and encouraging and promoting local initiatives towards community ownership (e.g., crime prevention, youth groups and community development).

The Criminal Courtwork Programme focuses mainly on providing services to the accused in the criminal division of Provincial Court. Services are provided in other provincial courts or higher courts if requested. Where a specialized young offender courtworker is not available, an estimated 20% of the Criminal Courtworker's time is spent on young offender matters. Services to victims, witnesses and families of the accused are also made available.

NCSA is currently completing a manual for the Criminal Courtwork Programme combining reference information and programme service policies, standards and procedures.

NCSA believes the family is important to sustaining cultural and value systems. This belief led NCSA to expand the role of the Criminal Courtworker to provide family courtwork services in the early 1970s.

The Family Courtwork Programme focuses on the family, with special emphasis on the resolution of problems and the maintenance of a cohesive family unit where possible. While offering services similar to Criminal Courtworkers, Family Courtworkers also supervise parent/child visits, represent clients at public assistance appeal hearings, conduct home visits, and counsel individuals, couples and families.

Family Courtworkers work closely with the courts to provide specific information about the clients' unique circumstances and to provide awareness of Native family life, traditional parenting and Native cultural values and beliefs.

Young Offender Courtworkers assist clients both in and out of the courtroom by ensuring that the youth and the families understand the young offender's legal rights and responsibilities. Services are similar to those of other courtwork programmes, and assistance is provided through all stages of the judicial process. Emphasis in the programme is placed on family interaction and involvement.

Family Support Prevention Programmes

Funded through the provincial Department of Family and Social Services, the Family Support Prevention Programme provides services in accordance with the Child Welfare Act to children who are, or are at risk of being, in need of protection. Family Support Prevention workers focus on the child and his or her family by collecting information about, referring, counselling, advocating for and providing liaison services on behalf of families in need. Weekly consultation of all new referrals, case planning, case management and case conferencing services are provided for each family.

A specialized youth worker provides similar services to youth in need of protection services and their families. Additional services for youth include special activities (e.g., summer camps, cultural awareness field trips) and individual services (e.g., counselling, advocating) to meet the needs of older children. Workers maintain an average case load of 20 children and youth and their families.

Elders Crisis Intervention Programme

An increasing number of Native families are experiencing family disruption and breakdown as a result of the many interrelated problems and stresses facing them. In December 1992, NCSA began a pilot programme to provide a high-impact, intensive intervention programme tailored to meet the needs of dysfunctional Native families in a non-threatening, culturally sensitive manner. The programme targets Native families who are at risk of having their children apprehended, thus avoiding dissolution of the family unit.

A project team consisting of a Native Elder, the Family Intervention Worker, a Social Worker[6] and the family members will assess the immediate needs of the family. If determined appropriate, the Family Intervention Worker will be temporarily placed in the home (up to 10 days) to live with the family and ensure child safety. The project team begins immediate and appropriate intervention services under the direction of an Elder.

Once the family situation is stabilized, the Family Intervention Worker leaves the home and appropriate referrals are made to the network of NCSA programmes to ensure continuity of services. Follow up by the Elder and the Family Intervention Worker continues until needs have been addressed.

Family Life Improvement Programme

The Family Life Improvement Programme (FLIP) began in Edmonton in 1978. One of NCSA's most successful programmes, FLIP furnishes clients with the necessary tools to improve themselves and enrich the quality of their family lives. The increased self-esteem and personal growth of clients create long-term improvements in family and personal relationships and open doors to a whole world of positive life opportunities.

Attendance is open and continuous admissions are accepted. FLIP encourages individuals, and where applicable their spouses and families, to attend together.

The programme runs four afternoon sessions per week for ten weeks. During this time, clients are encouraged to explore issues such as family relationships, all forms of abuse, child development, the welfare system, self-esteem and sexuality through discussions, films, group activities and other resources.

FLIP is currently offered in many locations throughout the province.[7] Programmes in Edmonton and correctional institutions are offered on a full-time basis, while others are operated part-time. FLIP II, focusing on skill development and behavioural application, is currently being offered and further developed in Edmonton, with plans to introduce the programme to other areas in the near future.

Federal Liaison Programme

In 1972, NCSA offered the first Native liaison programme for a federal correctional institution in Canada. Today, the programme provides support, information and assistance to Native individuals serving time in federal institutions. The programme focuses on assisting the Native offenders to maintain contact with the outside world, hence the term 'liaison' programme.

Liaison programme workers, called Native Programme Coordinators, provide a variety of services to both offenders and institutional staff. These services include counselling offenders; assisting and supporting offenders in parole planning and hearings; language interpretation; facilitating contact between offenders, their families and the community; coordinating Native Awareness Training and visits by Elders; facilitating positive communication between offenders and institutional staff; and involvement in life skills programmes, alcohol and drug abuse programmes, Native Brotherhood,[8] sweat lodge ceremonies and pow-wows.[9]

Elders Programme

Offenders have the right to religious teachings, ceremonies and practices while serving their sentences. NCSA introduced the Elders Programme to Alberta correctional institutions in response to a demand for traditional Native cultural and spiritual activities for Native offenders.

Elders are role models and advisers to both offenders and institutional staff. Elders explain the significance of spiritual rituals such as sweat lodges and pipe ceremonies, provide individual and group counselling, assist offenders to cope with institutional life, provide opportunities for personal and spiritual development and instruct institutional staff on Native culture.

Westcastle Minimum Security Forestry Camp

Westcastle Forestry Camp is a minimum security correctional facility created by NCSA in 1980 to offer an alternative to institutional incarceration for Native offenders. The camp is situated 35 kilometres outside the nearest community.

Offenders are paid an allowance to work on forestry and maintenance projects contracted through provincial and local governments and special projects negotiated through local organizations.

Offenders are offered Native cultural activities, addictions and personal counselling, awareness workshops, various recreational and organized leisure activities and a post-release employment referral service.

Westcastle has capacity for 20 offenders. Offenders are transferred from provincial correctional centres and are primarily of Native descent.

Stan Daniels Centre

In April 1987, NCSA assumed responsibility for the operation of the Grierson Community Correctional Centre (GCCC) in Edmonton, Alberta. A minimum security correctional institution, GCCC was renamed the Stan Daniels Centre in 1991. It is the first correctional facility to be operated by a non-profit Native organization in Canada.

A primary objective of the centre is to reduce incarceration and recidivism rates among Native offenders. Programmes focus on providing Native offenders with the skills and knowledge required to reintegrate into society and include family violence programmes for male abusers, Native cultural and spiritual teachings by Elders, addictions counselling, job readiness training and the NCSA Family Life Improvement Programme.

The centre has a capacity for 64 residents and houses federal and provincial offenders on various stages of conditional release. This initiative by NCSA to operate a correctional facility has proved successful and necessary to meet the needs of Native offenders at all stages of the criminal justice system.

Adult and Young Offender Probation Supervision

The Adult Probation Supervision Programme provides increased flexibility compared to standard probation programmes. Probation workers are trained to use their understanding of the unique needs of Native individuals on probation as the foundation for their probation supervision approaches. Workers actively promote involvement by Native communities in taking responsibility for community members who have broken the law.

NCSA Courtworkers offer Adult Probation services throughout the province through the Criminal Courtwork Programme and one specialized Adult Probation Officer.

The Young Offender Probation Programme provides similar services, with emphasis on community and family involvement during the young offender's supervision.

Parole Programmme

The NCSA Parole Programme has been operating since 1982 and offers direct supervision to Native individuals on various forms of conditional release. Supervision standards are consistent with those of the Provincial Parole Supervision Programme.

Parole Officers ensure that offenders abide by the conditions of their release, prepare community assessments and act as the offenders' advocates by providing support and assistance for the clients' reintegration into society. The supervision approach of NCSA is sensitive to the unique needs of aboriginal clients.

Fine Option Supervision

Fine Option Supervision provides an alternative to imprisonment for offenders who are unable or unwilling to pay their fines. Offenders work off their fines by performing community service on projects such as maintenance of community property and services to the elderly. A fixed hourly rate is applied directly to the outstanding fine amount.

The Fine Option Supervision Programme is offered by three NCSA offices on an ongoing basis. Other offices throughout the province offer the programme on a needs basis.

Young Offender Open Custody Group Homes

NCSA operates two young offender open custody group homes. Kochee Mena, meaning 'try again' in Cree, is an urban home which opened in 1988. The Sam Laboucan group home is a rural home that began operation in 1989. Both centres focus on preparing Native young offenders for independent community living. A major component of the programme is the Native cultural traditions and values taught by Native Elders. Youth are provided with the opportunity to participate in pipe ceremonies, pow-wows, and sweat lodges.

In-house independent living skills programmes promote the development of skills such as cooking, cleaning, personal hygiene, problem solving, decision making, personal growth and constructive use of recreation and leisure time. A tutor is available on a weekly basis, and a psychologist provides assessment and counselling services as required.

Community-based programming focused on education and employment is strongly emphasized. Resources such as the public school system, alcohol and drug counselling services, and employment counselling agencies complement the in-house programmes.

Youth Programmes

NCSA offers youth programmes in three aboriginal communities through the Family Courtwork Programme. The primary objective of the programme is to decrease the number of local youths in conflict with the law. Services include youth drop-in centres, young offender support groups, dances, field trips, Elder involvement, winter and summer survival camps led by Elders, various topical workshops and seminars, school liaison, educational sessions, role modelling, counselling, special events, field trips and recreational activities.

The programme focuses on youth ranging from eight to twenty-two years of age who are often from alcoholic, abusive or otherwise unstable homes.

Community Sentencing Panels

Community Sentencing Panels are currently operating and being developed in a number of communities throughout Alberta. The panels are organized through the efforts of the community and local NCSA staff.

The panels enable community members to become actively involved in the lives of community youth and their families by offering guidance and encouragement for leading healthy lifestyles. Panels are comprised of well respected community members, normally Elders, who have a desire to influence positively the lives of the youth. The Community Sentencing Panels focus on increasing community involvement in the justice system and reducing the recidivism rate among young offenders.

The panel receives referrals from sources such as the courts, social services or community members to meet with youth experiencing difficulties in their lives (e.g., conflict with the law, alcohol abuse, school problems, home stresses) and their family. Through a cooperative discussion in a traditional meeting format, the panel is able to work together to determine appropriate action to resolve the situation. Where a crime has been committed, the recommendation of the panel is taken to the youth court Judge who considers the panel's recommendations in sentencing.

The panel follows the case closely through visits and additional meetings to monitor progress and provide support. NCSA and other organization representatives offer information and advisory services to support the work of the panels. In some locations it has become standard practice for the Judge to refer all cases to the Community Sentencing Panels for their input prior to sentencing a young offender.

Community Workshops

Workshops are primarily coordinated by local courtworkers in their respective communities and cover such topics as child welfare issues, the criminal justice system, family violence, suicide prevention, Native cultural awareness, legal aid and drug and alcohol abuse.

Many workshops are offered in partnership with agencies such as the John Howard Society, local police, alcohol and addictions services organizations and government departments.

Addictions Programme

The Addictions Programme, funded by the provincial government of Alberta, Alcohol and Drug Abuse Commission, began in December 1990. The programme provides an opportunity for individuals and families to address prevention, intervention, follow-up and aftercare needs for their alcohol and drug abuse problems.

The Addictions Programme emphasizes intervention through one-to-one counselling, couples and family counselling, pre-treatment consultation, referrals to treatment centres and aftercare. Referrals to the programme come from courts, other agencies and through self referrals.

As part of the addictions programme, NCSA cooperated on the development and implementation of a programme focusing on alternatives to alcohol, drugs and physical abuse. The programme 'Initiatives Toward Conquering Alcohol and Drug Abuse' was geared towards youth and women, although services were open to all individuals.

STRUCTURE OF NCSA

Staff Development

Recognizing the importance of staff development, NCSA started its own staff training department in 1975. This has helped the organization to gain world-wide recognition as a leader in issues dealing with Natives and the justice system. Staff development has enabled NCSA to turn ideas and programme concepts into services that meet the unique cultural and personal differences of its various clients.

The number of courses has expanded considerably since 1975. The current course calendar offers 26 topics, including NCSA and the Law, Criminal Courtwork I and II training, Supervisory Training, Self Awareness, and NCSA's highly acclaimed Native Awareness Training.

Many organizations and individuals have benefited from NCSA training, and requests are constantly being received for the services of the NCSA training department.

Legal Education Media Department

Since 1976 the Legal Education Media Department has been producing audio-visual programmes. These productions provide staff and clients with relevant and up-to-date information regarding the justice system as it relates to the Native people and community.

Productions are distributed on VHS video tapes and are available from NCSA for a nominal charge. Messages and information provided through these videos are geared toward Native people. Production staff are predominantly of Native descent, thus the underlying themes of Native values and lifestyles are clearly expressed.

Over 50 productions have been completed by the media department, including such topics as financial management for low-income consumers (*Money Matters*), recounting old legends as told by a Native Elder (*Old Legends for Young Ears*), rights of children (*The Questions Kids Are Asking—Children's Civil Rights*), role of the Children's Advocate (*Someone to Listen—The Role of the Children's Advocate*), a documentary on family violence and abuse from a Native female perspective (*Honouring Our Voices*) and key sections in the Landlord and Tenant Act (*Movin' In, Movin' Out*). Current projects include a video detailing the work of Community Sentencing Panels (also called 'Youth Justice Committees'), a children's story about accepting individual differences (*Bert the Buffalo*), and an in-depth look at family violence from the male perspective (*Rage*).

Most videos include a brief *User's Guide* to assist the viewer and/or workshop coordinator. The Legal Education Media Department also produces the NCSA Newsletter for province-wide distribution.

Research Department

The Research Department is located in Edmonton and was established in 1978 to investigate and provide ongoing information on the law and administration of justice as they relate to Native people. It is one of the few Native-run, non-government research groups in Canada to provide this service. The Research Department is funded by the Alberta Law Foundation. Information provided by the Research Department is used for community education, law reform recommendations, improving client services, public relations, staff training, programme planning, community development, monitoring and evaluations.

The Research Department has produced hundreds of submissions, analysis, research studies, discussion papers, evaluations, pamphlets and other materials about Native people and the criminal justice system. Projects include *A Family Affair*, an examination of family violence from the Native female perspective; *Courtwatch*, sentencing practices in the Edmonton Criminal Courts; *Court Interpreters*, the current status of Native court interpretation in Alberta; *Bail Study*, reasons for differences in granting bail; *Fail to Appear*, why Native people fail to appear for court; *Bail Hearing Study*, a consideration of whether Native people are treated differently under the bail system; an information package on how to conduct research in Native communities; and an evaluation model for Native criminal justice programmes. Submissions were also sent to the Landlord and Tenant Act Review, Task Force on Federally Sentenced Women, Task Force on Alcohol and Family Life and Edmonton Policing Task Force. All research documents are available to the public.[10]

Library

All Research, Legal Education Media and NCSA information materials can be obtained through the NCSA library. The library, funded by the Muttart Foundation, offers three levels of dynamic and proactive services: traditional information services including reference requests and interlibrary loans; value-added services including abstracting, translation and bibliographic services; and current awareness services including newsletter bulletins, table of contents listings and summary reports.

The library houses the most extensive and up-to-date Native materials collection in Northern Alberta. While focusing on legal and social education materials, the library also maintains extensive information on all aspects of Native life, including Native culture and history.

PATHWAY TO SUCCESS

NCSA believes that community development is the pathway to success. In 1992, the government requested NCSA to develop a programme to increase the awareness and access to the federal government Canada Employment and Immigration Commission (CEIC) programmes and services within the aboriginal community. NCSA developed an operations manual to assist aboriginal groups to become more familiar with CEIC's programmes. Cross-cultural training programmes were developed for CEIC staff. Aboriginal labour market information was researched and compiled to assist aboriginal communities plan and develop training for their people. Aboriginal communities were assisted in developing comprehensive financial accounting and evaluation systems.

NCSA is extensively involved in community development projects. Through a core funding arrangement, NCSA dedicates staff and resources to help communities develop infrastructures necessary to ensure programme survival, assess community needs, develop and implement new initiatives and to evaluate and improve existing programmes and services. NCSA works in partnership with Aboriginal communities, government departments and various organizations to respond to requests for assistance. Services similar to these have been provided by NCSA since its inception; however, dedicated funding has allowed NCSA and aboriginal communities to make significant steps towards community healing.

Some projects include Community Sentencing Panels, a pilot project to help Native people eliminate dependency on social assistance, an inner-city youth alternative measures programme, an inner city violent crime project, male and female halfway houses, Elders treatment approaches to family violence, the Urban Elders Council for youth in need, a post-censual survey of aboriginal people in Alberta, Elder Crisis Intervention, courtworker programmes in other provinces and countries, a traditional parenting practices programme, a translators legal terminology handbook, an unwed mother's programme, a judicial interim release (bail) programme and healing centres.

CONCLUSION

NCSA is currently focused on two objectives: improving current services and exploring new initiatives focused on youth and families. In partnership with communities everywhere, NCSA is venturing into uncharted territory. The willingness and support of the provincial and federal government to pursue new initiatives and the growing support of other Native organizations underscore the growing acceptance and determination of all Canadians, Native and non-Native people alike, to resolve existing problems.

While recognizing the magnitude of work yet to be done, evidence suggests that significant differences have been made in the circumstances of Native people as a result of NCSA's work. The Kirby Report (1973: 35) began by stating that 'Native Courtworkers contribute much in assuring Native people more equitable treatment in the provincial justice system. The work of the services has been recognized both by the Courts and the police.' Others indicate that 'NCSA has also shown that Native organizations can develop the organizational and financial expertise to effectively operate these kinds of programmes' (Morse 1982). Griffiths and Verdun-Jones (1989: 562) states that 'Native courtworker programmes have become an integral part of the criminal justice system and have generally received high marks from judges, lawyers, and other criminal justice personnel, as well as from native clients'.

Ross (1992) noted that the magnitude of the job to overcome years of victimization and prejudicial treatment against Native people and the merging of two distinct cultures must be recognized. As stated in the words of NCSA's founder Dr. Chester Cunningham:

The 1960's were a time of awakening for Aboriginal people and their organizations. They were fed up that nothing was done about the revolving-door syndrome of the criminal justice system and the effect it was having on their people. The Aboriginal people decided that they had to take matters into their own hands, but was that possible? ... I say—let's be cautious, let's be ready, let's not play political games, let's not make promises that can't be kept ... [with] a little bit of time, this thing can be done (Cunningham 1992).

NOTES

1. The Canadian correctional system places individuals sentenced to less than two years of imprisonment under provincial jurisdiction, while those sentenced to

greater than two years are under federal jurisdiction.

2. The first Friendship Centre opened in Winnipeg in 1959. The Friendship Centres focused on providing a drop-in and programme centre for Native people.

3. Edmonton is the capital of the province of Alberta.

4. Chester Cunningham has received numerous awards and recognitions for his work with NCSA, including an honorary Doctorate of Laws in 1989 from the University of Alberta and The Order of Canada in 1993.

5. Native peoples in Canada are distinguished by their cultural and linguistic attributes as well as their legal status (Morse 1982). Status Indians are Native people who are registered under the Indian Act. Non-status Indians are those who identify themselves as Native but who are not registered under the Indian Act. Métis are of mixed Indian and European ancestry (Griffiths and Verdun-Jones 1989).

6. Social workers are highly trained case workers employed by the provincial Department of Family and Social Services.

7. FLIP is currently offered in various Native communities and two provincial correctional institutions.

8. Native Brotherhood is a Native cultural and support organization whose members are serving time in correctional institutions.

9. Sweat lodges and pow-wows are traditional Native practices among certain aboriginal groups in Alberta.

10. Publications are available through the Native Counselling Services of Alberta, Library, 800 Highfield Place, 10010-106 Street, Edmonton, Alberta, T5J 3L8, Canada.

REFERENCES

Alberta Board of Review (1973) *Native People in the Administration of Justice in the Provincial Court of Alberta*, Report No. 4, Edmonton: Queen's Printer.

Canadian Corrections Association (1967) *Indians and the Law*, Ottawa: Canadian Corrections Association.

Cawsey A. (1991) (See Task Force on the Criminal Justice System.)

Cunningham, Chester (1992) 'Foreword', in Robert A. Silverman and Marianne O. Nielsen (eds.) *Aboriginal Peoples and Canadian Criminal Justice*, Toronto/Vancouver: Butterworths.

Dempsey, Hugh A. (1986) *The Gentle Persuader. A Biography of James Gladstone, Indian Senator*, Saskatoon: Western Producer Prairie Books.

Griffiths, Curt T. and Verdun-Jones, Simon N. (1989) *Canadian Criminal Justice*, Toronto and Vancouver: Butterworths.

Kirby Report (See Native People in the Administration of Justice in the Provincial Court of Alberta.)

Laing Report (See Canadian Corrections Association *Indians and the Law*.)

Morse, B. W. (1982) 'The Original Peoples of Canada', *Canadian Legal Aid Bulletin*, Special Issue, Part 1, 5: 1, 1-16.

Morse, B. W. (ed.) (1985) *Aboriginal Peoples and the Law: Indian, Métis and Inuit Rights in Canada*, Ottawa: Carleton University Press.

Native Counselling Services of Alberta (1982) 'Native People in the Criminal Justice System: The Role of the Native Courtworker', *Canadian Legal Aid Bulletin*, Special Issue, Part 1, 5: 1, 55-60.

Native Counselling Services of Alberta (1991) *Annual Report 1990-91*, Edmonton: NCSA.

Nielsen, Marianne O. (1992) 'Introduction', in Robert A. Silverman and Marianne O. Nielsen (eds.) *Aboriginal Peoples and Canadian Criminal Justice*, Toronto/Vancouver: Butterworths.

Ross, Rupert (1992) *Dancing with a Ghost*, Markham: Octopus Publishing Group.

Schmeiser, Douglas A. (1974) *The Native Offender and the Law*, Ottawa: Information Canada.

Silverman, Robert A. and Marianne O. Nielsen (eds.) (1992) *Aboriginal Peoples and Canadian Criminal Justice*, Toronto/Vancouver: Butterworths.

Task Force on the Criminal Justice System and Its Impact on the Indian and Métis People of Alberta (1991) *Justice on Trial*, Vol. 3, *Working Papers and Bibliography*, Edmonton: The Task Force (Chief Commissioner of the committee preparing the report was A. Cawsey).

2 HEALING THE HURTS

7

HONOURING NATIVE WOMEN: THE BACKBONE OF NATIVE SOVEREIGNTY

Elsie B. RedBird

WOMEN AND SOVEREIGNTY

A people is not defeated until the hearts of its women are on the ground.
—Chief Seattle

What is 'sovereignty'? It is a term that non-native peoples do not understand, refuse to accept or ignore. In August 1992, I listened to the presentations of academics who spouted their paper wisdom to an international audience at the University of Wellington in New Zealand.[1] When a non-native academic declared that the word 'sovereignty' is useless, a Maori sister and I rose to correct him. We told the professor and the audience that sovereignty is very much alive in the minds and hearts of native peoples; that we know what it is, because we feel it each day of our lives. The embarrassed presenter protested that he did not mean to put down native peoples, but we saw that he did not understand the emotional content of sovereignty to us as native peoples.

Non-natives often see sovereignty as only a political concept. Their debates, held on local, national and international levels, exhibit limited thinking. They control policy, and the policy they declare revolves around the nature and extent of power they will *allow* native peoples. What nonsense! We have power as human beings, as is demonstrated by our ability to survive over the past five hundred years and grow strong again (Thornton 1987).

Sovereignty is not limited to political power or authority. As David Lujan, director of the Tonantzin Land Institute, correctly puts it, sovereignty embraces the spiritual, natural and social existence of native peoples within the world family of nations (Native American Studies Center 1993: 6). I join the twenty-year struggle by indigenous peoples to focus international attention on atrocities which continue to assault them (ibid). In reality, it is a 500-year struggle, which commenced in 1492. David Lujan asserts—and I agree—that native peoples must maintain international solidarity if they are to attain their goals of nurturing spiritual, natural and social existence and obtain protection in the world human rights regime (ibid). To do so effectively, there must be solidarity among and with native women.

To achieve it, we must understand the present status of native women in the context of a broad approach to sovereignty. I express these views to honour and support *all* the native women in our world: to honour Indians, Native Americans (including Alaska Natives, Hawaiians and the peoples of American territories or possessions in the Pacific), Maoris of New Zealand, Aborigines of Australia and the women of all places. I acknowledge my sisters who identify themselves with Spanish cultures and who may deny or be unaware of their indigenous roots. We all share the same problems, and we all look to the same Earth Mother, whether we call her 'Changing Woman' (Navajo), 'Thought Woman' (Keres), 'Clay Lady' (Santa Clara) or 'White Buffalo Calf Woman' (Sioux) (LaFromboise, Heyle and Ozer 1990: 458). She may be 'Our Lady of Guadalupe' or another woman deity. Whatever we call Her, She is our Mother. I use the case of American Indian women to describe the disparate impact of non-native policy on native women. Some policies specifically targeted Indian women (e.g., the Dawes General Allotment Act of 1887), and while others did not mention Indian women, they had the effect of hurting them more than Indian men. An analysis of what happened to Indian women is relevant to the situation of all native women.

What is the status of American Indian women in the present day? We are ignored and invisible. The Smithsonian Institute is publishing its multi-volume *Handbook of North American Indians*, and in 1988, it published the *History of Indian-White Relations* (Washburn 1988). It has no article on women, and the terms 'women' and 'Indian women' are absent from the index. Indian women and other women of colour have been largely ignored in the history of the American West (Deutsch 1991). Further, the historical record is unreliable, because of European stereotyping of women and misperceptions of their identity and roles (Riley 1984a). On 23 June 1993, Senator Pete Domenici (of New Mexico) introduced a bill to create a special Office of Indian Women and Families to identify their needs, make them a priority, and gather resources to serve them (Domenici 1993). He spoke about 'invisible women' in his speech in the Senate:

> Due mainly to their strong cultural traditions, it is often difficult to determine the impact of these Federal efforts on the living standards of Indian women and their families. Indian women remain an enigma to most of us ...
>
> Yet, there remains the fact that we have a difficult time identifying many of the indicators of social well-being for Indian women precisely because the contributions of Indian women remain undervalued and overlooked in the policies and programs of the Bureau of Indian Affairs and other Federal agencies with programs designed to help all Indian people (ibid: S 7761).

Sovereignty is the spiritual, natural and social existence of native peoples. Their cultures are alive. There is a native women's knowledge—their special way of looking at life. Throughout the history of European (or 'white') contact in the Americas (Indian-white relations) Indian women have been subjected to discriminatory treatment, and policies on Indians have had a disparate impact on Indian women. Many policies destroyed the family, and thereby hurt Indian women more severely. Women have been the target of direct atrocities, including sexual and labor exploitation, slavery, violence, disease, neglect and discrimination. They have also been the target of more subtle atrocities, which upset their place in native communities through the destruction of traditional law and customs, economic roles and families. Indian women were targets in the past and they are targets today.

In July of the Year of Indigenous People (1993), I took my family to visit Fort Sumner, New Mexico, the place where my Dine' People were held in captivity from 1864 through 1868. It was an emotional event for me, as I took my daughters to see the place where our ancestors executed their treaty of alliance with the United States of America. We were greeted with respect by a park ranger, and the tranquility of the place nourished our pilgrimage. We left the site of Fort Sumner in peace to go home. The 'Old Fort Sumner-Billy the Kid Museum' is close to the fort site. The sign out front told of exhibits about the area and invited people to see Billy the Kid's grave. Inside, a display case held the skulls of two Navajos, which the label said were gathered by schoolchildren in the fields nearby and given to the museum. When my daughters and I left the collection room and went into the gift shop, the sign over the women's room read 'SQUAWS'. That showed us what New Mexico thinks of Indian women—it allows a licensed tourist attraction to display our dead for money, and it endorses the use of racial epithets against us. Billy the Kid, a psychopathic killer, gets respect and honour in his place of rest, but my people do not.[2]

I will describe the history of Indian women and their treatment by European cultures to show the impact of five centuries of Indian policy. I will identify contemporary international and national policy approaches to resolve the problems those events created. I will then recommend steps to strengthen native women and the sovereignty of their groups. There are strategies to promote a new solidarity among native women throughout the world to assure their survival in the family of humankind.

EUROPEAN ATTITUDES AND POLICIES TOWARDS WOMEN

What were the first words written by a European after seeing native peoples? Columbus wrote: 'Presently they saw naked people' (Todorov 1984: 34). The sexual attitudes of Columbus and his followers laid foundations for European policy and the social climate of the New World to follow (Piedra 1982).

Columbus wrote that '[t]hese were the handsomest men and the most beautiful women whom he had hitherto encountered', and another writer described what Columbus and his crew first saw: 'All the women were lovely. One might have supposed one was seeing those splendid naiads or those nymphs of the spring so celebrated in Antiquity. Holding up palm fronds, which they carried while performing their dances, accompanied by songs, they knelt and presented them to the *adelantado* [governor]' (Todorov 1984: 36).

On the second voyage to the Americas, Columbus captured 1,600 Tainos in Hispanola and put 550 of 'the best males and females' in chains to take back to Spain (Sale 1990: 138). 'Of the rest who were left the announcement went around that whoever wanted them could take as many as he pleased; and this was done' (ibid). The author of that account, an Italian nobleman, wrote about his choice and what he did with her:

> While I was in the boat, I captured a very beautiful Carib woman, whom the aforesaid Lord Admiral gave to me, and with whom, having brought her into my cabin, and she being naked as is their custom, I conceived the desire to take my pleasure. I wanted to put my desire into execution, but she was unwilling for me to do so, and treated me with her nails in such wise that I would have preferred never to have begun. But seeing this (in order to tell you the whole event to the end), I took a rope-end and thrashed her well, following which she produced such screaming and wailing as would cause you not be believe your ears. Finally we reached an agreement such that, I can tell you, she seemed to have been raised in a veritable school of harlots (ibid: 140; Todorov 1984: 48-49).

The nobleman, Cuneo, wrote his pornographic narrative to titillate a friend. No doubt the women's 'harlotry' was the product of a severe beating with a length of rope. It was a rape, and compliance in rape comes from violence. Columbus gave out women to his followers 'as readily as he distributed little bells to the native chiefs' (Todorov 1984: 49), and he began the pattern of slavery and rape which followed. In 1519, a group of Dominicans made a report to a Spanish minister which showed how the settlers were treating women in the Carib islands: 'Some Christians encountered an Indian woman, who was carrying in her arms a child at suck; and since the dog they had with them was hungry, they tore the child from the mother's arms and flung it still living to the dog, who proceeded to devour it before the mother's eyes ... When there were among the prisoners some women who had recently given birth, if the new-born babes happened to cry, they seized them by the legs and hurled them against the rocks, or flung them into the jungle so that they were certain to die there' (ibid: 139). The report related the conduct of mine foremen towards their workers:

> Each of them had made it a practice to sleep with the Indian women who were

in his work-force, if they pleased him, whether they were married women or maidens. While the foreman remained in the hut or the cabin with the Indian women, he sent the husband to dig gold out of the mines; and in the evening, when the wretch returned, not only was he beaten or whipped because he had not brought up enough gold, but further, most often, he was bound hand and foot and flung under the bed like a dog, before the foreman lay down, directly over him, with his wife (ibid).

Some complain that these reports were exaggerations, resulting from the rivalry with humanists who wanted to protect Indians slandered by Spanish settlers.[3] There are accounts written by the men themselves, like the boasting of Cuneo and Bernal Diaz's story of the conquest of Mexico. Diaz tells us what the followers of Cortez wanted as their reward for the taking of Mexico: 'They were in fact concerned only to furnish themselves with some fine Indian women and to take a certain amount of booty' (Todorov 1984: 58):

Cuauhtemoc and all his captains complained to Cortez that some of our leaders who happened to be in the brigantines, as well as several who had fought on the highways, had carried off the wives and daughters of a great number of chieftains. They asked him to show mercy and to order that these women be returned. Cortez replied that he would have great difficulty taking them away from his comrades who already set great store by them, that he had sent for them, furthermore, and had them brought before him; that he would see if they had become Christians, declaring further that if they wished to return to their fathers and their husbands, he would make every effort to see that they did so (ibid).

Of course, when Cortez examined the captives, he then told the Aztec leaders that the women did not want to return, and some were already pregnant (ibid).

Sexual exploitation and rape also spreads disease. Sexual diseases were most likely the third leading cause of Indian mortality in America, and a major contributor to a decline in the American Indian population from more than 5 million in 1492 to about half a million in 1900 (Thornton 1987: 44, xvii). The debate over the pre-Columbian population is fierce, but historian Francis Jennings accepts a population peak of ten million Indians north of the Rio Grande in the year 1200 (Jennings 1993: 88-89). Sexually transmitted diseases killed people, made them sterile and caused pregnancy loss, contributing to depopulation (Thornton 1987: 54). Indian women suffered the double loss of their own bodies and their children.

The experience of women in Spanish America is not simply the story of slavery and resulting rape. Europeans vented their repressed sexuality in the Americas, where they had freedom and licence to brutalize women without consequences. They combined lust with law to justify the liberties they demanded after conquest. The Spanish held three views of Indian societies: First, that Indians were entitled to their own institutions and laws (Borah 1983: 28). The basis for that conclusion was that Indians, being human, possessed reason and the right to their own law and government. Some of the colonizers and their advocates attempted to justify their conduct by claiming that Indians were 'not human', but given the sexual exploitation, 'no participant urged that Spaniards having sexual intercourse with Indians be punished for the then-monstrous sin of bestiality' (ibid: 27).

The papal bull of 2 June 1537, *Sublimis Deus*, put the question to rest by declaring that Indians *were* human and entitled to their liberty and property (Borah 1983: 27). The second school of thought was that of 'one society' (ibid: 29). All Spaniards were under the Crown, and the Americas were the personal property of the King, who could manage them according to his will. The third was the notion that there were 'two republics', so Indians and Spaniards could organize two separate commonwealths with their own laws, customs and system of government (ibid).[4] The 'one society' position eventually prevailed, despite extensive experiments with native self-government under Spanish law. Clerics argued the basic human right of Indians to have the power of secular rule, but settlers eventually overcame the law (Haring 1975: 38-68, 314-325; Hall and Weber 1984). At the end of the Spanish empire, the new 'liberal' republics, based on the same values of 'liberty, equality and fraternity' as the United States, abolished special laws and privileges for Indians and thereby perpetuated modern revolution.[5]

That history tells us something about the foundations of European policies towards native peoples; something which is still important today. The cant of conquest is control. If the conqueror can justify control, then the licence to exploit follows. In the case of American Indians, the justification for conquest was the asserted barbarity of Indians and the need to both Christianize and civilize them. If Indians were 'barbarians' who lacked the ability to obey natural law, then that justified their conquest and control—by any means. That opened the door to exploitation.[6]

At the centre of it all lies male European attitudes towards Indian women. Indian woman is a metaphor for America. Classical allegories of the continents depict America as an Indian woman. On 20 May 1541, the Bishop of Santa Marta wrote to the King to suggest that land must be 'wrested from the power of these unnatural fathers [Indians] and given to a husband who will treat her with the reasonableness she deserves' (Todorov 1984: 171).

America is a woman; an *Indian* woman. Settlers abused Indian women and used the Americas any way they as 'husband' desired. They settled the Americas with violence against women, influenced by both the metaphor and the attitude of Europeans towards women. Violence against both women and the land is a lasting legacy of European thought about the control of the feminine force.

The Spanish set the stage, but their activities and policies were not unique. The same atrocities were repeated by the English, French and other invader-immigrants, in a pattern of brutal conduct against Indian women. The English shared many of the same paternalistic and patriarchal attitudes towards women (Drinnon 1990: 27-28; Bolt 1987: 253). The *pater* (father) root of those two words implies male authority. Paternalism is an ideology of power and the use of force. It elevates people to positions of authority over others, and once they are in place allows them to control the lives of their 'inferiors'; this is the foundation for excesses of authority or tyranny. The *pater* in 'patriarchal' defines the line of authority through a male figure; it means 'rule by the father'. When that rule is abused within a family, it is sexual tyranny (Sagan 1986: 293-94). The primary difference between traditional native systems of law and government and those of the modern state is that in so-called 'primitive' systems, power and authority are spread throughout the community as a whole, and there is no concentration of power (ibid: 236). Many Indian societies have kinship systems where everyone shares power, and Indian clans are legal institutions (Barkun 1968: 18-20).

The modern 'state' and particularly the 'liberal state' which enshrines individualism, elevates the individual over the community. In a male-dominated society, only a select group of men rule. They are the 'husband' with power over the 'wife'. If America, seen as an Indian woman, is the wife, then the Great White Father is the husband. Too often, he is an abusive husband. While the United States is a republican democracy, which should foster true equality and opportunity, the reality is that its law and government are hierarchical, and power is concentrated in the hands of very few. They have privileged positions of power and abuse it, because their own interests come before those of native peoples. (Two contemporary examples are religious freedom and gaming.)

At the beginning of settlement in North America, Indian women were important resources. They were needed for sex, labour, marriage, diplomacy, trade and new communities. Sexual exploitation continued, as before, but marriage with Indian women was an instrument for trade and settlement. There were marriages for diplomatic purposes and for trade along water-trade routes (Bolt 1987: 254-55). Traders married Indian women for companionship and labour. Without them the early trade economy would not have been possible. The women made moccasins, hauled canoes, hunted and fed the hunters and traders. Later, they were abandoned when the traders went home or newcomer (white) women outnumbered Indian women (Van Kirk 1980). In other areas, racial attitudes towards Indian women inhibited interracial marriage, and righteous colonists enacted miscegenation statutes to prevent marriage with Indian women (Bolt 1987: 254-55).[7] Indian women were essential to the hunting and trade economy of the frontier, and were pushed out when immigrants settled. National expansion ('manifest destiny' and 'the vanishing frontier') made Indian women redundant.

Indian women have always been on the edges, and they were marginalized in history. They were on the fringe of white society. It ignored them, misunderstood them or intentionally put them down (Drinnon 1990: 177-78, 226-

27; Riley 1991; Smith 1987: 63). American Indian policy consciously set out to destroy their traditional authority.

The major protections for Indian women are their families and their law. They are the core of the family, particularly in societies which are organized around women (i.e., matrilineal societies) (LaFramboise, Heyle and Ozer 1990: 457-61; Bolt 1987: 255-60). Traditional religion and politics protected them, and they were always at the centre of those forms of human activity (Bolt 1987: 264-69). To break down Indian society, white society had to get at Indian women to destroy Indian families, the core of society.

One of the major atrocities against Indian women is sexual abuse. It is practised by white men, along the lines of the historical pattern,[8] and by Indian men. Sexual abuse, which includes rape, is an act of violence against women as women. There are rape-prone societies, where rape is a means of social control to threaten and punish women (Zion and Zion 1993: 407-08). Many native societies are rape-free, or comparatively so. They are the societies where women have high status as respected and influential members of the community, essential equality exists, and there is a female deity (ibid). One of the tactics used to destroy Indian government was the destruction of women's values by dissolving the institutions which nourished them. One means of destruction was the missionary movement, which attacked and weakened native religions with female deities (Bowden 1981).

Traditional Indian law protected women. It had practices which non-Indians misunderstood and continue to misunderstand. They include brideprice, polygamy, the distribution of goods to relatives upon death (with protections for widows), traditional divorce and other aspects of family law. In the 1880s, a group of authoritarian (male) clergymen, law professors, lawyers and businesspeople—the 'Friends of the Indian'—gathered to determine the future of American Indians (Prucha 1973: 1-9). By that time, American Indians had been confined to reservations, and the group was formed to decide what to do about this; how to finally 'civilize' American Indians. In 1883, the Bureau of Indian Affairs created the Court of Indian Offenses, which outlawed traditional legal protections for Indian women by making them a crime (ibid: 300-05). Shortly thereafter, Congress passed the Major Crimes Act of 1885 to subject Indians to federal jurisdiction and overcome traditional criminal law.

Congress enacted other laws which affected the status of Indian women in their own societies. On 8 August 1888, it created statutes to deal with marriages between Indian women and white men. The statute on white men marrying Indian women (codified at 25 U.S.C. § 131) provides that a white man who married an Indian woman could not acquire 'any right to any tribal property, privilege, or interest whatever'. An Indian woman who married a white man (25 U.S.C. § 182) became a citizen of the United States (whether she wanted to or not). Many states had rules of evidence which prohibited people of colour (including Indians) from testifying against a white person, so 25 U.S.C. § 183 permitted testimony to prove a common-law marriage, that is, by 'general repute, or of cohabitation as married persons'. Children born of such marriages were entitled to inherit tribal property, under 25 U.S.C. § 184 (enacted in 1897).

On the surface, these laws protected Indian nations by ensuring that whites could not become 'Indians' by marriage and that Indian women could enjoy the blessings of non-Indian law. Beneath the surface, those statutes were aimed at destroying tribal sovereignty. Some Indian nations wished intermarriage because of strict tribal sanctions against incest. When there were too few clans to permit intermarriage, Indians brought in outsiders to expand the clans. Where whites married in, they could not legally join the Indian nation as one of its citizens. The statute regarding Indian women becoming citizens subjected them to the backward rules of American law of the time, which essentially stripped married women of their rights (Scharff 1991: 62, 63; Kanowitz 1969: 35-99). The statutes preempted Indian nation domestic relations law and subjected Indian women to white law, without their consent.

One of the most disastrous American Indian policies was the allotment of Indian nation lands for individual ownership. That practice, required by the Dawes General Allotment Act of 1887, not only destroyed Indian land bases, it assaulted kinship relations and social identity:

Individual ownership was intended to transform Indians who lived under varied kin systems into male-headed, monogamous nuclear families. One way in which federal administrators pursued that end was to give Native Americans new, patrilineal names on the allotment rolls. Imagine the confusion and anguish Indians felt as the government and Anglo settlers not only shattered their way of living on the land, but also ignored or attacked what Indians understood as family (Scharff 1991: 62, 64-65).[9]

Even if the bureaucrat who parcelled out the lands was a woman, there was little sympathy for the fact that families were being destroyed. Sitting Bull, the great Lakota leader and man of religion, was a visionary. He spoke with Alice Fletcher, a white woman who later administered the Dawes Act to help 'restore' Indian manhood, and told her to 'take pity on my women ... The young men can till the soil, supply the food and clothing. They will take the work out of the hands of women. And the women ... will be stripped of all which gave them power' (Deutsch 1991: 58, 59-60).

When white law destroyed Indian law, it destroyed Indian family and society. It destroyed Indian women. What were the effects of that policy? According to the 1982 report of the National Advisory Council on Criminal Justice, these were the results:

The displacement of Indian sovereignty by the encroaching Anglo-European system of laws and values has had pernicious debilitating effects to the present.

The legacy of this dispossesion is graphically revealed in current criminal justice statistics. American Indians have, by far, the highest arrest rate of any ethnic group. Their arrest rate is consistently three times that of blacks and ten times that of whites. As many as 80% of Indian prisoners are incarcerated for alcohol-related offences, a rate twelve times greater than the national average. The major crime rate is 50% higher on reservations than in rural America. The violent crime rate is eight times the rural rate, murder is three times the rural rate, and assault is nine times as high. Furthermore, the percentage of unreported crime on reservations is higher than anywhere else; thus, the situation is actually worse than the statistics portray, according to a 1975 Task Force Report on Indian Matters by the Department of Justice (National Minority Advisory Council on Criminal Justice 1982: 131).[10]

How are Indian women victimized? While a recent study by the National Research Council asserts that Indian women have less than a one in 100 chance of death by homicide (Reiss and Roth 1993: 62), that may not be the true risk. The most recent Indian Health Service statistics (Indian Health Service 1992) shows that Indians are more likely to die of accidents (Table 4.15; female, Table 4.17), suicide (Table 4.20; female, Table 4.21), homicide (Table 4.22; female, Table 4.23) and alcoholism (Table 4.24; female, Table 4.25) than other racial groups. While the rates for Indian women are lower than those for Indian men, they are generally higher than the national average.

A study of New Mexico death certificates shows that in that state, Indian women had the highest homicide rates of three groups (non-Hispanic white, Hispanic and American Indian) (Becker, et al. 1993: 132, 135). The age groups at greatest risk are Indian women aged 25 to 34 (young married women) and women between the ages of 45 and 54 (ibid: 137). New Mexico has the second highest injury mortality rate in the United States (behind Alaska) and a death rate from injuries which is 60% higher than the U.S. rate (Sewell et al. 1993: 119).

The ten leading causes of death for Indian women in New Mexico between 1958 and 1982 (in order of percentages) were traffic crashes (50.01%), homicide (8.7%), fires and burns (5.3%), falls (4.5%), suicide (3.5%), exposure or neglect (1.8%), poisoning (1.4%) and other unintentional injury (16.7%) (ibid: 123). Many of the deaths were associated with alcohol. In 1986, blood alcohol levels were present in the bodies of 51% of the victims of auto crashes (Chavez et al. 1993: 108, 113). It was present in the blood of 49% of homicide victims and 42% of suicides (ibid).

New Mexico ranks second in the nation in alcohol-related mortality, and its Indians 'consistently had higher alcohol-related mortality rates than did Hispanics or non-Hispanic whites from 1958 through to 1982' (ibid: 115). Alcohol is also involved in the deaths of Indian men and women by excessive cold and exposure (Sewell 1993: 123). These figures are only a sampling from one state, but they show that women are victimized by alcohol, homicide and accidents. The source of victimization is the destruction of Indian families and policies which weakened Indian women's roles.

Sexual assaults continue, whether they are perpetrated by white men or Indian men. A 1979 news report stated that rape was the number one crime in the Navajo Nation (Allen 1986: 191), and a survey of Indian women seen in a five-state Indian Health Service psychiatric service centre shows that 80% experienced some sort of sexual assault (Cross 1982: 18). Despite evidence that Indian nations had low sexual assault rates in pre-contact times (e.g., Zion and Zion 1993: 407, 411-13), Indians learned the ways of paternalism, patriarchy and the violence which accompanies those modes of control over women.

This survey of historical patterns of Indian affairs policy, attitudes towards Indian women and the treatment of Indian women shows that they were (and are) the victims of European culture. White policies towards Indians had a disparate impact on Indian women, and we must have a new human rights policy to protect them. Women are the keystone of Indian families, and true sovereignty depends upon the vitality of those families.

INTERNATIONAL HUMAN RIGHTS POLICY[11]

The story of Indian rights in international law begins with the papal bull *Sublimis Deus*, promulgated in 1537 (although the rights it declares have origins in medieval law) (Stogre 1991: 22, 23). The bull declared that Indians are capable of reason and are thus entitled to fundamental rights: 'that they may and should freely and legitimately, enjoy their liberty and the possession of their property; nor should they be in any way enslaved; should the contrary happen, it shall be null and of no effect' (ibid: 23).

This is the foundation of the right of native peoples to sovereignty, although it has been denied in many countries. Indian rights precede modern international law, and human rights law should incorporate the ultimate holdings of the bull as one of the first human rights. The right of Indians to their 'liberty' is the right of freedom to survive as groups. Indian 'tribes' (which I prefer to call 'Indian nations') are made up of families, with women being the nucleus of these families.

Until recent times, native peoples were deemed to have very few rights in international law, but given modern advocacy for native rights, the situation is changing (Zion 1992: 191, 198). The sovereignty model, which comes from canon law, international law and Spanish law, and the two republics theory did not make its way into the United Nations Charter (although native groups continue to advocate that position). Human rights law for native peoples is evolving, where perhaps there will be less hesitance to acknowledge group rights and where native groups will be accorded self-determination, liberation, and equality; peace and security; use of wealth and resources; development; and environment (i.e., 'collective rights') (Sieghart 1983: 367-76).

The original rights of native peoples *as* native peoples have become 'minority rights'. Native peoples were accorded rights and protections in the 1919 Treaty of Versailles (ibid: 377) and the Covenant of the League of Nations. The International Covenant on Civil and Political Rights (ICCPR) was adopted by the United Nations in 1966 and came into force on 23 March 1976 (ibid: 25). The United States of America ratified this in 1992. Article 27 of the International Covenant on Civil and Political Rights guarantees that: 'in those States in which ethnic, religious or linguistic minorities exist, persons belonging to such minorities shall not be denied the right, in community with other members of their group, to enjoy their own culture, to profess and practise their own religion, or to use their own language' (United Nations 1966: 376).

These are five aspects of the right to enjoy culture: 1) freedom of expression; 2) educational policy; 3) promotion of literature and the arts; 4) dissemination of culture; and 5) preservation of customs and legal traditions (Capotorti 1979: 57-68). Given the broader definition of sovereignty, all those areas (and the remainder of article 27) are important. Freedom of expression includes the ability of Indians to *be* Indians. Educational policy is particularly important, and all native groups are attempting to control their own schools. Many young people are entering literature and the arts to explore their own native identities, and they are also joining programmes designed to disseminate their culture. Political sovereignty is protected by the inclusion of the rights to preserve customs and legal traditions. It represents the ability to have, and to make, law and to use traditional methods to implement it, and the means to preserve and strengthen the strongest elements of culture.

Native peoples do not appreciate having rights as 'minorities', because this implies that a generous state has taken pity on them. Native rights are fundamental rights which arise from their existence. They are not an act of charity. Despite this, the right to culture deserves further examination as a focus for solidarity and advocacy. It is a broad term, and it encompasses every aspect of native life. Indian life and fundamental values are included in the concept of culture, and they are a foundation for new international human rights law for Indians (Zion 1992). Where do Indian women's values fall in such an approach?

INDIAN WOMEN'S VALUES

Indian women have their own values; their own separate women's knowledge (Bell and Ditton 1980: 6-7). Women's traditional wisdom is passed down through the generations, and women preserve it in their language, stories, ceremonies and teachings. It embraces values which regulate the way women raise and teach their children, relate to each other in networks and relate to work. Women have distinctive approaches to life, including reproductive strategies, survival techniques, work and roles in society (Martin and Voorhies 1975). Despite domination or repression by men, native women are strong in their societies, and male dominance is effectively a myth (Leacock 1981). Left alone by outside law and policy, Indian women have the ability to use their own knowledge to address the basics of life.

Native women have reproductive freedom and use their knowledge to regulate family size and health.[12] George Catlin, an American artist, visited Indians of the upper Missouri in 1832 (Jennings 1993: 348). One of his illustrations bore this caption:

> A Sioux woman, wife of the chief, with her boy, four years old, at the breast: an occurrence not infrequent among the North American Indian tribes. This unnatural habit, and the premature age (12 and 14) at which the young women marry, are no doubt the principal causes of the paucity of children borne by the Indian women, who are very seldom the mothers of more than three or four (ibid: 355).

When Catlin wrote, mothers in Italy suckled children five and six years old for the same reason—to prolong time between births (id). Catlin saw Indian women's knowledge in action, although he did not recognize what he saw, and it involved more than spacing the birth of children. Life in Sioux country was hard, because of the harsh plains environment. Winters were severe, and the Sioux Nation moved across the plains in a hunting economy. Sioux women knew that their children had to be strong to survive, and that the family size should be small. Breast milk is a source of protein, and it would enable a small child to survive until the child was strong enough to go through times of periodic hunger. Having a few children assured that each would live, and that the family unit was small enough to be viable in a hunting economy. A mobile population required new family units to act as groups within the community, and young marriage enabled youthful families to form and take their place in the economy. Women's knowledge assured family and group survival in ways which adapted to the environment.

Language is also women's knowledge, because they are the first teachers of the language, and control who will learn it. Language is one of the most important aspects of sovereignty, because it carried the values, concepts and ways of looking at life that define the group and make it unique. To the extent that women are denied the right to know and pass on the language, this destroys the group.[13]

Religion is women's knowledge. Women have their own ceremonies to learn and pass on spiritual wisdom. Indian nations which have female deities use puberty ceremonies to teach the dignity of women to all. In many of them, women become the deity which is honoured, often as an apparition of Mother Earth. Mother Earth is the source of life, and respect for Her ways is essential to survival. Native peoples are concerned about Her as their environment, and international environmental and development policies acknowledge the need to respect both native cultures and their environments (World Commission on Environment and Development 1987: 114-16).

Native women know best how to protect themselves in relationships, families and clan systems. Given the destruction of their traditional law, they have learned how to form new alliances for protection (Lamphere 1989: 431-56). In modern times, they integrate traditional and contemporary demands in a positive and culturally consistent manner using retraditionalization—the extension of traditional caretaking and cultural transmission roles which are vital to survival (LaFromboise, Heyle and Ozer 1990: 469). To the extent the ability to form protective associations or retraditionalize is inhibited or repressed, cycles of violence persist. Contemporary problems of alcoholism, family violence, and child abuse are learned behaviours. They come from intergenerational post-traumatic stress or the social climate created by the violence outlined here (Duran, Guillory and Tingley 1993). People who are the victims of such stress transmit it to their children—by personal example, teaching or conduct toward them. This is what creates the cycle of violence, and it can be broken by rehonouring Indian women's roles and knowledge.

CONTEMPORARY AMERICAN INDIAN POLICY

To date, the best and *only* American Indian law to benefit Indian women has been the Indian Child Welfare Act of 1978 (Public Law 95-608, 25 U.S.C. §§ 1901-1922). It is important because of the historical pattern it attempts to correct. It is *not* simply a law that keeps Indian children out of the hands of state judges.

Columbus began the practice of taking women and children for slavery, and Cortez firmly established it. It was brought to the American southwest by their followers. The usual excuse for refusing to return a woman or a child was that she or he had become a Christian and did not wish to return home. We, as native people, were told to take the master's word for it. My ancestors were taken as slaves by the Spanish and their families were told the same thing. That was a major cause of war, conflict and friction until after our Treaty of 1868. In modern times, slavery evolved. This time, the Great White Father took our children to reprogramme them in boarding schools. Indians are aware of the modern concepts of concentration or re-education camps, mass relocation, ethnic cleansing and the machine gun, because those vicious tools were first used on Indians. The Great White Father has his helpers—non-native social workers. They went into our communities and declared the horror of what they saw—alcoholism, child abuse and family violence. Rather than acknowledge what created those destructive forces, the Great White Father's helpers chose the easiest option—they took our children. Soon, a baby market developed. Given stereotypical images of Indians and romantic notions about them, Indian children were a desirable commodity. State officials met the demands.[14] The Indian Child Welfare Act makes it possible for Indians to grow up knowing their own families and cultures.

Finally, Congress did turn to the sources of the violence the social workers deplored. In 1990, it enacted the Indian Child Protection and Family Violence Prevention Act (Public Law 101-630, codified at 25 U.S.C. §§ 3201-3211), including an Indian Child Protection and Family Violence Program for Indian nations, to be funded at a level of $30 million per year for five years (§ 3210). The Great White Father's true concern about child abuse and family violence is reflected in what his Bureau of Indian Affairs did to implement this law. A 28 October 1993 Senate Committee on Indian Affairs oversight hearing disclosed that the BIA did not *begin* to write the regulations required by the act until 1 July 1993, and it failed to ask for an appropriation to implement the Indian nation programmes. The Senate committee did not use its oversight power to catch the bureau's inexcusable negligence.[15]

During the course of the hearing, Senator Pete Domenici commented that the situation could be cured through the passage of his Senate Bill 1149, The Office of Indian Women and Families Act of 1993. His comment has merit. The proposed Office would put a staffer directly under the Assistant Secretary of the Interior for Indian Affairs to form a working group, which would identify all available sources of federal funding for Indian women and families, and set inter-agency priorities to implement programmes. The idea comes from the Agency for International Development, which identifies sources of support for less developed nations on an international level. The merit of the idea is that it elevates awareness of women and family needs and acknowledges Indian nations as less-developed nations, but nations nonetheless.

EMPOWERING NATIVE WOMEN

The writings of European colonizers show that they recognized the power of Indian women in their societies, and that Europeans consciously set out to destroy it (Jaimes and Halsey 1992: 319-23). The missionaries may have thought that their ways were more 'civilized' and beneficial (they were not), and the military strategists likely knew precisely what they were doing. To destroy Indian enemies, they needed only to destroy the role of women. If the erosion of sovereignty comes from disempowering women, its renewed strength will come from re-empowering them.

'Empowerment' has become a buzzword. Its overuse and misuse trivializes an important idea. Conservatives attempt to seize the word for their own agendas, along with 'family values'. Republican termination strategies of the 1950s almost destroyed American Indian nations, and the 'family values' policies of the Right today attempt to perpetuate the attitudes which caused atrocities against native peoples in the first place. The new conservative dogma is attractive, but those who voice it have no intention of returning true power to native communities.[16]

All the stereotyping, misconceptions and abuse of Indian women come from the fact that they were not allowed to speak for themselves, express their own identities or participate in the development of policies which affected them. As shown, they were a resource to be exploited and treated as less than human. The Domenici approach is limited, because Indian women need to have the effective ability to promote their own interests, but it is a start. There should be some means to make the interests of Indian women a priority and finally to marshal resources to deal with their problems.

The concept must go further. Federal monies for grants to address child abuse, domestic violence, women's education, women's economic development and other programmes should be managed by women. Women's organizations or institutions should receive those monies directly to operate programmes for child support enforcement, domestic violence restraining orders, victim assistance and discrimination remedies. It is not enough to earmark monies to benefit women and families; women must be the instruments of change themselves.

Intervention is another aspect of the Great White Father/Great White Husband Syndrome. The Indian Child Protection and Family Violence Protection Act increases the federal government's presence in Indian Country and 'federalizes' family conduct:

> When the legalized fine print is read through the present attempt by the government is not only to intervene within the practice of domestic violence but also to continue the historical process of systematically forcing the Native lifeworld into the control of bureaucratic systems. The bill mandates that any discovery of abuse towards children must be reported to the FBI therein throwing the family into the federal court and prison system (Duran, Guillory and Tingley 1993: 3).

Self-determination, self-governance, and sovereignty are not the fantasy of proud and once-independent peoples. They are the reality. No amount of intervention by white fathers will cure the conditions they created. Even where central government monies are returned to native peoples (to compensate for stolen lands and resources or otherwise), the established order should not be followed. The approach of 'people who do things for others' along police and social work lines simply does not work (Barsh and Henderson 1976: 25-60). Instead, let the people who are suffering take the resources to do things for themselves. This is true empowerment.

'Empowerment' is a sacred word to me. I address changes in the political structure which we need to empower women, but there is another aspect which makes this a ceremonial process. Women's strength comes from their prayers, ceremonies, inner wisdom and teachings. As we practice traditional knowledge, we grow stronger as women. My language, religion and culture were taken from me as a child when I was put into boarding school. I felt alienated from my own culture, but when I returned to it by relearning the language, religion and ways of the Dine', my personal strength grew. As I take on projects, I draw upon the inner strength that comes from traditional empowerment. All the programmes and initiatives I advocate must go hand-in-hand with traditional empowerment. Without it, we cannot regain our sovereignty.

We cannot go back to 1492; it is too late to repel the invaders. (As the bumper sticker says, 'Indians had lousy immigration laws'). However, we can attempt to restore some of the basic values of native societies, including the role of women. It is not enough to pay attention to them now through special programmes from the top down. Traditionally, men and women stood in good relations to each other, sharing special roles. These values must be restored, because they embody survival skills. Doing so will promote the genuine sovereignty which comes from the family and clan—the basic institutions of native society.

NOTES

1. Commission on Folk Law and Legal Pluralism Conference, held by the Law Faculty, Victoria University of Wellington, New Zealand, 27-30 August 1992.

2. I made a complaint about this to the New Mexico Office of Indian Affairs, and I await action on it.

3. I do not intend to enter the debate over the Las Casas 'Black Myth', which the English deliciously employed in propaganda. One may dispute specific events and numbers, but the pattern of genocide is apparent. It was not limited to the Spanish.

4. When I visited New Zealand in 1992, I found a Maori 'two republics' approach.

5. Why is it that the right to revolution, as announced by Jefferson, Lincoln and Grant and endorsed by Justice Douglas, is denied to Indians? Was Richard Nixon an advocate of Indian rights, or did he announce his progressive Indian policies out of fear of an Indian uprising (given the AIM era)? What will be the lessons of the recent 'uprisings' in Canada, which produced the Royal Commission on Aboriginal Peoples (whose justice sessions I attended in Ottawa in 1992).

6. The European literature which said that Indians had 'no law or government' and that they practised 'barbaric' ways, contrary to natural law, was propaganda used to justify misconduct. Isn't it amazing that so many of the accounts by conquistadores, explorers and traders follow the same patterns? Contemporary literature and media continue the same pattern.

7. My former husband, James W. Zion, tells of reading through 1860s issues

of the *Montana Post* (Virginia City, Montana Territory) and coming across accounts of Indian-white marriages. The *Post* (whose editor was a lawyer) argued against the adoption of California miscegenation law, which prohibited marriages with Indians. A few issues later, it reported (without editorial comment) the visit of a Catholic priest to Fort Benton and the marriages between males with Anglo names and women with obviously Indian names.

8. There is insufficient space here to describe some of the horrible sex murders of Indian women in modern times. Indian women are particularly prone to rape and murder by non-Indian psychopaths.

9. Navajo women used a sneaky tactic to get around 'head of household' (i.e., male) land allocation. They sent their men to the agency office to claim their allotments under the women's war names (Zion and Zion 1993: 419 n.95). Women are not always defenceless.

10. These figures should not be accepted without an understanding of what they do *not* tell us. Most numbers on Indian crime and victimization use national crime figures, which come from police reports on crime or surveys of victims. Many Indian nations do not contribute data to the national bases. The figures may have more to do with the behaviour of Indians outside their native territory than behaviour within Indian country. FBI and Justice Department enforcement of federal law is lax, and the figures for Indian country crime could be low. The U.S. government has never provided Indian nations the means to assess their own crime rates in a meaningful way.

11. This is only a summary survey of international human rights law. Native leaders publish many positions on the subject, and the literature is too large to review here.

12. I do not enter the debate over abortion. Whether or not it is sanctioned by state law, it exists. Native women make their own decisions about themselves, their children and their families. Native women have the right to determine whether abortion should be legal, and if the women in a given society practised it traditionally, they will continue to do so. If they did not, they won't.

13. In a recent Social Security disability claim case, a Navajo women explained why she did not speak English. When she was a child, she attended a mission school. She dropped out because all the nuns taught her was how to scrub floors and clean rooms. She left school when they had her clean toilets. In my own case, I spoke my language as a child, but it was taken from me in a Bureau of Indian Affairs boarding school.

14. I stand on this assertion even over the protests of social worker friends. The statistics on the taking of Indian children and placement for adoption clearly show the existence of a baby market. Now that Indian children are less available in the United States, people are turning to Asia as a source of 'cute little brown children'. Many residents of New Mexico are Navajo descendants, although they may not know it.

15. President Bush's signature message on the act shows that he was tempted

to veto the bill, due to budget reduction, but instead he signed it, saying he would move to repeal the law. That wasn't done, but the reason for the Bureau's failure to act prior to 1993 is obvious.

16. Despite the passage of the Indian Self-Determination and Education Assistance Act of 1975, which follows an empowerment model, the Nixon, Reagan, and Bush administrations cut funding for Indian nation programmes and made certain there was no effective federal commitment to revitalizing Indian government. The Bush administration blocked funding and shifted Indian policy to the Office of Management and Budget. There has been a lot of lip service and a lot of hypocrisy by both political parties.

REFERENCES

Allen, P. G. (1986) *The Sacred Hoop*, Boston: Beacon Press.

Barkun, M. (1968) *Law without Sanctions*, New Haven: Yale University Press.

Barsh, R. L. and Henderson, J. Y. (1976) 'Tribal Courts, The Model Code, and the Police Idea in American Indian Policy', in L. Rosen (ed.) *American Indians and the Law*, New Brunswick: Transaction Books, 25-60.

Becker, T. M., Wiggins, C. L., Key, C. R. and Samet, J. M. (1993) 'Suicide and Homicide, Racial and Ethnic Patterns of Mortality in New Mexico', in T. M. Becker, C. L. Wiggins, R. S. Elliott, C. R. Key and J. M. Samet (eds.) *Racial and Ethnic Patterns of Mortality in New Mexico*, Albuquerque: University of New Mexico Press, 132-44.

Bell, D. and Ditton, P. (1980) *Law: The Old and the New: Aboriginal Women in Central Australia Speak Out*, Canberra: Aboriginal History for Central Australian Aboriginal Legal Aid Service.

Bolt, C. (1987) *American Indian Policy and American Reform*, London: Unwin Hyman.

Borah, W. (1983) *Justice by Insurance*, Berkeley: University of California Press.

Bowden, H. W. (1981) *American Indians and Christian Missions*, Chicago: University of Chicago Press.

Capotorti, F. (1979) *Study on the Rights of Persons Belonging to Ethnic, Religious and Linguistic Minorities*, New York: United Nations.

Chavez, L., Becker, T. M., Wiggins, C. L., Key, C. R. and Samet, J. M. (1993) 'Alcohol-Related Mortality', in T. M. Becker, C. L. Wiggins, R. S. Elliott, C. R. Key and J. M. Samet (eds.) *Racial and Ethnic Patterns of Mortality in New Mexico*, Albuquerque: University of New Mexico Press, 108- 117.

Cross, P. (1982) 'Sexual Abuse, a New Threat to the Native American Woman: An Overview', *Listening Post: A Periodical of the Mental Health Programs of Indian Health Services*, 6: 1/2, 22.

Deutsch, S. (1991) 'Coming Together, Coming Apart—Women's History and the West', *The Magazine of Western History*, Montana: 41: 2, 58-61.

Domenici, P. (1993) 'Office of Indian Women and Families Act', *Congressional Record*—Senate: S 7761-7764, 23 June 1993.

Drinnon R. (1990) *Facing West*, New York: Schocken Books.

Duran, E., Guillory, B. and Tingley, P. (1993) *Domestic Violence in Native American Communities: The Effects of Intergenerational Post Traumatic Stress*.

Hall, G. E. and Weber, D. J. (1984) 'Mexican Liberals and the Pueblo Indians, 1821-1829', *New Mexico Historical Review*, 59: 1, 5-32.

Haring, C. H. (1975) *The Spanish Empire in America*, San Diego: Harcourt Brace Jovanovich.

Indian Health Service (1992) *Trends in Indian Health 1992*, Washington: U.S. Department of Health and Human Services.

Jaimes, M. A. and Halsey, T. (1992) 'American Indian Women: At the Center of Indigenous Resistance in North America', in M.A. Jaimes (ed.) *The State of Native America*, Boston: South End Press, 311-44.

Jennings, E. (1993) *The Founders of America*, New York: W. W. Norton.

Kanowitz, (1969) *Women and the Law*, Albuquerque: University of New Mexico Press.

LaFromboise, T. D., Heyle, A. M. and Ozer, E. J. (1990) 'Changing and Diverse Roles of Women in American Indian Cultures', *Sex Roles*, 22: 7/8, 455-76.

Lamphere, L. (1989) 'Historical and Regional Variability in Navajo Women's Roles', *Journal of Anthropological Research*, 45: 4, 431-56.

Leacock, E. B. (1981) *Myths of Male Dominance*, New York: Monthly Review Press.

Martin, M. K. and Voorhies, B. (1975) *Female of the Species*, New York: Columbia University Press.

National Minority Advisory Council on Criminal Justice (1982) *The Inequality of Justice*, Washington: Government Printing Office.

Native American Studies Centre, University of New Mexico (1993) 'International Testimonial on the Violation of Indigenous Sovereignty Rights', *NAS Newsline*, 3: 3, 5-6.

Piedra, J. (1982) 'Loving Columbus', in R. Jara and N. Spadaccini (eds.), *Amerindian Images and the Legacy of Columbus*, Minneapolis: University of Minnesota Press, 230-65.

Prucha, F. P. (1973) *Americanizing the American Indians*, Lincoln: University of Nebraska Press.

Reiss, A. J. and Roth J. A. (eds.) (1993) *Understanding and Preventing Violence*, Washington: National Academy Press.

Riley, G. (1984a) 'Some European (Mis)perceptions of American Indian Women', *New Mexico Historical Review*, 59: 3, 237-66.

Riley G. (1984b) *Women and Indians on the Frontier, 1825-1915*, Albuquerque: University of New Mexico Press.

Riley, G. (1991) 'Western Women's History—A Look at Some of the Issues', *The*

Magazine of Western History, Montana: 41: 2, 66-70.

Sagan, E. (1986) *At the Dawn of Tyranny*, New York: Vintage Books.

Sale, K. (1991) *The Conquest of Paradise*, New York: The Penguin Group.

Scharff, V. (1991) 'Gender and Western History: Is Anybody Home on the Range?' *The Magazine of Western History*, Montana: 41:2, 62-65.

Sewell, C. M., Becker, T. M., Wiggins, C. L., Key, C. R., and Samet, J. M. (1993) 'Injury Mortality', in T. M. Becker., C. L. Wiggins., R. S. Elliott., C. R. Key and J. M. Samet (eds.) *Racial and Ethnic Patterns of Mortality in New Mexico*, Albuquerque: University of New Mexico Press, 118-31.

Sieghart, R. (1983) *The International Law of Human Rights*, Oxford: Clarenden Press.

Smith S. (1987) 'Beyond Princess and Squaw: Army Officers' Perceptions of Indian Women', in S. Armitage and E. Jameson (eds.) *The Women's West*, Norman: University of Oklahoma Press, 63-75.

Stogre, M. J. (1991) *The Development of Papal Teaching on Aboriginal Rights: 500 Years of Catholic Social Teaching*, Rerum Novarum Series.

Thornton, R. (1987) *American Indian Holocaust and Survival*, Norman: University of Oklahoma Press.

Todorov, T. (1984) *The Conquest of America*, New York: Harper and Row.

United Nations (1966) *International Covenant on Civil and Political Rights* (adopted by General Assembly resolution 2200 A [XXI], 16 December).

Van Kirk, S. (1980) *Many Tender Ties*, Norman: University of Oklahoma Press.

Washburn, W. E. (volume editor) (1988) *History of Indian-White Relations*, *Handbook of North American Indians*, Vol. 4, Washington: Smithsonian Institution.

World Commission on Environment and Development (1987) *Our Common Future*, New York: Oxford University Press.

Zion, J. W. (1992) 'North American Indian Perspectives on Human Rights', in A. A. An-na'im (ed.) *Human Rights in Cross-Cultural Perspectives*, Philadelphia: University of Pennsylvania Press, 191-220.

Zion, J. W. and Zion, E. B. (1993) '"Hazho' Sokee"—Stay Together Nicely: Domestic Violence under Navajo Common Law', *Arizona State Law Journal*, 25: 2, 407-26.

8

'A Fitting Remedy': Aboriginal Justice As a Community Healing Strategy

Marcia L. Hoyle

INTRODUCTION

This chapter highlights the theme of community resources for the development of alternative justice models in Canada's First Nations. In particular, it refers to preliminary research in a mid-sized, semi-urban Anishnabek (Ojibway) reserve in the province of Ontario. This community is one of seven Anishnabek reserves that make up Mamaweswen, the North Shore Tribal Council, situated on the North Shore of Lake Huron, Ontario (Map 8.1). This two-year project, which in 1984 had just begun, takes an anthropological perspective on contemporary and customary legal and conflict resolution behaviour and philosophy as resources for the building of an alternative justice system. The project is collaborative and participatory in design, and its eventual outcome will be a foundation for the development and implementation of a community-based justice programme.[1] It is necessary, however, to situate the discussion of this particular project within the larger framework of aboriginal justice programmes as part of a general movement for Native self-government and the revitalization of tradition, and the healing metaphor in which this book is currently cast.

It has been widely acknowledged for some time now, not only by Canada's aboriginal people but increasingly by both the federal and provincial governments, that there is a pressing need to implement some form of culturally appropriate alternative to Canada's present justice system. The alienating and discriminatory system that has resulted in unequal access to justice for aboriginal people, and their over-representation in courts and carceral facilities, has been extensively documented over the last two decades (Havemann et al. 1985; Coyle 1986; Jackson 1988; Province of Manitoba 1991; Province of Alberta 1991; Lajeunesse 1991; Rudin and Russell 1991; Warry 1991). It has taken repeated expressions of these fundamental inequities, and the recent political activism of aboriginal people to have at last brought affairs to the stage where justice systems designed

MAP 8.1
Location of North Shore Area, Lake Huron, Ontario

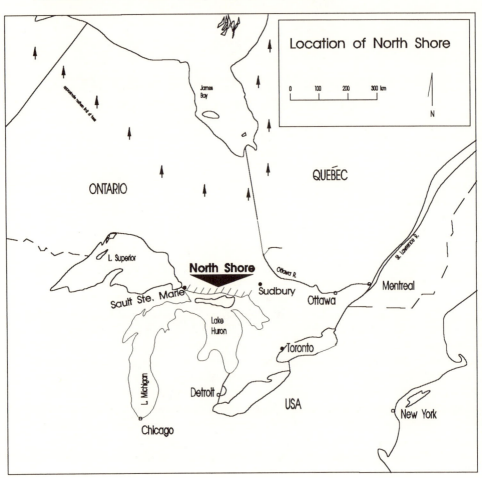

and implemented by aboriginal people themselves are a genuine possibility.

Nations is a priority both at the level of aboriginal national organizations and at the level of particular communities. Nevertheless, the perception of Canada's current system as discriminatory and unresponsive to indigenous peoples' needs is only one of the motivations behind the search for workable alternatives to the Eurocentric, adversarial model of law currently entrenched in Canada. A change in the legal system is necessary also as a means of reintegrating conflict resolution into the life of the community, in ways which are harmonious with Native cultural values and will help achieve the goal of aboriginal self-government.

Self-determination and self-government are the two closely linked and overarching frameworks within which many aboriginal groups are working towards a revitalization of traditional values and practices. Self-determination, in the aboriginal view, entails 'jurisdiction over aboriginal lands and over those aspects of the lifestyle of aboriginal peoples that influence directly economic, linguistic, cultural, educational and other related matters' (Asch 1984: 35), and is believed to be possible through the achievement of self-government.

To put this in historical perspective, we need to realize that first the colonial British government, and later the Canadian government, instituted policies and practices that have systematically denied this jurisdiction, while maintaining a high degree of centralized bureaucratic control over aboriginal lives. Treaties were signed that ceded land to the Crown and in exchange usufructuary rights for hunting and fishing were promised. Autonomy was lost through encapsulation on reserves that could not sustain traditional economies, and by control of daily life through the federally legislated Indian Act (1876). Aboriginal rights and resources have subsequently been eroded and challenged, to the point where Canada's indigenous populations have existed, for more than a hundred years, in a state of what Ponting (1986) calls 'internal colonialism'.

While the past few years have been marked by a change in government practice and public sentiment that seems to support aboriginal self-government, efforts to have the concept entrenched in the constitution and to achieve self-government on a significant scale have been continually frustrated (Asch 1984; Clark 1990; Morse 1988). Despite these frustrations, however, there is more commitment than ever before to finding workable models of self-government that will enable the First Nations of Canada to govern themselves in ways appropriate to their present reality, a reality that is often characterized by a tenacity of core cultural values that have persisted in the face of these nearly overwhelming challenges to their integrity.

JUSTICE AS HEALING

Recently, as part of the move towards aboriginal self-government, a potent and engaging metaphor has become central to the public discourse in Canada concerning approaches to changing the social, economic and cultural reality of aboriginal peoples: the *healing* of communities through the combined revitalization of traditional culture and the creation of new institutions. The Canadian Royal Commission on Aboriginal Peoples, for example, in its present three-year round of consultations, has pinpointed 'healing' as one of the four 'touchstones for change' (Royal Commission on Aboriginal Peoples, 1993a: v) that are to be the guiding objectives for the future of aboriginal peoples' relations with the Canadian state.

This talk of healing in official and academic circles represents the fact that the Royal Commission, and the government it represents, have heard the repeated, urgent calls by indigenous peoples that the government take action to address the endemic pathologies in aboriginal communities in Canada.   As far as justice reform is concerned, this call for a healing of aboriginal communities has now merged with First Nations' people's conviction that their self-determination must include the development of justice systems that can act to promote and further the healing process.   One aboriginal participant at the recent round of talks of the Royal Commission on Aboriginal Peoples expressed the connection this way:

[N]o health issue, no justice issue and no social issue can be 'cured' if it is approached in piecemeal fashion.   Each must be addressed as part of a chain linking oppression and self-destruction.   And 'healing' must come, not from the outside, not from the short-term health and social programmes designed in Ottawa and elsewhere, but from aboriginal people, their traditions and values (Royal Commission on Aboriginal Peoples 1993a: 53).

This discursive phenomenon represents the appropriation of the healing metaphor by non-aboriginals concerned with legal reform in Native communities. It does not signal a new approach to justice by aboriginal peoples themselves; community healing is acknowledged as having been the central goal of traditional law since pre-colonial times.   In formerly small band societies such as the Cree/Ojibway, the shaman or religious leader fulfilled the dual role of healer and principal channel of social control (Kinietz 1974).   Dispute resolution and law, through the mechanisms of confession, compensation and reconciliation performed in a small community context, and often mediated by the Elders, were aimed at restoring harmonious relations between persons and at keeping the community in harmony with natural and spiritual elements.   A healthy community was one characterized by internal and external harmony.

Despite the attrition of the shamans' role, and the diminishing role of the Elders, as a result of colonization and acculturation, and the further appropriation of conflict resolution and social control by the dominant state, the healing paradigm has once again surfaced in aboriginal discourse as an expression of a holistic approach to social ills.   A leader from a small northern reserve told the Royal Commission: 'We are communities in the fullest sense of the word. We operate almost as a family where we all have obligations and rights ... We do not punish; rather we seek to heal' (Royal Commission on Aboriginal Peoples 1993b: 9).

Healing has perforce taken on a new urgency, however, as aboriginal communities and individuals are torn apart in a profoundly deeper and broader scope than in traditional times.   New models of legal process and conflict resolution for Native communities will need to take a broad and comprehensive approach to attend to broken individuals and suffering communities. Writer Boyce Richardson encapsulates the state of affairs accurately:

What we want is self-reliance, self-control, internal growth. We want to start a process of healing. We want to contribute to North American society, through better education, higher rates of employment and literacy, less dependence on welfare, and finally through a determined attack on the youth suicides, family abuse, alcoholism and social dissolution that blight so many of our communities today (1989: 5).

SELF-GOVERNMENT AND THE REVITALIZATION OF TRADITION

Any discussion of current aboriginal life in Canada must try to strike a balance between assessing the continuity of central cultural values and practices, and the colossal effects of European colonization. In addition, the diversity of both pre-contact and present social forms and the differential effects of colonialism on different areas of what is now Canada must be appreciated in order to avoid using the term 'indigenous' as just another essentialist category. The term 'aboriginal peoples' refers to Inuit, Dene, Métis, and Indian populations. Those who designate themselves 'Indian' have been arbitrarily categorized by the colonial government into 'status' (legally defined) and 'non-status', and further distinguished (for legal purposes) into treaty and non-treaty Indians. Most aboriginal people living on reserves are status Indians, constituting 'bands', a political creation of the colonial government, made to facilitate bureaucratic control (Map 8.2).

Contemporary Cree and Ojibway communities represent a diverse range of social, economic and political forms and practices that reflect both pre-contact differences in cultural patterns, environment and economy and differential exposure to European influence and domination. The area traditionally inhabited by the Cree and Ojibway extends from the eastern shores of Labrador, along the St. Lawrence River Basin and the Gaspe Peninsula, to regions around the western shore of Hudson Bay, the north shores of Lake Superior and Lake Huron and the Lake Winnipeg basin (Brown 1989: 208). The general Northern Algonquian cultural pattern has traditionally been a hunting and trapping economy characterized by small kin-based groups operating on a seasonal round of small hunting groups in the winter, and larger summer gatherings for trade, fishing and ceremonial purposes (Brown and Wilson 1989). The hunting economy is still basic to some communities and has been recently revitalized in others where resources are available (Feit 1989).

The political life of these former, small kin-based groups was loosely organized, with no overarching authoritative leadership; rather, leaders were recognized for their competence and wisdom, and individuals possessed a great

MAP 8.2
Aboriginal Communities in the Province of Ontario

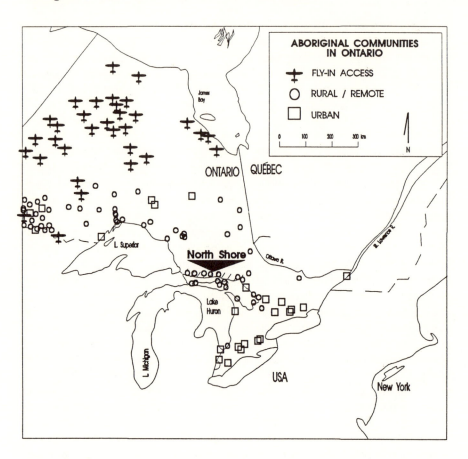

deal of personal autonomy (Brown 1989). An ethic of sharing and reciprocity has
been recognized as a fundamental Cree/Ojibway value (Brown and Wilson 1989;
Feit 1989). First European contact for some members of the Northern Algonquian
group was early in the sixteenth century, while others continued relatively
unaffected until early in this century (Brown and Wilson 1989: 138). Similarly,
the present degree of integration with the modern industrial state varies
significantly between communities and from one region to the other. In the
province of Ontario, for instance, reserve communities such as those along the
North Shore (Map 8.1) have had significant and long-standing interaction with the

settler population, dating from the early seventeenth century, while many of the band populations in the far north of the province continued relatively unaffected until about sixty years ago.

Still, there are some generalizations that can be made about the effects of European expansion and the eventual political incorporation of all aboriginal groups into the capitalist economy of the Canadian welfare state. In general, the colonial processes of deterritorialization and the concomitant loss of hunting territory and encapsulation on reserves, the involvement in European trade and economy, an imposed form of government replacing traditional forms of leadership, the European attempts at 'civilization' expressed in missionization, and education, and government administration of daily life through the Indian Act (1876) were the main agents of disruption of aboriginal ways of life.

Challenges imposed by the modern welfare state have been urbanization, swings in government policy between overtly assimilationist and devolutionist, educational policies and programmes, and the socio-economic decline in reserve communities that possess an insufficient land base for economic viability. The combined effects of these processes have created many reserve communities characterized by high unemployment and welfare dependency, poverty, shocking suicide rates, poor health and educational standards, loss of aboriginal languages and traditions, a high incidence of alcoholism and related violence, and conflicts over political legitimacy.

While the Indian Act has been responsible for a high degree of institutional surveillance and what Foucault (1980) calls disciplinary power over status Indians, it is nevertheless perceived by many status Indians as offering protection from provincial governments, with whom they have no special, fiduciary relationship as they do with the federal government (Gibbins and Ponting 1986). Differences in opinion over whether to abandon the act have created fracture lines within communities. Because the constitutional status of the 'existing' rights is still ambiguous, many status Indians (those defined as 'Indian' by the Indian Act) feel that it would be too great a risk to trust that their historic treaty rights would be honoured without the protection of the Indian Act. Aboriginal rights have, since 1982, been written into the Canadian constitution, but have yet to be defined. Aboriginal politicians who advocate full sovereignty within the nation-state of Canada do so on the basis that rights were never abrogated. Aboriginal conceptions of sovereignty, however, comprise full jurisdiction within aboriginal territory, including the legislative authority to pass laws.

The colonial government was, to a significant degree, successful in its goal of suppressing existing forms of aboriginal law and the values on which traditional legal process was based. The blame for current conditions on reserves and in urban centres is placed squarely on the shoulders of the government: 'In our view the serious conditions of alcohol and drug dependency, family violence, child abuse, unemployment, incarceration, housing and educational deficiencies, disease and violent death that are found today in so many First Nations communities are a measure of the extent to which government-defined and -imposed programmes have undermined our values' (Richardson 1989: 33).

In Anishnabek First Nations, at least, the indigenous justice form has atrophied, and the Anishnabek and other First Nations now face the task of creating legal systems anew from the various elements at hand.   Individual communities diverge widely in their perceptions of the emancipatory potential of this change and the urgency with which they feel the need to confront the issue, but there is a widespread and deeply felt sense that the revitalization of traditional values will be the key to community healing.   This goal poses a considerable challenge to communities like those on the North Shore that have been profoundly changed by their long-standing interaction and integration with the dominant society.

A HYPOTHETICAL COMMUNITY CASE STUDY

If we take this discussion down to the community level and posit, not a 'typical' community, but a more or less aggregate type, it will focus the discussion of aboriginal attempts to surmount the obstacles created by the colonial and post-colonial past. Let us say that this is an Ojibway community of approximately 500 people living in Northern Ontario. Because their ancestors signed the Robinson-Huron Treaty in 1850 with the British colonial government, they are designated as both 'status Indians' and 'treaty Indians' by the Canadian government. This means that they have been under the direct jurisdiction of the colonial administration, and then the federal government which has been guided by the Indian Act since 1876, and that the government has certain obligations to honour the treaty that was signed. Their local government consists of a chief and one band councillor for every hundred people, elected every two years. This is a form of government instituted and legislated through the Indian Act, which stipulates the frequency, form and rules of elections for chief and council. If the community wants a different form of government, they must achieve it through changes to the Indian Act, or the negotiation of a self-government agreement with the federal and provincial governments.

The articulation with the Canadian justice system has been a particularly debilitating one for this community. The high rate of alcohol dependence (an artefact of contact) and unemployment have contributed to family violence and juvenile delinquency, and police in the adjacent, mainly non-aboriginal town exercise their discretionary powers to arrest reserve members frequently. Community members are aware that their experience in the district Euro-Canadian court is alienating in the extreme, due to basic value and language differences and the very real awareness that they are being dealt with by an alien jurisdiction. The dissatisfaction and oppression of community members become expressed in the assertion that 'traditional law' would be a more authentic way of handling their problems of social control and conflict.

When discussions begin at band council to propose reinstituting 'traditional law', several obstacles become apparent. The first is a problem of jurisdiction. Since sovereignty has not been achieved from the Canadian state and the jurisdiction of traditional aboriginal law is not recognized in the constitution, an agreement for limited jurisdiction needs to be negotiated with both the federal and provincial governments. But before the state and province will enter into negotiations, the band must prepare documentation outlining the 'traditional law' which they want to institute. The next problem is a problem of definition.

Since 'traditional law' was a means of social control for a small, kin-based, semi-nomadic hunting group, it was based on a system of individuals who respected each other's autonomy to a high degree, and who were more or less homogeneous in religious values that were closely integrated with the hunting ritual complex that was basic to life. Shamans acted as a community force of social control. Law was not codified, so to try to articulate what law *is*, has become a dilemma.

If it is then decided that, rather than attempt a definition of law, it might be possible to delineate broad value statements out of which codes of conduct and modes of intervention could be drafted, it must then be decided what those values are. Here the possibility of success may be increased. But an obstacle immediately becomes apparent; most of the community members are Roman Catholic, a legacy of the early missionizing in the area. Their value statements reflect Christian ideology. But several younger members reject Christianity as a hegemonic ideology, and want to subscribe to traditional values. Nevertheless, it may well become apparent that there is a significant degree of consensus on basic values; that those who embraced Christianity maintained many basic Ojibway value orientations, and that some underlying principles of a legal order can be outlined. Someone may point out in the midst of the discussion that no 'traditional' values have been expressed over private property. Yet one of the persistent problems on the reserve has been the vandalizing of homes and community property, and the theft of boats and fishing equipment. Encapsulated within a capitalistic system, and influenced by Christian missionaries and Christian ideology, communities have inculcated private property values and a notion of individual rights that will need to be incorporated into the proposed traditional law.

The next step might be to discuss specific modes of intervention. This runs up against the fundamental value orientation of non-interference adhered to by most members of the community. Nevertheless, if a 'traditional' legal system is to be negotiated with the government, it needs to conform to standards of the mainstream justice system to the extent that some specific recommendations are put forward. The suggestion may be made that a court system such as that in the Navajo nation in the United States might be implemented. But the problem is pointed out that the court system is a Western model, not one based on 'traditional' values and forms of restitution.

Discussions of 'traditional law' have made it apparent that elders, those respected in the group for their competence and wisdom, were the community members with legitimate authority in the past. When it is suggested to the elders, however, that they be responsible for disciplining young offenders who have been vandalizing community property, they reject the proposal, stating that the young people no longer respect their authority. Many of the youths of the reserve have been away to school in nearby towns, away from the authority of family and community, or have already served prison sentences. Some of them feel that their education has given them a wisdom superior to that of the elders. Moreover, some of the elders speak only Ojibway, and most of the youths, having been educated in English schools, speak only English.

The discussions of community problems have led to the perception that a major proportion of the crime and conflict is due to alcohol abuse and unemployment. How can a legal system true to Ojibway values deal with that? The justice committee and band council may then begin to focus on prevention and healing strategies for alcohol abuse rather than punitive techniques, true to what they have identified as a basic Ojibway orientation towards harmony and healing in response to community conflict. If these treatment strategies are based on contemporary Native spirituality, the Christian segment of the community may oppose it.

The problem of unemployment falls to a separate realm, and will require economic strategies for community development consonant with community values surrounding land and resources. One likely strategy for economic advancement would be to expand the land base. That will mean reopening treaty negotiations to reclaim land that was illegally claimed by the Crown. That, in turn, will require political reorganization, the aid of outside legal expertise, and increased links with the regional Native political network. Another likely project might be renegotiation of treaty fishing rights, and the promotion of either individual or communal viable small businesses.

PROBLEMS AND POTENTIAL IN ONE COMMUNITY

There is so little accurate information about traditional values surrounding Native law in Canada (Coyle 1986) that the task of model-building from a base of traditional values is a formidable one (cf. Brodeur, LaPrairie and McDonnell 1991). Moreover, it can neither be assumed that 'tradition' is a satisfactory base for modelling a justice system or that every aboriginal community would want such a focus. Native communities across Canada vary tremendously in the degree to which customary practices have been retained, changed or forgotten. Many aboriginal communities are characterized by fractious disputes over the role of 'traditional' values and practices in the ordering of daily life. These disputes often follow along generational and religious lines. It is likely that in most cases, particularly that of semi-urban reserves, the final product will be a blend of values and strategies that reflect contemporary Native experience and the dynamism of cultural meaning codes as they interact with those of the dominant society.

The community in which my present research is based, a semi-urban Anishnabek (Ojibway) reserve with a population of just over 1,000, has been dramatically affected by its close contact with Euro-Canadian society. Its proximity to an urban environment, past history of political control through federally appointed Indian agents, the movement of many community members between the two environments in work, education, marriage, and conflict with the Canadian criminal justice system, have allowed the erosion of many traditional values and the language that served as a medium for those values.

Many of those values may persist; the long-term, in-depth research in which this community is presently engaged is intended to discover what these may be. Practices have changed, but how have the values and ideas that guided those practices changed? Any attempt to build a justice system on what are thought to be 'traditional' ways will ignore what may be fundamental changes in value patterns. By the same token, the attempt to apply a ready-made model based on Western legal concepts and values will fail to take into account which elements of a customary philosophy of law have persisted in the face of structural changes in Native society, and the wide diversity among reserves.

The political leadership of this reserve community has already begun to move towards self-government in areas other than law, such as education, health and social services, but law and conflict resolution is and will be the least straighforward of all these areas. In any legal system of the future in this place, police are a given. There have been 'special constables' on the reserve for more than thirty years. Their role was first as adjunct to the federal, then provincial, police; now they are enforcers of band by-laws, Indian Act infractions and provincial and federal law. These law enforcers are trained by provincial police and operate under the same legislative umbrella. Part of our research is to examine their historic and present role in the community and the perceptions, both their own and those of others, of that role. Research in other areas has indicated that community-based aboriginal police are often in conflict over their dual role as members of the community's kinship structure and as enforcers of a foreign law (Havemann 1992: 114).

The existence of an already-constituted police presence in the community will mean that the attempt to develop an autonomous legal system will require a re-evaluation and reworking of their role in line with the articulated philosophy and goals of a new system. This will no doubt be a sensitive and difficult task requiring a great deal of political skill and community cooperation, and placing a tremendous strain on already stretched human resources in the community. Likewise, if a future legal system is to achieve the holistic, healing ideal being expressed in current discourse, there will need to be an integration of present social services already operative on the reserve, such as a family violence prevention and treatment facility, child welfare service and an alcohol abuse treatment programme.

Most of these services are indigenized versions of nationally conceived programmes. They will need to adapt and change in order to become more effective in dealing with the whole individual in context, and to express Native concepts of intervention and treatment. An ex-offender from the community who, in his words, 'did my homework in the joint', speaks despairingly of the problems Native offenders encounter in trying to get help in the community:

> When a native person plans his or her future from the confines of their cell, their best hopes rest with trying to conform to the non-native approach, because he or she knows well enough that the support on the street is tied directly to A.A. [Alcoholics Anonymous] or other programmes ... Parole officers and boards realize this and encourage our people to take that route. No matter how much we've improved ourselves through our learning, our culture and traditions, they'll see it as the wrong way, based on the fact that few native communities have support groups set up ... Many of us have failed time and time again and the will to keep trying fades away.

This particular community is navigating virtually uncharted waters in setting out to define and develop its own socio-legal framework. I say this, not because alternative justice models are untried in First Nations communities, but because most of what has been tried has been based on a Western model of law rather than generated in and by communities themselves, or because what fits in one context may be entirely foreign in the next. This became apparent quite strikingly at a recent meeting of First Nations leaders concerned with justice issues. A representative of the Gitksan-Wet'suwet'en from the West Coast of Canada described the recent revival of their traditional justice system, which is based on their matrilineal house and clan kinship structure.[2] They have extensively documented the kinship connections of their population and have it available on a computerized data base, so that when an individual facing criminal charges is referred to them by the police, they can determine house and clan membership and hence involve the extended kin network in the processing of the case. The offender becomes the responsibility of his or her house and clan. Together, a council of house members works with the offender and victim to determine appropriate action in each case. The main goal is to provide restitution to the victim and to reintegrate the offender into the community. Representatives of the Gitksan-Wet'suwet'en government report that the process is more strenuous and requires more commitment from offender and community than the present judicial system, and often takes a longer period of time. The process is completed with a 'shame feast' in which compensation is paid to the victim and their house, after which the case is closed.

Members of Northern Ontario Cree/Ojibway communities, after hearing of the Gitksan-Wet'suwet'en programme, expressed vivid interest in the apparent early success of the system, and indeed, it seems to express what many see as the 'ideal' revival of traditional law in contemporary aboriginal society. Moreover, the Gitksan-Wet'suwet'en are eager to share the knowledge and experience of the process through which they have gone to institute this system, as a model for other aboriginal groups.

Nevertheless, there are several factors that underlie their apparently smooth transition to a revived traditional law. One of these is that the house and clan system have remained central to Gitksan-Wet'suwet'en society despite the effects of colonialism. Their location on the resource-rich far northern coast of British Columbia kept contact with the colonizers at a minimum, and despite government and missionary attempts to outlaw such practices as the potlatch feast, the Gitksan-Wet'suwet'en have been able to sustain greater cultural continuity than the Ojibway, who occupied central areas and whose lands were coveted by European settlers. In addition, these matrilineal groups, who remained in large, stable villages well supported by a rich resource base, differ markedly in social structure from the Cree/Ojibway, who subsisted in small bands in a much harsher climate. Those contemporary Cree/Ojibway individuals, who are consciously trying to revive tradition, seek out Elders who may be able to tell them their clan membership. But the clan system is far from viable today, and was likely never as crucial for these sub-Arctic hunting groups as for the coastal, sedentary peoples. The point is that the formal aspects of a legal system arise in part from social structure, and any attempt to base an autonomous justice system on the house/clan system of another aboriginal group could prove dysfunctional for the Cree/Ojibway, despite similar value orientations. Hence, the importance of developing models at the community level, that are responsive to local context, draw realistically on local human resources and speak to local experience is clear.

CREATING MODELS IN COMMUNITIES
AND THE ROLE OF RESEARCH

There has been a persistent inclination in Canada towards adoption of ready-made system models for aboriginal legal autonomy. One has to ask why this has been the case, when 'home grown', community-based options may be equally effective and may in addition contribute in a significant way to community development. The application of ready-made solutions may be a particularly attractive option for researchers, the Canadian government, and First Nations communities in the area of indigenous justice systems. The adoption of systems already in use, like the U.S. tribal courts, can be implemented quickly while saving the work of designing a new programme. The question to be asked, however, is at what social and cultural costs? What will be more effective is the more strenuous, and certainly more long-term task, of creating models from the resources which already exist in the community. This is an option which is now seriously being considered by aboriginal leaders on the North Shore—leaders who are concerned with the revitalization of regional culture and with self-governing institutions which are authentically Anishnabek.

There are a number of existing systems to which Native communities can turn, if they wish simply to transplant a foreign model onto Native soil. The present Canadian policing and court systems could be emulated and run by Native personnel; however, indigenization of the institutions of the dominant society falls short of achieving true autonomy, and can in reality constitute an extension of state control (Havemann 1992). In the case of policing, this indeed seems to be the state of affairs in the province of Ontario at the present. An agreement for a major indigenization programme, funded by the federal and provincial governments until 1996, has just recently been ratified.[3] This short-term solution can be a powerfully seductive option for reserves needing immediate help for the pervasive juvenile delinquency, vandalism, family violence and alcohol-related offences that traumatize communities.

Other than policing, some of the Alternative Dispute Resolution models, such as mediation panels and victim/offender reconciliation, would be viable options. It is interesting to note, by the way, that many of these conflict resolution methods made their way into North American society via anthropological reports of dispute resolution in 'face-to-face' societies, and as an alternative to the often alienating effects of the adversarial judicial system; thus we may now have come full circle.

Those alternatives that have already been implemented in selected aboriginal communities (with varying degrees of success) within present legislative parameters include:

1.   Justice of the Peace courts (also known as Section 107 courts) whose roots are in the use of the former Indian agent as local law enforcer, but which now employ Native personnel. This option has been widely under-utilized, and many appointed JPs are inactive (Ontario Native Council on Justice 1982).

2.   Attempts to increase cross-cultural understanding by training of Euro-Canadian police and justice personnel and legal education of aboriginal citizens. This is a necessary but not sufficient step in improving the current situation; it cannot replace the move towards autonomy.

3.   The institution of special Native constables on reserve with limited powers.

4.   Diversion programmes that interrupt the processing of offenders through the system by suggesting alternate sentencing or treatment.

5.   The Native courtworker programme, whose function is to facilitate Native offenders' passage through the dominant system chiefly through education about rights and amelioration of the language difficulty experienced by the majority of Native people in their encounter with the present court system.

One of the established models, looked to as an alternative to Euro-Canadian law, is the tribal court of the United States. Since at least the mid-seventies, these Native courts have been promoted in Canada as a viable alternative for aboriginal communities who seek to develop their own form of justice. This idea has become quite firmly established, and seems to be the favoured option by government, members of the academic community and aboriginal leaders (Morse 1980; Prov.of Alberta 1991; Prov.of Man. 1991). For example, along the North Shore it is not uncommon for aboriginal people to be familiar with the Navajo justice system in use in the southwest United States; indeed, many tribal council and reserve government officials have taken tours to evaluate this American model.

While the U.S. tribal court model could offer considerably more autonomy to Native communities than the programmes just listed, it is certain, based on its stated policy, that the federal government would find this a more attractive option than local development of community-specific programmes based on Native sovereignty. The tribal court's appeal could be attributable to a number of factors, the most salient of which is that a Western judicial model could be preserved, albeit with Native actors playing the requisite roles. This kind of legal exclusivism exhibits what Strathern calls a 'naturalist' interpretation of Western law as that which serves universal human needs for regulation (1985: 114). Such a position either ignores the fundamental disjunction between Native and Western conceptions of justice (Nader 1984; Coyle 1986; Bellioti 1988; Rudin and Russell 1991), or suggests that aboriginal people need to abandon their philosophy of law.

A further advantage to the tribal court model from the government point of view would be that it is more amenable to government control. American tribal courts were instituted by the U.S. government and since their inception have been subject to a gradual erosion of jurisdictional authority by government legislation (Morse 1980; Rudin and Russell 1991). Tribal courts that achieve legitimacy through legislation are more vulnerable to control by the government in power.

The possible disadvantages of adopting a Western court system into Native communities in Canada are many, on both a philosophical and a pragmatic level. The court, which expresses a judicial model, is a form emphasizing individualism rather than the communal values, and a proving of guilt rather than the harmony-seeking solution expressive of a Native worldview. In addition, Native conflict resolution emphasizes legal process rather than substantive law (Warry 1991). Form can order function in this instance by defining participants' structural positions and leading them to, in Arno's words, 'discuss their relationship through modalities afforded by a legal or customary institution of control communication'(1985: 44). Moreover, the court, in isolation, will not provide the holistic approach to families in the context that has been repeatedly expressed as desirable by aboriginal leaders and front-line workers.

A major difficulty with this state of affairs is that the court model itself is never questioned. Depending on the degree to which traditional norms and values have persisted in Native communities, they may be undermined by a court model. Each community seeking its own justice system should be evaluated regarding the extent to which people's accumulated experience of the Western court system has altered their relational patterns when conflict arises and to what extent the alien system has been resisted. The move to self-determination in law may in fact show an enduring resilience of Native interaction patterns in the face of the interactional modes of the dominant society (Arno 1985; Rudin and Russell 1991). If there are communities who wish to institute the Western court model, one of the factors may be that the legal norms and values of the dominant society have been incorporated to a sufficient degree for consonance between this relational model and conflict resolution as practised in the community.[4] Research in particular communities will discover these patterns.

The extent to which reserve communities presently use communal mechanisms to resolve conflicts may be severely hampered by the adoption of the tribal court framework. Indigenous conflict resolution strategies emphasized community ownership of the conflict (Lajeunesse 1991; Warry 1991); state monopoly of social control 'atrophies public opinion as control and places remedies beyond the reach of complainants' (Nader 1984: 639). Thus Western-style courts rob Native communities of a central cultural process, that of reconstituting culture (Partridge 1987: 221) by expressing cultural norms through conflict resolution.

In addition to the philosophical bases on which to approach the American tribal court model cautiously, there are pragmatic considerations as well. One of these is that the scale on which Native justice systems will be operative in Canada has yet to be negotiated. The Navajo court in place in the United States, for example, is a tribal court system covering a large population and geographical area. There is yet to be extensive discussion in Canada as to whether justice systems will operate on the level of reserve, tribal council or national level. If justice systems operate at the reserve level, the diversity of resources of particular reserves needs to be taken into account. A court model would not be appropriate or manageable in many cases.

Alternatively, it may be that First Nations communities would be willing to adopt a court model for certain categories of dispute and not for others. This may be the case where people have often refused to acknowlege the jurisdiction of Euro-Canadian law (for example, in matters related to natural resource management) or have resisted reporting conflict to Canadian authorities (for example, in instances of family violence). Research into the various blends of informal and formal justice in particular communities will discover these patterns. To date, this type of research has been very rare in Canada, but is obviously crucial for an understanding of the appropriateness of courts for various communities.

I propose that researchers attend to the generation of appropriate models at the community level, rather than promote the adoption of particular models into which local content is inserted. The readiness to employ a court model shows a lack of faith in the creativity of communities in developing conceptual frameworks of their own, and often a reluctance to do the hard work of model building from the ground up. There is no doubt that it is the job of the community to determine the appropriateness of any model. A central role of the researcher is to provide the forum and the stimulus for community dialogue on the issue, and to add an external viewpoint to the 'native science' (Colorado 1988) already extant in the community. The generation and implementation of appropriate justice systems, therefore, poses methodological challenges for the social scientist and requires a shift toward research that is collaborative and applied in nature (cf. Warry 1990). This kind of participatory research has its roots in Freire's (1988) model of education for action, and seeks to make manifest the knowledge already present in the community (Hall 1979). In the process, reflective action can lead to community development.

What are the resources other than established models that are available to Native communities who choose to develop their own system of culturally appropriate justice? The essential building blocks of any justice system are the knowledge, experience and creativity of the members of society, the conflicts of the community, and tradition. Community-based, participatory research can be a potent tool for mobilizing these resources into reflexive action. The participatory research relationship represents a combination of what Lockhart (1982) refers to as 'insider' and 'outsider' knowledge. It provides for the interaction of insider knowledge of 'community process dynamics', with outsider knowledge of the larger context within which newly initiated projects will operate.

A community demonstrates a diverse range of experience and knowledge along generational, political, religious and other axes. The Elder and the young college graduate, the pipe carrier and the Pentecostal perceive the world through different lenses. In the North Shore community in which this research is taking place, for instance, the number of residents who are aware of and interested in self-government issues *qua* self-government issues represents a small proportion of the population. Other members of the community who have experienced the same oppression, disadvantage and discrimination, express their anger or discontent in less politicized, perhaps more personal, ways. Some local leaders have made it a priority to raise community awareness of self-government through seminars and workshops, and similar initiatives have begun at the regional tribal council level; however, there is still a considerable amount of fear of change in many communities. A consensual choice among justice options will, of necessity, be the result of long-term community discussion and debate, if it is to be representative. Moreover, the integration of justice programmes with other social services will lead to the integrated, holistic approach expressed by aboriginal leaders across the country. Many have expressed a belief in the crucial importance of the education of Native children. An ex-offender from this North Shore community explains this:

Our people believe in working for future generations. Seven generations. Go to the children and teach them, so they will grow up believing in this way, so they can pass it on. For too long we've wasted energy on trying to see gains in a big hurry. Take time and put faith in what we teach our young ... Take our time and do it right the first time. In seven generations we'll see if we did good.

The resurgence and redefinition of 'tradition' are an essential part of contemporary Native cultural and political identity at the personal and societal level. There is a desire to be authentically Anishnabek, but a still inchoate sense of what that is. This reconstitution of Native culture highlights the way in which tradition is forever changing through cultural contact. A community-based justice system must find and use the links between traditional ideas of law and present reality.

The past three or more decades have been characterized by aboriginal peoples finding new ways to meet the challenges of the modern period through political organization and the revitalization of cultural traditions. Habermas (1990: 33) writes, regarding the relationship between the 'life-world' and the 'system', that the 'life-world has to become able to develop institutions out of itself which set limits to the internal dynamics and to the imperatives of an almost autonomous economic system and its administrative complements'. It is this challenge that faces aboriginal communities in their interaction with the dominant Canadian state. Communities have the task of developing and mobilizing the human resources which constitute their 'life-world' to meet this challenge and begin the healing process.

NOTES

1. The project is funded by the Social Sciences and Humanities Research Council of Canada, and The Fund for Dispute Resolution (under The Network: Interaction for Conflict Resolution).

2. This is a provincially funded project that has been underway since early 1992 and is expanding. Representatives reported that provincial police now divert the majority of cases to the traditional system, if the basic criteria are met of admission of guilt and permission of the victim.

3. This is a multipartite agreement between the Canadian and Ontario governments and the First Nations of Ontario (Ontario First Nations Policing Agreement, March 1992).

4. See Long's 1990 discussion of institutionalization.

REFERENCES

Arno, Andrew (1985) 'Structural Communication and Control Communication: An Interactionist Perspective on Legal and Customary Procedures for Conflict Management', *American Anthropologist* 87: 40-55.

Asch, Michael (1984) *Home and Native Land*, Toronto: Methuen.

Belliotti, Raymond A. (1988) 'Our Adversary System: In Search of a Foundation', *Canadian Journal of Law and Jurisprudence* 1: 1, 19-34.

Brodeur, J. P., LaPrairie, C. and McDonnell, R. (1991) *Justice for the Cree: Final Report*, The Grand Council of the Cree (Quebec), Cree Regional Authority.

Brown, Jennifer (1989) 'Northern Algonquians from Lake Superior and Hudson Bay to Manitoba in the Historic Period', in R. Morrison and C. R. Wilson (eds.) *Native Peoples: The Canadian Experience*, Toronto: McClelland and Stewart, 208-236.

Brown, Jennifer and Wilson, C. R. (eds.) (1989) 'The Eastern Subarctic—A Regional Overview', in R. Morrison and C. R. Wilson (eds.) *Native Peoples—The Canadian Experience*, Toronto: McClelland and Stewart, 134-171.

Canada, Department of Justice (1991) 'Aboriginal People and Justice Administration: A Discussion Paper', Ottawa.

Clark, Bruce (1990) *Native Liberty, Crown Sovereignty. The Existing Aboriginal Right of Self-Government in Canada,* Montreal: McGill-Queens University Press.

Colorado, Pam (1988) 'Bridging Native and Western Science', *Convergence* 21: 2/3, 49-67.

Coyle, M. (1986) *Traditional Indian Justice in Ontario: A Role for the Present?,* Toronto: Ontario Native Council on Justice.

Feit, Harvey (1989) 'Hunting and the Quest for Power: The James Bay Cree and Whitemen in the Twentieth Century', in R. Morrison and C. R. Wilson (eds.) *Native Peoples: The Canadian Experience*, 171-207.

Finkler, Harald (1988) 'Legal Anthropology in the Formulation of Correctional Policy in the Northwest Territories, Canada', in B. W. Morse and G. R. Woodman (eds.) *Indigenous Law and the State*, Dordrecht, Holland: Foris, 413-20.

Foucault, Michel (1980) *Power/Knowledge: Selected Interviews and Other Writings 1972-1977,* trans. Colin Gordon, Leo Marshall, John Mepham and Kate Soper, New York: Pantheon.

Freire, Paulo (1988) *Pedagogy of the Oppressed,* New York: Continuum.

Gibbins, Roger and Ponting, J. R. (1986) 'Historical Overview and Background', in J. R. Ponting (ed.) *Arduous Journey*, Toronto: McClelland and Stewart.

Habermas, Jurgen (1990) *The Philosophical Discourse of Modernity: Twelve*

Lectures, Frederick G. Lawrence (tr.), Cambridge, MA: MIT Press.

Hall, Budd L. (1979) 'Knowledge as a Commodity and Participatory Research', *Prospects*, 4: 4, 393-408.

Havemann, P., Couse, K., Foster, L. and Matonovich, R. (1985) *Law and Order for Canada's Indigenous People: A Review of Recent Research Literature Relating to the Operation of the Criminal Justice System and Canada's Indigenous People*, Regina: Prairie Justice Research.

Havemann, Paul (1992) 'The Indigenization of Social Control in Canada', in Robert A. Silverman and Marianne O. Nielsen (eds.) *Aboriginal Peoples and Canadian Criminal Justice*, Toronto: Butterworths.

Jackson, Michael (1988) *Locking Up Natives in Canada: A Report of the Committee of the Canadian Bar Association on Imprisonment and Release*, Ottawa: Canada Bar Association.

Kinietz, W. V. (1974) *Chippewa Village: The Story of Katikitegon*, Bloomfield Hills, MI: Cranbrook Institute of Science, Bulletin No. 25.

Lajeunesse, Therese (1991) *Cross-Cultural Issues in the Justice System: The Case of Aboriginal People in Canada*, Manoa, HI: University of Hawaii at Manoa, Programme on Conflict Resolution.

Little Bear, Leroy, Boldt, M. and Long, J. A. (eds.) (1985) *Pathways to Self-Determination: Canadian Indians and the Canadian State*, Toronto: University of Toronto Press.

Lockhart, Alexander (1982) 'The Insider-Outsider Dialectic in Native Socio-Economic Development: A Case Study in Process Understanding', *Canadian Journal of Native Studies*, 2: 1, 159-68.

Long, J. Anthony (1990) 'Political Revitalization in Canadian Native Indian Societies', *Canadian Journal of Political Science*, 23: 4, 751-73.

Morse, Bradford (1980) *Indian Tribal Courts in the United States: A Model for Canada?* Saskatoon: University of Saskatchewan Native Law Centre.

Morse, Bradford W. (1985) *Aboriginal Peoples and the Law: Indian, Métis and Inuit Rights in Canada,* Ottawa: Carleton University Press.

Morse, Bradford W. (1988) 'Indigenous Law and State Legal Systems: Conflict and Compatability', in B. W. Morse and G. R. Woodman (eds.) *Indigenous Law and the State*, Dordrecht, Holland: Foris.

Morse, B. W. and Woodman, G. R. (eds.) (1988) *Indigenous Law and the State*, Dordrecht, Holland: Foris.

Nader, Laura (1984) 'The Recurrent Dialectic between Legality and its Alternatives', *University of Pennsylvania Law Review,* 132: 621-45.

Ontario Native Council on Justice (1982) *The Native Justice of the Peace: An Under-employed Natural Resource for the Criminal Justice System*, Toronto: Ontario Native Council on Justice.

Partridge, William L. (1987) 'Toward a Theory of Practice', in E. Eddy and W. L. Partridge, (eds.) *Applied Anthropology in America* (2nd ed.), New York: Columbia University Press, 221-36.

Ponting, J. Rick (ed.) (1986) *Arduous Journey: Canadian Indians and Decolonization,* Toronto: McClelland and Stewart.

Province of Alberta (1991) *Report of the Task Force on the Criminal Justice System and Its Impact on the Indian and Métis People of Alberta,* Edmonton: Province of Alberta.

Province of Manitoba (1991) *Report of the Aboriginal Justice Inquiry of Manitoba: The Justice System and Aboriginal People,* Winnipeg: Queen's Printer.

Richardson, Boyce (ed.) (1989) *Drumbeat: Anger and Renewal in Indian Country,* Ottawa: Assembly of First Nations.

Royal Commission on Aboriginal Peoples (1993a) *Focusing the Dialogue,* Discussion Paper No. 2, Ottawa: Canada Communication Group.

Royal Commission on Aboriginal Peoples (1993b) *Public Hearings, Overview of the Second Round,* prepared by Michael Cassidy, Ginger Group Consultants, Ottawa: Canada Communication Group.

Rudin, J. and Russell D. (1991) 'Native Alternative Dispute Resolution Systems: The Canadian Future in Light of the American Past', Toronto: Ontario Native Council on Justice.

Schmalz, Peter S. (1991) *The Ojibwa of Southern Ontario,* Toronto: University of Toronto Press.

Strathern, Marilyn (1985) 'Discovering Social Control', *Journal of Law and Society* 12: 2, 111-34.

Warry, Wayne (1989) *An Evaluation of the Ontario Native (criminal) Courtworker Programme,* SPR Associates, for the Ontario Federation of Indian Friendship Centres, Ottawa: The Ministry of the Attorney General and the Department of Justice Canada.

Warry, Wayne (1990) 'Doing Unto Others: Applied Anthropology and Native Self-Determination', *Culture* 10: 61-73.

Warry, Wayne (1991) 'The Eleventh Thesis: Applied Anthropology as Praxis', paper prepared for the 1991 Meetings of the Society for Applied Anthropology.

Zion, James W. (1988) 'Searching for Indian Common Law' in B. W. Morse and G. R. Woodman (eds.), *Indigenous Law and the State,* Dordrecht, Holland: Foris, 121-48.

9

Addressing Aboriginal Crime and Victimization in Canada: Revitalizing Communities, Cultures and Traditions

Curt Taylor Griffiths and Charlene Belleau

INTRODUCTION

The discussion in this chapter focuses on the resurgence of traditional cultural practices in addressing issues of crime and justice in Canadian aboriginal communities. These developments are occurring against a larger political backdrop of the constitutional recognition of an inherent right to aboriginal self-government, the assertion of control by aboriginal bands and communities over all aspects of community life and the revitalization of aboriginal communities and cultures.[1] Increasingly, the focus of federal and provincial government policy initiatives and aboriginal bands has been on identifying ways in which this inherent authority and the capacity to exercise it can be restored. This includes the administration of justice. Reversing the historical, world-wide trend which has resulted in the destruction of indigenous cultures and communities, Canada's aboriginal peoples have become more aggressive in pursuing land claims and in exerting pressure on federal, provincial and territorial governments to transfer power and control for administering aboriginal lands and affairs to bands and communities. Concurrently, there has been a revitalization of aboriginal cultures and communities and an increasing interest in incorporating traditional cultural practices into aboriginal-controlled justice structures and programmes which would serve as an alternative to the Anglo-Canadian criminal justice system (Griffiths and Verdun-Jones 1993; Silverman and Nielsen 1992).

These justice initiatives are designed to provide alternatives to the Euro-Canadian justice system, which is viewed by many aboriginal people as incapable of addressing the needs of aboriginal victims, communities, and offenders and which, in the past, has functioned only to increase the dependency of aboriginal peoples on governments. More specifically, it has been argued that the conflicts between basic tenets of Euro-Canadian culture and aboriginal culture and the different models of law and justice adhered to by Euro-Canadian society and aboriginal society preclude the delivery of effective justice services to aboriginal persons.

To fully understand the context within which aboriginal peoples in Canada are developing and implementing justice programmes, it is necessary to consider, albeit briefly, the historical and contemporary experience of Canada's aboriginal peoples with the law and the criminal justice system.[2]

The Legacy of Euro-Canadian Colonization

Any discussion of aboriginal peoples, crime and victimization must consider their political position and socioeconomic condition in Canadian society, which are, in large measure, a consequence of their colonization by Europeans and of Canadian government policies that have exerted control over virtually every aspect of aboriginal life (Berger 1991; Dickason 1992; Getty and Lussier 1988). The introduction of Euro-Canadian culture resulted in overwhelming change in aboriginal culture and, in many cases, its near destruction.

The impact of the policies of successive federal governments on aboriginal peoples is evidenced in their marginalized position in Canadian society. This is reflected in pervasive poverty, high rates of unemployment and reliance upon public assistance, low levels of formal education, high death rates from accidents and violence, increasing rates of family breakdown and high rates of victimization. These patterns of crime and 'trouble' are reflected in the findings of innumerable task forces and commissions of inquiry.[3]

Census data from the province of Saskatchewan (Wolff 1991), for example, reveal that:

- one-half of the aboriginal people residing on reserves had never been to high school and few had completed Grade 12;
- only 38% of reserve residents over the age of 15 were in the labour force;
- the average income of reserve residents was less than one-half that of persons living off the reserve; and,
- 25% of reserve families were headed by a single parent, compared to 11% of families off the reserve.

Information provided to the Indian Justice Review Committee (Linn 1992a: 6.8) in the province of Saskatchewan indicated that:

- the suicide rate on the reserves was three times that for the provincial population as a whole; and
- an estimated 30-40% of the aboriginal population was involved in alcohol abuse, as compared with an estimated 6% of the general population in the province.

While there have been measurable improvements in the condition of status aboriginal peoples, including a decline in infant mortality rates, a rise in annual income and an increase in life expectancy, on nearly every quality of life indicator at the individual and community levels, Canada's aboriginal peoples fall far short when compared to non-aboriginals (Canada 1989). Particularly vulnerable are aboriginal youth, aged 15 to 24, who are most susceptible to violent and accidental death, suicide, and alcohol and substance abuse (Krotz 1990; Shkilnyk 1985; York 1990).

ABORIGINAL CRIME AND CRIMINALITY

It is likely that the marginal socioeconomic position of many aboriginal people, as well as the consequences of the loss of culture and community through the process of colonization, have contributed significantly to the pervasive crime and 'trouble' which afflict many communities. Among the more *general* attributes of aboriginal crime which can be gleaned from the research studies conducted to date are:

1. *The rates of crime on aboriginal reserves and in aboriginal communities, particularly in the northern regions of Canada, are higher than the rates for the general population.* The crime rate among Canada's registered aboriginal peoples is nearly two times the national crime rate. In comparison with non-aboriginals, aboriginal people commit more violent crimes and fewer crimes against property (Hyde and LaPrairie 1987).

2. *Many aboriginal communities are afflicted by high rates of violence, particularly assaults.* The violent crime rate for aboriginal bands is three and one-half times the national rate. In many jurisdictions, aboriginal people are charged with higher rates of violent crime than non-aboriginals. In the province of Saskatchewan, for example, violent crimes comprised 25% of all Criminal Code offences committed on the reserves, while the figure was less than 10% for other communities in the province (Wolff 1991).

3. *Alcohol is involved in a high percentage of aboriginal crime.* In many areas of the country, alcohol is involved in over 95% of the offences which are committed. There are aboriginal communities in which nearly 100% of the adult residents, and many of the youth, are involved in extensive alcohol abuse (Shkilnyk 1985; York 1990).

4. *There is considerable variation in the patterns of crime across aboriginal communities and reserves.* Even within the same jurisdiction, aboriginal communities evidence different patterns of crime. This variation has been documented in studies conducted in Nishnawbe-Aski Nation communities in northwestern Ontario (Auger et al. 1992), in the northern regions of the province of Quebec (LaPrairie and Diamond 1992), and in the Eastern Arctic (Griffiths et

al. 1995). Among the factors which may be related to the crime rate in communities are the enforcement practices of the police, the extent to which community residents and victims call the police, the attributes of the individual communities, including their leadership, the persistence of culture and traditions, and the degree to which the community has assumed responsibility for addressing its problems (LaPrairie 1991).

Aboriginal Peoples in the Criminal Justice System

One outcome of the colonization process was the imposition of 'white' law upon aboriginal peoples, beginning a pattern of conflict which continues to the present time (Moyles 1989; Schuh 1979). Little attempt was made by Euro-Canadians to accommodate the laws and methods of social control that aboriginal peoples used to maintain order, prevent crime and respond to individuals whose behaviour transgressed acceptable boundaries. Rather, the criminal justice system, represented initially by the Royal Canadian Mounted Police and later by criminal courts and corrections services, became another mechanism by which aboriginal peoples were brought under the control of, and became increasingly dependent upon, the federal, provincial and territorial governments.

In most jurisdictions across Canada, aboriginal people are over-represented in the criminal justice system from the arrest stage to incarceration in correctional institutions (Griffiths and Verdun-Jones 1993). Information gathered by the Manitoba Aboriginal Justice Inquiry (Hamilton and Sinclair 1991), for example, revealed that, while aboriginal peoples comprise 6% of the total population in the province of Manitoba, more than 50% of the inmates in correctional institutions were aboriginal.

Further, in comparison with non-aboriginal accused, aboriginal persons were more likely to be denied bail, were more likely to be held in pre-trial detention, more likely to be charged with multiple offences, spent less time with their lawyer, and were twice as likely to be incarcerated upon conviction than were non-aboriginals. Similar findings have been reported by commissions of inquiry in the provinces of Alberta (Cawsey 1991) and Saskatchewan (Linn 1992a; 1992b). There is evidence that, in many jurisdictions in Canada, the over-representation of aboriginal peoples in the criminal justice system is due to 'a mixture of discrimination on the part of the justice system and actual criminal behaviour on the part of Aboriginal people' (Hamilton and Sinclair 1991: 87).

The over-representation of aboriginal youth in the justice system is often more pronounced than that of aboriginal adults or non-aboriginal youth. Figures from the province of Alberta (Cawsey 1991: 6.6), for example, indicate that:

- there has been a significant increase in the numbers of aboriginal youths charged with offences;

- aboriginal young offenders are less likely to be referred to alternative measures programmes which keep them out of the formal youth court;
- all things being equal, aboriginal youth are more likely to receive a disposition of confinement in a correctional facility than their non-aboriginal counterparts; and
- aboriginal youth spend longer periods of time in custody than non-aboriginal youth for the same offences.

Over the past two decades, there have been an increasing number of initiatives taken by federal, provincial and territorial governments to address the conflicts with the law experienced by aboriginal peoples and to reduce the over-representation of aboriginal peoples in the criminal justice system. These have included the development of Indian Special Constable programmes, Native courtworker and Justice of the Peace programmes, and a variety of initiatives in the corrections field. These initiatives were designed to increase the numbers of aboriginal persons working within the justice system, which, in turn, would result in the design and delivery of more culturally appropriate programmes and services.

Despite the initial support of these initiatives by aboriginal and non-aboriginal politicians and leaders, there has been no appreciable reduction in the difficulties which aboriginal people encounter with the law nor any decrease in the high rates of arrests, convictions and levels of incarceration in correctional facilities found in many jurisdictions. Nor have these government-sponsored initiatives had any appreciable impact on crime and trouble in the communities. This suggests that merely making administrative adjustments to the existing criminal justice system, through such policies as 'indigenizing' the system by hiring more aboriginal police officers, probation officers and corrections workers, will not be sufficient to address the needs of aboriginal communities, offenders and victims. A major obstacle is the set of basic principles upon which the Canadian criminal justice system operates. More fundamental structural changes are required, including the increased use of non-adversarial strategies such as reconciliation and negotiated justice for resolving disputes and the devolution of justice services and programmes in order to facilitate the substantive involvement of aboriginal bands and communities in the design and operation of justice programmes and services.

Aboriginal Victims of Crime

The needs of aboriginal victims of crime are also receiving increased attention. A pronounced feature of life in many aboriginal communities, one which has direct implications for the development of programmes and services for the victims of crime, is pervasive violence and abuse directed towards women and female adolescents. Materials presented to the Manitoba Aboriginal Justice Inquiry (Hamilton and Sinclair 1991) suggest that one in three aboriginal women in the province of Manitoba were abused by their male partners. And among the findings of a study conducted by the Native Women's Association (1989: 18-21) in the province of Ontario were:

- 85% of the women surveyed indicated that family violence occurred in their community;
- 80% of the women had personally experienced family violence;
- a high percentage of the women who were victims of violence sustained severe physical injury;
- alcoholism was identified by nearly 80% of the women as the main cause of family violence; and
- large numbers of women who are the victims of family violence did not seek assistance or make use of services for battered women.

These revelations led the commissioners in the Manitoba Aboriginal Justice Inquiry (Hamilton and Sinclair 1991: 481) to conclude that: 'Violence and abuse in aboriginal communities has reached epidemic proportions'.

There are, in many areas of the country, inadequate services available to aboriginal women who are victims of violence, including a lack of emergency shelter services and 'safe' houses and services for children who have been the victims of and/or witnesses to family violence and abuse. Information provided to the Manitoba Aboriginal Justice Inquiry (Hamilton and Sinclair 1991), for example, revealed that there was only *one* shelter for aboriginal women in that province and this was situated in the city of Winnipeg. For aboriginal women in the province of Manitoba, as well as in the other provinces and territories in Canada, the only option to continued victimization is to leave their home community. This is not a viable alternative for most aboriginal women, given strong family and community ties and the hesitancy to leave children and friends. Further, it has been argued that victim assistance programmes developed in and for the 'southern', urban areas of the country and for administration within the framework of an adversarial criminal justice system may have little relevance to aboriginal victims, particularly those residing in remote and rural areas (Griffiths and Yerbury 1991).

These points were highlighted by the Northwest Territories Task Force on Spousal Assault (Bayley 1985: 10):

There is a common thread running through the problems associated with spousal assault, whether it occurs in Yellowknife [the capital of the Northwest Territories], Gjoa Haven or Clyde River [small aboriginal settlements]. However, solutions which may work in larger communities may not be so easily transferrable to small native communities. At the same time, there may be in those communities closely knit family and cultural ties which will give rise to solutions which might be unworkable in larger, more fragmented communities.

Euro-Canadian versus Aboriginal Culture, Law and Justice

The problems that Aboriginal people have with the criminal justice system are
... a result of the implicit convictions of white society embodied in Canadian
law. The end result is a clash of cultures ... For Aboriginal people ... the
criminal justice system does not embody their implicit convictions (Cawsey
1991: 9.1).

In contrast to White society's linear/singular worldview, the Indian and Métis
worldview can be characterized as cyclical/wholistic, generalist, and process
oriented (Cawsey 1991: 9.3)

Many of the difficulties that aboriginal people experience with the criminal
justice system can be traced to the conflict between the 'world view' of aboriginal
peoples and that of Euro-Canadians (Ross 1992). The major components of Euro-
Canadian culture and aboriginal culture are outlined in Table 9.1. These
differences extend to the models of law and justice pursued by Euro-Canadian and
aboriginal societies.[4]

Westernized, adversarial systems of criminal justice, centred on 'winners' and
'losers', have retribution as their primary objective, while traditional aboriginal
law and justice are based on a restorative model (Barkwell 1991; Brodeur, La
Prairie and McDonnell 1991). The basic tenets of the Euro-Canadian retributive
model of law and justice and those of the aboriginal restorative model of law and
justice are outlined in Table 9.2.

Traditional aboriginal systems of customary law were based on the principle
of the least amount of interference with the rights of the individual and had, as a
primary objective, not a determination of guilt and the imposition of punishment,
but the restoration of peace and harmony within the group. Among the more
informal sanctions employed were gossip, mockery, derision and shunning.
Formal sanctions included song or drum duels (among the Inuit), banishment,
various corporal punishments, and in rare instances, death. As Cawsey (1991:
9.5) notes: 'In White society, law and justice are largely matters of public law
while among the traditional Aboriginal societies, law and justice were largely
private'.

In traditional aboriginal society, for example, restitution was designed to
provide reparation to the injured party. Lost or damaged equipment, for example,
would be replaced or repaired by the person or persons responsible for that
condition. The victim was recompensed and order was restored. The two parties
would have face-to-face contact with one another. The modern application of
restitution, however, removes this contact and the state, through the criminal

TABLE 9.1
The Foundations of Euro-Canadian Culture and Aboriginal Culture

Euro-Canadian Culture	Aboriginal Culture
1. God created the universe, the earth and everything in it.	The Creator made everybody as equals including humans, plants and inorganic life.
2. God created humans in His own image and gave them dominion over everything.	Everybody is interrelated with everybody.
3. God had a chosen people that He blessed to show the true way for all others.	Existence consists of energy and is expendable.
4. Creation is divisible.	The energy quotient of creation is rechargeable through ritual. Man is subordinate to and a mere part of creation.
5. Individuals are more important than the group. Nations exist to protect and provide for individuals.	The group is more important than the individual. Aggressive tendencies bring about disorder and imbalance.
6. Property is individually ownable, including land.	All land and resources belong to the group. Individual property is private but should be shared.
7. Knowledge is the learning of skills for a comfortable living	Attainment of the knowledge of other-than-human beings is power.
8. Accumulation of wealth is a sign of success.	Harmony and balance brings about happiness, order, beauty and health.
9. Social order is hierarchical.	Individuals are important and should be given freedom. Disorder is corrected through rehabilitative and restorative action.
10. The earth and everything on it is for the benefit of man.	Everything in the universe and on earth is alive and has a spirit. Other-than-human beings have knowledge that humans do not have.

Source: Cawsey, R. A. (1991) *Report of the Task Force on the Criminal Justice System and Its Impact on the Indian and Métis People of Alberta*, Edmonton: Attorney General of Alberta and Solicitor General of Alberta, 9.4-9.5.

TABLE 9.2
Euro-Canadian Law and Justice and Aboriginal Law and Justice

Euro-Canadian Law and Justice (The Retributive Model)	Aboriginal Law and Justice (The Restorative Model)
1. Crime is a violation of the state.	Crime is a violation of one person by another.
2. The focus is on establishing blame or guilt.	The focus is on problem solving and restoration of harmony.
3. Justice is defined by intent and process.	Dialogue and negotiation are normative. Restitution and reconciliation are used as a means of restoration.
4. Community does not play a leading role.	The community acts as a facilitator in the restorative process.
5. Action revolves around the offender. Accountability of the offender is put in punishment.	The offender is impressed with the impact of his/her action on the total order.
6. Offences are strictly legal and devoid of moral, social, political and economic consideration. Past behaviour is important.	The holistic context of an offence is taken into consideration, including moral, social, economic, political and religious and cosmic considerations.
7. Social stigma of criminal behaviour is almost unremovable.	Stigma of offences is removable through conformity.
8. Remorse, restitution and forgiveness are not important factors.	Remorse, repentance and forgiveness are important factors.
9. Offenders play a passive role, depending on proxy professionals.	Offenders take an active role in the restorative process.

Source: Cawsey, R. A. (1991) *Report of the Task Force on the Criminal Justice System and Its Impact on the Indian and Métis People of Alberta,* Edmonton: Attorney General of Alberta and Solicitor General of Alberta, 9.5-9.6.

courts, intervenes between the two parties. The offender is ordered to pay restitution in the form of cash to an officer of the criminal court, rather than providing services directly to the victim. This indicates the limitations of 'community' justice strategies sponsored by the criminal justice system (Griffiths and Patenaude 1990).

For aboriginal peoples, the primary objectives of social control and the imposition of sanctions are 1) resolution of the conflict, 2) restoration of order and harmony in the group or community, and 3) healing the offender, the victim and, if necessary, the community (Ross 1992). These tenets are illustrated in Table 9.3 which depicts a procedure and process proposed by an aboriginal community in British Columbia for responding to band members who have committed sexual abuse.

In contrast, Western justice systems are primarily reactive in nature: they respond to crime, focusing primarily on the behaviour of the individual offender and, in many cases, sanctioning offenders by removing them from the community, often for extended periods of time. The etiology of the criminal behaviour is rarely addressed, the needs and concerns of victims and communities are generally unmet. The response to crime has become, in many countries, a highly legal/technical/procedural process which has produced few positive outcomes.

This has led to increasing concerns about the relevance of the non-aboriginal justice system for aboriginal peoples. As Hamilton and Sinclair (1991: 22) note:

> The purpose of a justice system in Aboriginal society is to restore the peace and equilibrium in the community, and to reconcile the accused with his or her own conscience and with the individual or family who has been wronged. This is a primary difference. It is a difference that significantly challenges the appropriateness of the present legal and justice system for aboriginal people in the resolution of conflict, the reconciliation and the maintenance of community harmony and good order.

ABORIGINAL JUSTICE INITIATIVES

In recent years, aboriginal communities in Canada have become increasingly involved in developing community-based criminal justice services and programmes which are designed to better address the specific needs of community residents, victims and offenders (Griffiths 1989; 1990; 1992). This has included the development of reserve-based, aboriginal-controlled police forces and a wide range of community justice programmes and services centred on diversion and mediation. In addition, collaborative arrangements between aboriginal communities and criminal justice agencies have been established to create alternative mechanisms for justice delivery.

It is important to note that aboriginal-controlled initiatives may be, but are

TABLE 9.3
Dealing with Sexual Abuse in a Traditional Manner
(A Process of Active Intervention by the Community)

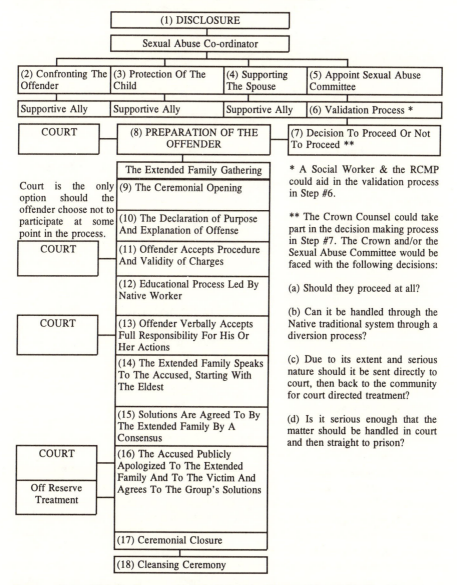

(1) DISCLOSURE

Sexual Abuse Co-ordinator

(2) Confronting The Offender	(3) Protection Of The Child	(4) Supporting The Spouse	(5) Appoint Sexual Abuse Committee
Supportive Ally	Supportive Ally	Supportive Ally	(6) Validation Process *

COURT	(8) PREPARATION OF THE OFFENDER	(7) Decision To Proceed Or Not To Proceed **

The Extended Family Gathering

Court is the only option should the offender choose not to participate at some point in the process.

(9) The Ceremonial Opening

(10) The Declaration of Purpose And Explanation of Offense

COURT — (11) Offender Accepts Procedure And Validity of Charges

(12) Educational Process Led By Native Worker

COURT — (13) Offender Verbally Accepts Full Responsibility For His Or Her Actions

(14) The Extended Family Speaks To The Accused, Starting With The Eldest

(15) Solutions Are Agreed To By The Extended Family By A Consensus

COURT

Off Reserve Treatment — (16) The Accused Publicly Apologized To The Extended Family And To The Victim And Agrees To The Group's Solutions

(17) Ceremonial Closure

(18) Cleansing Ceremony

* A Social Worker & the RCMP could aid in the validation process in Step #6.

** The Crown Counsel could take part in the decision making process in Step #7. The Crown and/or the Sexual Abuse Committee would be faced with the following decisions:

(a) Should they proceed at all?

(b) Can it be handled through the Native traditional system through a diversion process?

(c) Due to its extent and serious nature should it be sent directly to court, then back to the community for court directed treatment?

(d) Is it serious enough that the matter should be handled in court and then straight to prison?

Source: Oates, M.L.B. Terrace, British Columbia: Terrace Mental Health, 11.

not necessarily, premised on customary law. Most, however, do contain elements of traditional culture, involve community elders and have a strong emphasis on healing and restitutive justice. They tend to respond to offenders in a holistic fashion, considering a wide range of issues beyond the specific criminal behaviour. As importantly, the band and community have control over the programmes, a significant departure from previous arrangements whereby justice services were delivered by outside agencies and non-aboriginal personnel.

There are numerous examples of collaborative arrangements between aboriginal communities and the criminal justice system which are premised on traditional cultural practices:

The Teslin Tlingit First Nation (Yukon Territory) Community Justice Initiative. The Teslin Tlingit First Nation has implemented a number of alternative community justice structures. The intent is to create programmes and services which interface with the non-aboriginal criminal justice system and better meet the needs of the people in the community. The Teslin Tlingit Council Constitution sets out the roles of the leaders of each of the five Teslin clans, which includes serving as members of the Teslin Tlingit Justice Council. This council functions as a tribunal and passes sentence on offenders convicted in the Territorial Court in Teslin.

Bound only by the limits set by the judge of the Territorial Court of the Yukon and informed by submissions from the defence lawyer and the prosecution, the Justice Council imposes sentences which are appropriate for the treatment of the offender and for the restoration of harmony in the community. To date, 98% of all sentences handled by community members in Teslin have fallen within the limits set by the court. Those sentences which have gone beyond the limits set by the Territorial Court judge have been harsher than the sentence recommended by the prosecutor and/or the judge.

Once the sentence is passed, the clan leaders in the community are responsible for ensuring that it is carried out. This approach is beneficial because it involves every community member in ensuring that offenders obey the conditions of their sentence, and this helps increase the likelihood that the offender will be supported and that the conditions will be met. Unlike traditional non-aboriginal sentencing practices, the community of Teslin has a substantive role in the response to offenders. The use of clan leaders in sentencing is only part of the holistic approach to the administration of justice in the community. Proposals have been made to increase the authority of the Justice Council to adjudicate all summary conviction (less serious) offences.

Circle Sentencing. One of the more innovative approaches to sentencing is 'circle sentencing', which is being practised by provincial judges in the Yukon Territory and in several provinces. Circle sentencing involves all of the participants in a case—the judge, prosecutor, defence lawyer, victim, offender and community residents—sitting in a circular arrangement and discussing all facets of the case. The circle is designed to break down the formality of the court process and to provide a forum for the disposition of cases which is premised on healing, consensus building and returning to communities the responsibility for resolving conflicts.

The discussions surrounding the case centre not only on the offender and his or her behaviour, but also on the needs of the victim and the community. Community sentencing is an attempt to empower communities and to provide a mechanism for residents, aboriginal and non-aboriginal alike, to become directly involved in the delivery of justice services.

In cases adjudicated in sentencing circles, the judge sets an upper limit on the sentence which may be imposed. Informal discussion on the offender and his or her personal circumstances by participants in the circle follows. When the discussion has concluded, a consensus on the most appropriate sentence is reached and this is the disposition which is imposed on the offender. Circle sentencing not only empowers the community but also expands the information base from which sentencing decisions are made. In addition to considering the facts of the case and the circumstances of the offender, the discussions in sentencing circles often include a dialogue on problems that exist in the community and how these can be addressed and resolved.

Youth Justice Committees, Northwest Territories. Youth Justice Committees (YJCs) are composed of five to seven citizens from the community each of whom has an interest in assisting young persons in conflict with the law. Cases may be referred to the YJC at any time in the youth justice process by the R.C.M.P., Crown counsel, justices of the peace, or Territorial Court judges. Cases are resolved by consensus in discussions involving the committee, the youth, his or her parent or guardian and the victim. Among the dispositions which the YJC may impose are: requiring that the youth apologize to the victim; having the youth complete a number of community service hours; placing a curfew or other restriction on the youth; and/or removing the youth from their home. The YJCs appear to be most effective with minor and first-time offenders rather than with serious or chronic offenders (Finkler 1992).

The Aboriginal Court Model, Province of Manitoba. In Manitoba, an Aboriginal Court Model comprised of two systems for the hearing and disposition of cases involving aboriginal offenders on reserves has been created. The 'guilty plea' system involves elders and a community-based judge who will reach a decision through consensus in cases in which the offender pleads guilty. The 'guilty-not guilty' system is used in cases where the accused person pleads not guilty. It involves a Provincial Court judge who hears the case, and, should the person be found guilty, the community determines the sentence to be imposed. A requirement of the Aboriginal Court Model is that all persons involved in making decisions in both scenarios must speak the language of the community in which the case is heard.   The 'guilty-not guilty' model also involves community justice liaison workers who mediate between the community and the court.

Initiatives for Violent Offenders and Their Victims

Increasingly, aboriginal bands and communities are addressing the causes and consequences of violence, spousal assault, and sexual abuse in their communities, and this has provided an opportunity for the development of programmes and services which incorporate elements of traditional aboriginal culture. Aboriginal-controlled programmes for abusers and their victims, unlike those sponsored by 'outside' non-aboriginal justice and social service agencies, centre on healing and restitutive justice, rather than on punishment and retribution.   There is the recognition that many offenders were themselves victims of sexual abuse, either while growing up in their home community or while students in church-operated residential schools (Haig-Brown 1991).

Two of the more innovative aboriginal-controlled programmes for the victims and offenders of violence and sexual abuse are described here.

The Hollow Water (Province of Manitoba) Resource Group. This programme was initiated at the community level by several survivors of sexual abuse. An attempt is made to restore community, family, and individual peace and harmony. A healing contract is signed, and offenders apologize publicly to the victims and to the community for the harm that has been done. The response is one which is designed to consider the needs of all of the parties to the abuse—the victim, the offender and the community—and is directed beyond merely punishing the offender for a specific behaviour (Lajeunesse 1993).

The Canim Lake (Province of British Columbia) Family Violence Programme. This community-based, band-controlled family violence programme is designed for the management and treatment of adult and adolescent sex offenders as well as for the victims of sexual abuse. One component of the programme is the identification of sex offenders in the community who have not been detected by the police or otherwise subjected to sanctioning by the band. During an amnesty period, these individuals can contact the Family Violence Committee, and acknowledge responsibility for their offence(s); they are then, through a diversionary scheme, placed in a treatment programme without being subjected to criminal charges. The specific treatment interventions blend modern clinical techniques with traditional aboriginal healing practices and address the needs of the offender and the victim within a family and community context. To qualify for the treatment programme and as a condition of being diverted, the offender must sign a contract indicating a commitment to completing the treatment programme. Should the offender either reoffend or fail to complete the programme, the diversion status is revoked and the person is subjected to formal prosecution by the criminal justice system.

Community Justice Ceremonies

While many of the justice initiatives which have been developed involve collaborative arrangements between the criminal justice system and aboriginal communities (while incorporating elements of traditional cultural practices) there is an increasing number of instances in which individual aboriginal communities are responding to, and issuing sanctions on, offensive behaviour without any assistance from outside agencies or personnel. Such ceremonies often occur without the knowledge of criminal justice personnel and are generally of low visibility.

Illustrative of this type of event was a traditional justice ceremony and potlatch held in a small aboriginal village on the west coast of Vancouver Island in December 1993. During this ceremony, a man from the community who had sexually abused women in the community over a 35-year period of time faced his victims, their families and invited witnesses. Over the course of a day and evening, the offender spoke publicly to the assembly, asked the forgiveness of the victims and the community and apologized to the victims. A number of highly symbolic events occurred during the ceremony, including the washing of the victims feet by the offender and the burning of a mask that had been carved by the offender. These activities were designed to begin the process of renewal for the victims, the offender and the community. Following this, women from the community and from neighboring villages were asked to offer their support to the victims and to the community, as well as to speak directly to the offender. A feast was held and then the men in the assembly were asked to speak. Finally, a potlatch was held and blankets and gifts were given to the victims and their families, elders, visiting chiefs, persons who supported the victims and other witnesses in attendance.

This ceremony provided an opportunity for the victims of the sexual assaults to confront their abuser. It required the offender to fully disclose his crimes and to acknowledge full responsibility for his offences to the victims, their families and to the assembled witnesses. The ceremony also provided the basis for reconciliation and healing and functioned to strengthen the community (Griffiths et al. 1994).

Aboriginals in Urban Settings: A Unique Challenge

To date, the development of local justice programmes and services incorporating elements of aboriginal tradition and culture has occurred largely in rural and remote areas of the country and most often on aboriginal reserve lands. There are, however, large numbers of aboriginal peoples who reside in urban centres across the country, including Toronto, Winnipeg, Calgary and Vancouver and the rate of aboriginal in-migration to these centres continues to increase.

There has been little focus on the difficulties encountered by urban aboriginal peoples, the nature and extent of their conflict with the criminal justice system, or the potential for developing alternative justice services and programmes that might better address the needs of the urban aboriginal community. This is due to a number of factors which characterize the situation of the urban aboriginal: 1) the lack of an aboriginal land base; 2) the cultural and linguistic diversity of the urban aboriginal community; 3) the fact that urban aboriginal peoples are one of many cultural and ethnic minorities; and 4) the lack of an established framework within which policy and programmatic initiatives relating to urban aboriginal policing can be developed and implemented. There are notable exceptions to this paucity of urban programmes and services, including the Aboriginal Legal Services of Toronto Community Council Project.

The Aboriginal Community Council is a forum for hearing cases of aboriginal persons in conflict with the law. The project is funded by the Attorney General of Ontario and operated by Aboriginal Legal Services of Toronto. The programme is premised on the practice of diversion and is an attempt to allow the aboriginal community in Toronto to assume control over the response to, and the setting of sanctions for, aboriginal persons charged with offences in the city. The council, comprised of aboriginal volunteers, reaches decisions by consensus and has a number of dispositions to draw from, including fines, the payment of restitution to the victim, completion of a number of hours of community service, or referral to a treatment resource. An evaluation (Moyer and Axon 1993) of the project identified a number of positive attributes, including: 1) the programme was designed, and is controlled, by the aboriginal community; 2) the programme is offender based, rather than offence focused; 3) the project functions to facilitate offender access to urban programmes and services; 4) the project is holistic in its orientation; and 5) offenders participating in the project feel that their individual needs are met by the Community Council process. The findings of the independent evaluation suggest that the Community Council model holds considerable promise as one strategy to address the needs of the urban aboriginal community.

Community Justice and Justice for Crime Victims

There is little doubt that the community-based justice initiatives designed and delivered by aboriginal bands and communities are a positive development and have significant potential to address the needs of crime victims, criminal offenders and communities. Decentralized, community-based programmes and services, premised on a restorative model of law and justice and traditional cultural practices, function to empower communities to assume ownership of troublesome behaviour and individuals. Informal networks involving community elders and other key community members can be utilized with more positive outcomes than occurs with the intervention of outside criminal justice professionals, who may have little knowledge of the community, its culture and its residents. Programmes and services can be tailored to the specific requirements of the community, offenders and crime victims, and there is the opportunity, so often absent in adversarial justice systems, to address the causes of criminal behaviour as well as its consequences.

The necessity for alternative models of justice delivery is even more paramount in view of the evidence indicating the inability of government-sponsored programmes to reduce aboriginal conflict with the law and to adequately address the needs of victims, offenders and communities.

This optimism and potential, however, must not obscure several critical issues which aboriginal communities themselves are confronting as they move to assume increasing control over the delivery of justice services. Among the more significant (and potentially divisive) issues is ensuring that the rights of victims are protected within the community and that vulnerable persons, particularly women and female adolescents, who are often the victims of violent crime and sexual abuse, are adequately protected.

While the federal, provincial and territorial governments, under pressure from aboriginal political organizations, bands and communities, are pursuing policies which encourage the devolution of justice services to the community level, concerns have been raised about the ability of community justice initiatives to protect individuals vulnerable to criminal victimization. Even within small aboriginal communities, there are power hierarchies based on clan or family affiliation. This results in the views of some residents weighing more heavily in decisions regarding the administration of justice.[5]

Aboriginal women, in particular, have voiced concerns about the high rates of sexual and physical abuse in communities and questioned whether local justice initiatives provide adequate protection for the victims of violence and abuse and whether the sanctions imposed are appropriate. The concern is that attempting to address serious assaultive behaviour in the community, under the guise of traditional justice may be harmful to the victim, the community, and to the offender, who may not have access to professional, clinical treatment.

In a study of gender equality in the administration of justice in the Northwest Territories, Peterson (1992: 74) argued that 'while the efforts to expand the perspective of the administration of justice are very positive ones, there must be a degree of caution exercised. In receiving input from the community, there must be some assurance that the input received is truly representative of community opinion or values' (see also Nightingale 1991: 93). In consultations at the community level, Peterson (1992: 75) found that many aboriginal women expressed concerns that their voices were not heard, and a common complaint was that there was a willingness to hear from male elders and not from women:

> There must also be an awareness of the fact that there can be differences that develop along generational lines and that older people may evidence a tolerance of violence against women that is no longer acceptable to younger women. In seeking advice and input from communities these differences must be recognized. While it is appropriate to explore alternatives for addressing issues of violence, such alternatives must not become a mechanism for excusing violent behaviour.

The failure to address these critical points has led to situations in which justice initiatives by aboriginal bands have been first criticized by aboriginal women and then discredited in their entirety.

CONCLUSION

Canada's aboriginal peoples are assuming greater control over the design and delivery of justice services at the community and reserve levels. This is part of a general movement towards self-government and the assertion of aboriginal rights and sovereignty. It is also a consequence of the seemingly irreconcilable differences between the world view held by Euro-Canadians and aboriginals and the differing models which are reflected in the two systems of law and justice. Government-sponsored justice initiatives have been largely ineffectual in reducing the levels of conflict which aboriginal people in Canada experience with the criminal justice system or in meeting the needs of aboriginal victims, offenders and communities.

It is also finally being acknowledged that criminal behaviour is often only a symptom of deeper community and individual ills; and that there is a need to create non-adversarial forums for responding to criminal behaviour—forums which provide for substantive community participation. Aboriginal-controlled justice programmes and services, premised on aboriginal culture and traditional practices, hold great promise and can provide models which, perhaps, may be utilized by non-aboriginal communities as the search for more effective criminal justice strategies intensifies.[6]

NOTES

1. Approximately 3.6% of the total population of Canada is aboriginal. Aboriginal peoples in Canada are distinguished by their cultural and linguistic attributes as well as their legal status. Status Indians are aboriginal people who

are registered under the federal Indian Act. Non-status Indians are those who identify themselves as aboriginal but who are not registered under the Indian Act. Métis are of mixed aboriginal and European ancestry, while the Inuit (Eskimo) are a distinct cultural group who reside in the Northwest Territories, Labrador, and in the northern regions of the province of Quebec.

2. A definitive discussion of the patterns of crime and 'trouble' among aboriginal peoples is hindered by a lack of published research. Official criminal justice statistics generally include only status aboriginals. Few data exist on the involvement of Métis, Inuit, and non-status aboriginals in the criminal justice system, and only recently has attention been given to the difficulties encountered by aboriginal women and youth and by aboriginal victims of crime.

3. The concept of 'trouble' is useful in examining the difficulties afflicting aboriginal communities, as it is a far more inclusive term than crime, which has distinct legal connotations and limitations. Behaviours such as suicide, alcohol and solvent abuse, ongoing disputes between clans and families, and conflict in interpersonal relationships may be as disruptive and destructive as criminal activity, or more so.

4. The general nature of the present discussion obscures the complexities of aboriginal cultures and traditions and the wide variations. It is important to note that, even among aboriginal groups in close proximity to one another, there are often wide differences in cultural practices. There are, however, similarities in their approaches to the maintenance of order at the community level.

5. One of the difficulties in discussing community-based justice initiatives is that the terms 'community' and 'community-based' are used (and misused) to depict a wide range of justice programmes and services. There has not been, to date, any clear delineation of 'who' the community is, or what the criteria are for a programme or service, in order to be 'community-based'. In a study of the development and implementation of community-based justice initiatives in the Yukon Territory, Weafer (1986: 148, 150) found that: 'it is at times very difficult to perceive who exactly is the "community", and what the "community" needs are that a programme is supposed to attempt to meet. While a programme may be based in a community, this does not necessarily mean that the programme is realistically a "community-based" justice programme'.

6. A previous version of this chapter was presented in the workshop 'The Development of Victimology and Its Impact on Criminal Justice Policy' at the Eleventh International Congress on Criminology, Budapest, 22-27 August 1993.

REFERENCES

Auger, D. J., Doob, A. N., Auger, R. P. and P. Driben (1992) 'Crime and Control in Three Nishnawbe-Aski Nation Communities: An Exploratory Investigation', *Canadian Journal of Criminology*, 34: 317-38.

Barkwell, L. (1991) 'Early Law and Social Control among the Métis', in S. Corrigan and L. Barkwell (eds.), *The Struggle for Recognition: Canadian Justice and the Métis Nation*, Winnipeg: Pemmican Publications, 7-37.

Bayley, J. U. (Chair) (1985) *Task Force on Spousal Assault*, Yellowknife, Northwest Territories: Government of the Northwest Territories.

Berger, T. R. (1991) *A Long and Terrible Shadow: White Values, Native Rights in the Americas, 1492-1992*, Vancouver: Douglas and McIntyre.

Brodeur, J. P., LaPrairie, C. and McDonnell, R. (1991) *Justice for the Cree: Final Report*, James Bay, Quebec: Grand Council of the Crees.

Canada (1989) *Basic Departmental Data*, Ottawa: Indian and Northern Affairs.

Cawsey, R. A. (Chairman) (1991) *Justice on Trial, Report of the Task Force on the Criminal Justice System and Its Impact on the Indian and Métis People of Alberta*, Volume 1, Main Report, Edmonton: Attorney General and Solicitor General of Alberta.

Dickason, O. P. (1992) *Canada's First Nations—a History of Founding Peoples from Earliest Times*, Toronto: McClelland and Stewart.

Finkler, H. W. (1992) 'Community Participation in Socio-Legal Control: The Northern Context', *Canadian Journal of Criminology*, 34: 503-12.

Getty, I. A. L. and Lussier, A. S. (1988) *As Long as the Sun Shines and the Water Flows: A Reader in Canadian Native Studies*, Vancouver: University of British Columbia Press.

Griffiths, C. T. (1989) *The Community and Northern Justice*, Burnaby, British Columbia: The Northern Justice Society, Simon Fraser University.

Griffiths, C. T. (1990) *Preventing and Responding to Northern Crime*, Burnaby, British Columbia: The Northern Justice Society, Simon Fraser University.

Griffiths, C. T. (1992) *Self-Sufficiency in Northern Justice Issues*, Burnaby, British Columbia: The Northern Justice Society, Simon Fraser University.

Griffiths, C. T. and Patenaude, A. L. (1990) 'The Use of Community Service Orders in the Canadian North: The Prospects and Problems of "Localized" Corrections', in B. Galaway and J. Hudson (eds.) *Criminal Justice Restitution and Reconciliation*, Moarsey, New York: Criminal Justice Press, 145-53.

Griffiths, C. T. and Verdun-Jones, S. N. (1993) *Canadian Criminal Justice*, Toronto: Harcourt, Brace.

Griffiths, C. T., Wood, D., Saville, G. and Zellerer, E. (1995) 'Crime, Law and Justice in the Baffin Region: Preliminary Findings from a Multi-Year Study', in K.M. Hazlehurst (ed.) *Legal Pluralism and the Colonial Legacy: Indigenous Experiences of Justice in Canada, Australia and New Zealand*, Aldershot: Avebury.

Griffiths, C. T., Wood, D., Zellerer, E. and Simon, J. (1994) *Aboriginal Policing in British Columbia*, prepared for the Commission of Inquiry, Policing in British Columbia, Vancouver: Available from C. T. Griffiths.

Griffiths, C. T. and Yerbury, J. C. (1991) 'Native Indian Victims in Canada: Issues in Policy and Programme Delivery', *International Review of*

Victimology, 1: 335-46.

Haig-Brown, C. (1991) *Resistance and Renewal: Surviving the Residential School Experience,* Vancouver: Tillacum Library.

Hamilton, A. C. and Sinclair, C. M. (1991) *Report of the Aboriginal Justice Inquiry of Manitoba, the Justice System and Aboriginal People,* Volume 1, Winnipeg: Queen's Printer.

Hyde, M. and LaPrairie, C. (1987) *Amerindian Crime Prevention,* Ottawa: Solicitor General of Canada.

Krotz, L. (1990) *Indian Country—Inside Another Canada,* Toronto: McClelland and Stewart.

Lajeunesse, T. (1993) *Community Holistic Circle Healing, Hollow Water First Nation,* Ottawa: Solicitor General of Canada.

LaPrairie, C. (1991) *Justice for the Cree: Community, Crime, and Order,* James Bay, Quebec: Grand Council of the Crees.

LaPrairie, C. and Diamond, E. (1992) 'Who Owns the Problem? Crime and Disorder in James Bay Cree Communities', *Canadian Journal of Criminology,* 34: 417-34.

Linn, Judge P. (Chairperson) (1992a) *Report of the Saskatchewan Indian Justice Review Committee,* Regina: Government of Saskatchewan.

Linn, Judge P. (Chairperson) (1992b) *Report of the Saskatchewan Métis Justice Review Committee,* Regina: Government of Saskatchewan.

Moyer, S. and Axon, L. (1993) *An Implementation Evaluation of the Native Community Council Project of the Aboriginal Legal Services of Toronto,* Toronto: The Ministry of the Attorney-General (Ontario) and Aboriginal Legal Services of Toronto.

Moyles, R. G. (1989) *British Law and Arctic Men,* Burnaby, British Columbia: The Northern Justice Society, Simon Fraser University.

Nightingale, M. L. (1991) 'Judicial Attitudes and Differential Treatment: Native Women in Sexual Assault Cases', *Ottawa Law Review,* 23: 71-98.

Ontario Native Women's Association (1989) *Breaking Free—a Proposal for Change to Aboriginal Family Violence,* Thunder Bay, Ontario: Ontario Native Women's Association.

Peterson, K. R. (1992) *The Justice House—Report of the Special Advisor on Gender Equality,* Yellowknife, Northwest Territories: Department of Justice, Government of the Northwest Territories.

Ross, R. (1992) *Dancing with a Ghost—Exploring Indian Reality,* Toronto: Octopus Publishing Group.

Schuh, C. (1979) 'Justice on the Northern Frontier: Early Murder Trials of Native Accused', *Criminal Law Quarterly,* 22: 74-111.

Shkilnyk, A. (1985) *A Poison Stronger Than Love,* New Haven: Yale University Press.

Silverman, R. A. and Nielsen, M. O. (1992) *Aboriginal Peoples and Canadian Criminal Justice,* Toronto: Butterworths.

Weafer, L. F. (1986) 'The Development and Implementation of Community-Based Justice Programmes for Native and Northern Communities: The Justice of the Peace Programme in the Yukon', unpublished M.A. thesis, Burnaby, British Columbia: School of Criminology, Simon Fraser University.

Wolff, L. (1991) *Crime in Aboriginal Communities, Saskatchewan 1989*, Ottawa: Canadian Centre for Justice Statistics.

York, G. (1990) *The Dispossessed—Life and Death in Native Canada*, London: Vintage U.K.

10

'BODY, MIND AND SPIRIT': NATIVE COMMUNITY ADDICTIONS, TREATMENT AND PREVENTION

Maggie Hodgson

A fire is blazing in two Indian bands in British Columbia. The fire is the development of a community addictions treatment and healing model. One spark was ignited in the 1970s when the Chief of the Alkali Lake Indian Reserve decided his community could become sober and healthy by combining the traditional concept of in-residence treatment and the total involvement of community in the pre- and post-treatment process. His philosophy was 'the community is a treatment centre and a potential place of healing'. When he started this courageous task, 100% of his community was affected by alcoholism, and ten years later they had achieved 95% sobriety!

The second spark was lit approximately ten years later in another small British Columbia reserve called Tache. This community developed another model of the vision of the community being a treatment centre and a potential place of healing. They developed an on-the-reserve mobile treatment programme. This new model involved the whole community in the treatment process of the 25 people who attended the treatment programme in the band hall. They came from almost 100% alcoholism to 65% sobriety in three years! The fire has now leaped over provincial boundaries, and a small Indian band in Alberta is in the process of developing its own community vision of how it can build on the original philosophy that the community can be a treatment centre and a healing place.

To understand the profound impact of this process of collective thought and action of Alkali Lake Indian Community and the Tache Indian Community we refer to Emile Durkheim's theory on anomie. In talking about suicide in the 1800s, Durkheim explained anomie as a collective state of community without values and in a state of hopelessness which contributed to suicide. *Webster's Dictionary* defines anomie as: 'a lack of direction or purpose, aimless or rootless. The process of change tends to develop situations in which the old norms no longer restrain individual behaviour and new norms are either absent or unacceptable.'

Emile Durkheim's understanding of counteracting the state of anomie with the development of collective values or healthy societal norms, and the philosophy of the two Indian communities that the community is a treatment centre, both say the same thing. The root of the Indian communities' theory lies in the importance of the collective health of the extended family and community. The only difference is, Durkheim talked about anomie in the 1800s and Tache and Alkali both put into action a plan to counteract the state of anomie which existed in their communities 100 years later. Neither community had ever heard of Durkheim or his theory before.

In traditional thought, all healing is spiritual. While sociologists look at the development of societies, and the meaning within societies, it is important to recognize that these Indian communities developed meaning which was not only committed to a practical goal (sobriety) using the extended family system, but that these communities were also dedicated to a spiritual goal. That spiritual goal includes the belief that all things are related within the universe and that by honouring the spirit of ourselves and others we will become healthy; that when we are hurt through societal breakdown, through violence and losses, our spirit becomes hurt.

We have to work towards the healing of our spirits, and the spirit within our community structure, through our agents of healing—ourselves, family and friends and Indian leadership. Both communities directed the whole and individual efforts towards the good of the group. Both groups started with a vision of community health. Both groups utilized the major agent of change in the Indian community—the extended family—in the development of their vision. Both Indian communities included the body, mind and spirit in their community health plan. Their vision included the movement to incorporate values of faith in ourselves and our fellow man, trust in the potential for change, trust that they could rely on themselves to help themselves and others. It included the ability to share the resources, love, hurt, happiness, sorrow and kindness and to be kind to oneself, to believe in a power greater than oneself and to believe that the Creator or God is in all of us and our environment. This process involved the force or the power of the Creator and the manifestation of love in the community.

How did these two communities accomplish this movement from a state of anomie to a state of community sobriety and health? In our Indian society there is a model of wholeness, or what mainstream society refers to as the 'holistic' way of thinking. One form of holistic thinking is in the medicine wheel of involving seeing or vision, feeling or emotions, thinking or volition, doing or action. Those parts of the medicine wheel were used in the development of health in these two Native communities. While the communities did not set up a wheel and say 'this is what we will follow', they did in fact follow a healing model put forth through the visions and the direction of Native Elders for many centuries.

ALKALI LAKE HISTORY

Historically the Alkali Lake community was a hunting and trapping group. Its members lived and worked for the collective health and protection of the community. In the early 1900s, with the movement of the white population into Canada, the children of the Indian communities were moved into residential schools to facilitate the development of an educational system and to teach the children the religion of the group operating the residential school. The children were removed from their parents' homes from the ages of five to fifteen years. They were denied the right of speaking their own language and removed from their natural family support systems, primarily the extended family. In any culture the primary foundation of the culture is in the language and modelling of parents and community. Removing these children from their natural environment was profoundly damaging. Imagine taking a twenty-block radius in the city and removing all the children from the homes and placing them in another culture for ten years, where they spoke a new language and had minimal contact with their family and their own language. The result could be a community which suffers from a state of anomie. That is what existed in the Alkali Lake Indian Community in the early 1970s. There was a high rate of suicide, murder and vehicle accidents. There was a high rate of child neglect and physical and sexual abuse. There was family violence in every form. There was often a funeral a week. There was almost 100% welfare and unemployment.

Vision—'Seeing'

In the early 1970s a woman called Phyllis Chelsey came home to find that her daughter wanted to move in with her grandmother because of Phyllis' and her husband's drinking. Phyllis decided she wanted to quit drinking because she could not cope with the thought of her daughter moving out due to her drinking behaviour. She could *see* the results of her drinking and she *felt* the pain of knowing the results, the potential loss of her daughter and her love and respect. Phyllis went though a process of grieving for the loss of the friend of alcohol, the anaesthetic for her emotional pain. Her husband Andy experienced severe medical problems as a result of his drinking and witnessed his wife's decision to quit drinking. His motivation to quit drinking came when he was walking to work and saw two little kids walking to school dirty, ragged and hungry. When he asked them if they had had anything to eat that morning their reply was 'no'. He *saw* why he should quit drinking. He *felt* a deep sense of sadness at seeing those two neglected children. His vision and feelings provided the will to quit drinking, and he went to a support group for alcoholics. Andy continued to go to the same spot every day to watch the many neglected children walk to school. Those children were his motivation to continue to stay sober, one day at a time, for the first year. Imagine being the only two people sober in a community for a whole year. What determination. He kept his commitment to his vision by witnessing the pain of those children.

The first year, Phyllis and Andy held a Christmas party for those people who were willing to come sober. The only people who came were children, who were glad to have a hot meal for Christmas. While the children were eating, another woman walked in and announced, 'I quit drinking'. Both Andy and Phyllis brought the lady presents for her and her children. The lady said it was the best Christmas they ever had. They continue this tradition each year by having a community feast for New Year's Day. Now up to 500 people come to that sober feast. Andy started the development of his vision. When people became sober, they did everything they could do to support them by demonstrating their encouragement. They showed them love, their sharing and their kindness. They did everything they could to help the people feel good about being sober and provided support to motivate them to stay sober.

Andy witnessed the Chief and Band Council talking about addiction-related problems, but talking and drinking at the same time. He decided the way to change the community was to become a leader and to provide leadership in the development of community health through action. After becoming Chief he involved his fellow council members in the commitment to sobriety and community development.

The Chief and Band Council and other community members utilized a process of involvement, commitment, caring and 'tough love' to meet the challenge of working towards a healthy community. When they found that a band employee was stealing from the band because of addiction, they would give that employee the choice of going for treatment or being charged with theft. When people were abusing alcohol the Band Council would place those families on a voucher system instead of giving cash for them to drink. When people left their children alone they would go to the home and pick up the children and refuse to return the children until the parents went for treatment. They constantly reassured people they cared about them. They had the flow of alcohol slowed down by cutting down the vans bringing in bootlegged booze. The bootleggers were charged at the request of the Chief and council; one of the bootleggers was the Chief's mother. This action was based on the vision and awareness that there was a lot of enabling towards drinking behaviour being done by caregivers, child welfare workers, social assistance workers and family members. They stopped following the rules of addicted families—the rules of 'don't talk about the destruction that is going on in families'. When they saw the results of a man beating up his father, they gave him the choice of getting treatment or being charged.

Those methods of intervention were not carried out in isolation. Care and kindness was shown when they dealt with extended family and friends. They ensured they paid attention to the body, mind and spirit of the people when they were intervening in their drinking pattern. They offered support to those people when they would go to treatment. As a community, they would send the person a card with everyone signing it saying, 'we love you, hang in there, you will make it'. They would travel 55 to 200 miles to the treatment centre to honour that person for successfully completing treatment. They ensured that the children were kept in the community in relatives' homes when the parents went to treatment. They would, as a community, fix up and clean the home of the family away in treatment to enhance that person's excitement at returning to a home which was not in an untidy and neglected state of repair. When those people returned, they felt loved and cared for and certainly more comfortable.

Once there were a few more sober people, they expanded their vision about what the community life required if the people were to stay sober. They started the development of a locally-controlled store, opened by the two women who first became sober in the community. They set up a logging company and ensured that when people came back from treatment they had the opportunity to work as volunteers even if there were no jobs available. They ensured that there was a sense of purpose which no longer only belonged to Chief and council but to the whole community. *This vision saw the community as a treatment centre.* In this approach you do not send someone out to a treatment centre and forget about them for the 30 days they are away from the community and expect the treatment centre to be the miracle worker. The person being treated in the centre is in the beginning process of healing, and the balance of treatment is carried out in the community as a community responsibility. It is not only a responsibility but also an act of love when you extend your hand to that person. These principles are taught to some degree by Alcoholics Anonymous. Many of the principles of AA were followed and practised in the process of community support for the newly recovered alcoholic. However, AA does not become a catalyst for community and economic development.

Emotional Development—'Feeling'

Once there was a large group of people at Alkali Lake who had been successfully treated and were back in the community, the Chief and community leaders recognized and remembered their own pain from their early days of sobriety. They knew they had expanded on the number of people who knew about addictions. 'But now that I'm sober, how do I communicate with my spouse, my children?' 'Now that I'm sober, how do I live with seeing the people I have abused physically or sexually through the years?' 'How do I share my pain with my community peers about feelings I learned how to ignore and not feel?' They brought training companies in the human services field to the community to teach skills which would assist them in communicating with their children, their spouses, their Elders and employers. They had sobered up, but they had to learn more about alcoholism and how it affects them and their communities. They learned how to contradict the *'don't feel rule'*, the rule which destroys many a sober family. They worked on changing the *'don't talk rule'* to a *'talking circle rule'*. They shared the many losses each experienced, and grieved over those losses as a community, with community support in those healing and training sessions. They utilized the historic norms and revitalized the cultural value of the extended family.

They ensured that every man, woman and child participated in training in alcoholism awareness and in communications and counselling. Why? Because drug abuse reduces self-esteem, and people had to recognize the damage entailed in returning to alcohol and see how they could assist their neighbours. They followed the old Indian saying, 'We are all counsellors'. It is important that even the Elders had to take the training programmes, because many of them had been to boarding school and had lost the sense of value of self and others. Training focussed heavily on the development of the people and their emotions and communication between couples.

Mainstream treatment programmes bring together the nuclear family for counselling, maybe a Mom, Dad and two children. The extended family as it exists in the Native community includes a larger circle of people. To work with the extended family, Alkali Lake utilized their community as a treatment centre, thereby including everyone who was affected. That training process utilized Native trainers from Alberta, their own community members, non-Native trainers and the local community college. They utilized Native, Black, White and Oriental trainers. The reason I mention the colours of the people involved in the training process is that these four coloured peoples fit equally on the medicine wheel. Again, it was not a planned process but was very symbolic of the healing of feelings of low self-esteem, with everyone being equal. The heavy training process of the community continued for approximately five years. Within that time, Alkali Lake developed its own human relations training institute, which assisted their community members and provided assistance to outside communities.

Mind—'Thinking'

Alkali Lake facilitated the opportunity for band members to return to school if they chose to as part of their aftercare programme plan. In order to assist students to have appropriate accommodation in a larger centre when they were going to school, some families pooled their money to purchase a house which they rented to the students. This presented the opportunity for students to avoid living in run-down accommodations, which is where they had to live prior to the purchase of housing for them. The house gave students the opportunity to maintain a support system when they had to leave home to go to school to reach their academic goals. Academic resources required in their community were identified, and the Alkali Lake Band Council encouraged their community members to pursue their careers.

Spirit—'Spiritual'

Alkali Lake invited Elders from other regions to show them traditional ceremonies and started to partake in sweats or daily prayer ceremonies. They set up groups for both men and women. They opened all training sets with a prayer and closed with a prayer so their meetings would be spirit driven. They incorporated the spiritual ways into their actions via sharing, caring, honesty and turning their will over to the Creator on a daily basis, and with clear thought on the importance of that element of their development, as a community and as individuals within that community.

Action or Movement—'Doing'

People at Alkali Lake did not receive welfare cheques if they drank: instead, they received vouchers. This was the community's way of saying, 'We will not enable you to continue to drink and it is *not okay* if you continue to hurt yourself'. People had to work for their welfare, and in many instances it involved helping others in their community. They had community meetings where they discussed issues which were affecting the community as a whole. Some of these meetings were hot and heavy with anger. (Some of the people were scared of the change.) They held sober community dances where band members volunteered as the entertainment. Elders and children learned to dance and have fun together, and Moms and Dads learned how to dance sober. Children and families learned to have fun in the old way, with the involvement of the whole family. They looked at the children and identified what they wanted for them, and one of the things they decided was that they wanted the children to feel proud of being Indian. They wanted their children to learn to speak their language and to have access to their culture. They set out to do this via the educational system. A band member worked in the school as a counsellor to the children, and later became the assistant principal and then the principal. The local people started teaching their own language in the school, and there were traditional teachings from the few Elders left in their community. A cultural centre was built in the school. The children participated in the 'talking circles' as a means of rebuilding their trust in themselves and others; and developed a youth leadership corps.

The teachers coming into the community were advised that a condition of their employment was that they agree not to drink for 365 days a year, as they were role models to the students. The school had as many Native teachers as possible and moved to a community-controlled school. They were now moving into the realm of community health and taking care of their future through the development of their youth.

Fear with a Prayer—'Courage'

Dealing with issues which arose at Alkali Lake as soon as they surfaced was possible because the community trusted. Change was possible, and they had the support to change what was happening. With this belief in place, it was much easier than it would be in most communities to deal with the issue of sexual abuse when a member of the community was charged with incest. They immediately brought in a consultant to do an educational workshop on the signs and symptoms of sexual abuse. As soon as this workshop started it became very apparent that the community was experiencing another layer of healing, a deeper level of healing. People were trusting enough to say they had been abused and were willing to talk about it. This had a ripple effect, and the Chief and council met and decided they were going to have a community healing session. There was a new woman Chief who had witnessed the development of the community and believed in the community, and who had the ability to work on this new community healing problem. *Feel the energy!*

They hired five Native trainers, including the author, to work with the community in this process. One trainer worked in the school to present information on sexual abuse prevention called, 'Strong Kids, Safe Kids.' Another trainer conducted workshops in the community hall on community development. At this workshop information was given on the signs and symptoms of abuse and how to develop peer support groups. One trainer who is a Pipe Holder and a Sweat Holder held daily sweats to assist in the healing process by providing a focus of prayer and release of the toxins from the peoples' bodies due to the release of anger and deep grieving in the group process. Two other trainers, one a psychologist, worked with victims in a separate area. The participants became aware that the deep feelings of loss and anger which they felt about their own experiences of abuse were the same feelings many, many of their friends, their mother or brother, had also suffered due to physical and sexual abuse. Many talked of their deep shame and the guilt from holding in the repressed shame over the years. The important fact was that the whole community dealt with the issue of healing and wanting to get healthier.

Seven months later the community held another workshop for teenagers who had been abused both physically and sexually during the drinking years.

Many of the teenagers were drinking on weekends because of the abuse they had suffered. Many who were using alcohol or drugs were doing it to numb their shame and anger. They continue to work on this issue by following, with rigorous honesty, the *'talk rule'*, the *'trust rule'* and the *'feel rule'*. Maybe the next generation will be a healthier generation, with the community's commitment to health.

While I separate the sweat lodge and people going to church in the community as demonstrations of spirituality in the community healing process, true spirituality is manifested when each of the persons becomes involved in the healing process. The ceremonies mentioned are an opportunity to focus good energy, pray together and facilitate God's healing power. The World Health Organization does not talk too much about spirituality as an integral part of development of a healthy community model; but rest assured, it is the foundation. One other form of the spiritual movement within Alkali Lake was the continued expansion of their AA programme. After all, it is one of the most successful spiritual programmes in the world. It has fifty million members in the world. Like Alkali Lake, it is a self-help organization founded on principles of a spiritual nature.

Reaching Out—'Sharing'

In 1985 the Alkali Lake community developed a video about how they accomplished this miracle of 95% sobriety in ten years. Remember, this is a community which had come from a situation of 100% of the population being affected by active alcoholism. The video has been an inspiration to peoples across Canada and the United States. Alkali Lake continues as a community to work on the further development of the next layer of community healing. They are now going out to conduct workshops like those conducted in their community ten years earlier. The community members go to all parts of Canada and the United States in response to requests such as, 'Please come talk to our leaders and show us how we can do what you have done'. They are in the process of sharing their inspiration about the *community as a treatment and healing centre*.

TACHE INDIAN RESERVE—A MOBILE TREATMENT MODEL

Another example occurred on the Tache reserve. In 1981 the alcohol counsellor of this small community realized he was sending people out to treatment centres and when they returned to the community they were unable to remain sober. He decided that they had to bring treatment home, and that the whole community had to be involved.

He discussed the idea with the Tache Chief and Band Council. They supported the development and started the following process. To familiarize community members with the counsellors who would be coming to facilitate the treatment process he brought them in to conduct workshops on alcoholism. He worked on building trust and a good relationship. Through this process they would be willing to become involved as clients in the treatment process when it happened. He brought other trainers into the community to conduct workshops on alcoholism. He brought a trainer in to conduct peer counselling workshops and to develop support groups in different areas of the community. One other counsellor from the community and the director, Vincent Joseph, went to the treatment centre in Prince George to participate in the in-treatment programme as in-house counsellors to learn how a residential treatment programme operated.

When they were ready for the on-the-reserve treatment programme to commence, they utilized an existing facility within the community to conduct the treatment programme. The whole community agreed not to drink during the treatment process as an act of support and respect for the 26 people partaking in the programme. Only two members of the whole community violated that commitment, and it was a community with a very high rate of alcoholism. The community members got involved in the treatment of those 26 people by cooking food for them and babysitting their children. The community health representative and band social workers assisted in the support process. Elders came forward and taught songs and Indian games they had not shared prior to that time. The priest said Mass in the community to support the community in the development of their vision. 'Born-again' Christians prayed for the success of the community treatment process. People hunted and fished to help provide food for the feasts during the treatment, and the whole community held an honour feast for the participants of the treatment programme when they completed it. Paul Hanke, the developer of the model, says a key to the success of this model has been the inclusion of each community's culture.

Aftercare

The counsellors met with the Tache treatment participants on a regular basis. They provided both individual and group counselling. Their aftercare procedures included taking all the treatment members and their families on camp-outs. Therapy took place in the process of fishing and hunting, walking through the bush and talking. Those undergoing treatment continued to enjoy their natural environment and to get well. They had the benefit of both their peer support groups and AA groups for support. The follow-up inclusion of the family in the treatment process continued for a period of two years. The counsellors found the issue they had not addressed during the treatment process was how the children would feel with the sudden decision of the parents to start becoming responsible. By changing the process from the individual treatment of 26 people, to one which included the whole community in the treatment process and aftercare, they revolutionized the concept of treatment.

The programme incorporated the values of sharing, caring, respect and love in action. The results are impressive. After three years Tache had 65% sobriety. Again, it is a process of including the spirit, the body and mind. It requires having a vision, building feeling and trust. Of thinking about how it can be done and then doing it—action. During the treatment process, Tache adapted the treatment appropriate to the specific needs of the participating group. An example is their dealing with the question of parenting when it was raised as an issue which 50% of the participants were concerned about. They also dealt with the issue of couples' communications for the couples in the treatment process.

ANAHEIM LAKE—MOBILE TREATMENT

The National Native Alcohol and Drug Abuse programme funded the expansion of the programme, and in 1987 Vincent Joseph and his team went into Anaheim Lake to conduct mobile treatment. At that time 95% of the population suffered from active alcoholism. By involving the whole community in supporting the treatment process, Anaheim Lake reduced its drinkers to 5% of the community, that is, there was 95% sobriety after five months. Is there any other programme in Canada which can boast of such success?

During the treatment process, the treatment team hosted sober dances and skidoo races, the first sober skidoo races in that community. They involved the spirit of the people and the leadership in the process of changing community norms. Much attention was paid to the utilization of television and video in changing norms. Can you possibly think of a more powerful norm changer than leaders seeing that community health is everyone's responsibility? The World Health Organization would do well to come and observe the development of a community health model which involves body, mind and spirit, in practice, not only in theory.

A young Chief saw the Alkali Lake video of how people became sober and worked towards health by involving the whole community in the development of a sense of value of oneself and others. She also clearly understood that it was of primary importance that she be the role model to assist in this development. She went to treatment and believed it would help her community. When she arrived and participated, she found that first she had to help herself.

A community team worked on the development of a mobile treatment programme for the reserve. All members of Band Council passed a resolution that 'if you are going to be a member of this council, you must be a non-drinker'. Six months later that had happened. The community developed one English AA group, one Indian language AA group and one women's group. They now have a therapist working with team members and people returning from treatment and an intervention team which includes social services and other resource people. They are presently involving six young people in treatment for inhalant abuse at the request of the mothers and the grandmothers. They have involved economic development in the community healing process.

BROADER APPLICATION

Society as a whole will learn a lot about collective action in addictions if they pay attention to these phenomenal happenings. Can you imagine the cost saving of this process? Normally 30 people are treated at a total cost of approximately $30,000. But the cost of involving the whole community in the treatment process was around $10,000, and the results were 410 sober people out of a population of 450 within five months. 'Awesome!', as my daughter would say.

The concepts that the community is a treatment centre and that healing and developing a sense of health is everyone's responsibility have grown and are working. The models developed in British Columbia for helping the community reframe and reclaim their vision are effective. All of this can be confirmed in an old Hopi prophecy.

Hopi Prophecy

In the mid-1800s there was an old Hopi prophecy which went as follows:

Our Indian people are in a darkness and we will come out of our midnight into our day to be world leaders. This change will start when the eagle lands on the moon.

No one understood this business of an eagle landing on the moon. In the 1960s when the first space ship landed on the moon, the astronauts sent word back to the world, 'The Eagle has landed.' That week the first Indian Alcohol and Drug Programme was set up. The case examples presented here are manifestations of that prophecy. Native alcohol programmes have generated the rebirth of our culture. The prophecy is coming true.

The development within these communities changed the collective state of anomie with the development of a collective vision of the value of community health. North American Native alcohol programmes, like Poundmaker's Lodge and the Nechi Institute, have been the primary instruments of dealing with addictions prevention and treatment in a holistic way. They have been catalysts in the renewal of the Indian culture.

For good social change to happen it has to have a 'spirit' of healing, an energy, a vision and movement. The community involvement in body, mind and spirit wellness and the miraculous results in short periods of time are the futuristic model all sectors of society could learn from. *See the spark.*[1]

NOTE

1. This chapter refers to the work of the Nechi Institute on Alcohol and Drug Education. Nechi is a Native adult addictions counsellor training and research centre which trains staff of the 45 Native addictions programmes in the province of Alberta. The trainees come from various treatment, detox, halfway house, and walk-in counselling service centres. Nechi is jointly housed with Poundmaker's Lodge—a Native residential treatment centre—and there are 100 beds between the two organizations. This unique concept of having Native training and treatment within one facility was developed with the support of the Alberta government.

11

WE AL-LI 'FIRE AND WATER': A PROCESS OF HEALING

Judy Atkinson and Coralie Ober

INTRODUCTION

The programme now called We Al-Li evolved out of the need to help heal the individual, family and community pain and trauma resulting from colonial domination and power abuse. The concept behind We Al-Li came from the knowledge that where there is pain there must be healing. We Al-Li wanted to provide a healing approach to the needs of those Aboriginal and Torres Strait Islander people presently suffering post-traumatic stress disorder, a medical term which could better be called 'dispossession disaster trauma'. These terms are used to explain the 'dis-ease' and dysfunction of body, mind and spirit which inflict many colonized indigenous people. This chapter outlines the development of that programme and the concepts behind it.

Colonization: A Fatal Psychic Trauma

The Royal Commission into Aboriginal Deaths in Custody stated that those Aboriginal and Torres Strait Islander men and women who died in custody were not victims of isolated acts of violence or brutality but were victims of institutionalized and entrenched racism and discrimination which evolved out of the practices of colonization. The practices of colonization depend upon oppressive attitudes and behaviours which also encourage violence against women and children.

One of the oppressive behaviours of the colonizers was to remove children from their immediate and extended families. Generally, the reason for this government policy and action was that Aboriginal children, often living in situations of enforced poverty and dispossession with mothers or parents, were thought to be in need of 'proper care and education'. It has now been shown that many Aboriginal children who were removed from their families and placed in institutions or in foster homes were sexually, physically and psychologically abused in these institutions or foster families. There is still a denial by many people of the consequences of this kind of 'education'. For example, many will claim children must be taught cleanliness and particular work habits when young so they will grow up with such desired attributes. On the other hand, they also believe that those who are abused when young should just put these experiences behind them and become solid contributing citizens within Australian society. The pain and shame of these childhood experiences should be repressed and denied.

Furthermore, we have not yet begun to articulate or understand the cumulative, intergenerational impact on people who have seen or been subjected to extreme acts of violence. Children who saw their parents killed in massacres; their grandfathers, fathers, brothers and uncles beaten with hobble chains and stock whips; their grandmothers, mothers, sisters and aunties run down on horseback and raped; and their brothers and sisters torn from the fold of the family and never heard of again are now the grandparents of the present generation. Such people have seen: 'too much war, too much violence. Some of this violence can affect them, stick with them, like a rash on the soul. They carry this violence with them back to their communities and their homes and their lives and they begin to act in ways they have never acted before' (Nordstrum 1993: 35-36).

The present generation enacts the traumatic feelings of past experiences. Recent studies have explored the process whereby oppression and abuse is internalized by those who are oppressed or abused. Other studies document the results of oppression or abuse. Some see themselves as victims of a colonial past, while their own behaviours may be reinforcing that victimization as they perpetrate abuse on others. We can function as both victim and as perpetrator at the same time, and both these behaviours hold us in a place of not being able to move out of our victimization, of not being able to become fully empowered, self-actualizing, self-determining people. The colonizers themselves may be both abusers in their positions of power and yet be functioning from their own experiences of power abuse. People without inner power (spiritual strength) feel the need to have power over others. This understanding in no way denies the criminality of the abuse, but gives a context to its multidimensional and intergenerational effects. It emphasizes the essential need to break the cycle now, in this generation.

Within some Aboriginal and Torres Strait Islander communities, the level of abuse of women and children must be looked at with serious concern. Marcia Langton, Ah Matt and colleagues reported to the Royal Commission into Aboriginal Deaths in Custody: 'The death of women and constant assault, both sexual and physical, of women and children, in Aboriginal communities, far exceed in sheer numbers and the enormity of suffering the problems which custody and deaths in custody pose for men' (Langton and Ah Matt et al. 1991:

373).

In talking about the effects of sexual abuse and domestic violence, an Aboriginal woman described the different layers of pain: 'People get hurt physically—you can see the bruises and the black eyes. A person gets hurt emotionally—you can see the tears and the distressed face—but when you've been hurt spiritually like that—it's a real deep hurt and nobody, unless you're a victim yourself, could ever understand because you've been hurt by somebody that you hold in trust' (Atkinson 1990: 7).

Violence against women and children was a colonizing tool and has similar implications to the deaths in custody of young Aboriginal men. The Aboriginal and Torres Strait Islander Health Strategy Report says:

> Family violence has its origins in institutionalization, incarceration, loss of role, loss of parental and role models, low self-esteem, alienation, overt and covert discrimination, isolation, theft of land and loss of culture and language, loss of economic independence and enforced dependence on welfare, powerlessness, high levels of imprisonment, alcohol and drug abuse, poverty, high unemployment levels and low education attainment, and a history of childhood separation from parents—in one survey 65% of respondents had been separated from a parent during childhood and 47% had been separated from both parents (National Aboriginal Health Strategy Working Party 1989: 174-75).

Family violence is a product of individual, family and community dysfunction. Many families and communities oppressed by colonization show symptoms of dysfunction: that is, they are functioning with difficulty and in pain. This includes such physical, mental, emotional and spiritual pain as individuals and families experience in domestic violence; rape; child abuse and child sexual assault; self-inflicted injury, including motor vehicle accidents; suicides; the trauma of life-threatening diseases; and the ongoing grieving in relation to homicides, death through injury or illness, and unresolved pain. The ability to resolve and release this pain in grieving ceremonies has been denied because of the unremitting context and the sheer volume of the trauma over the years. Alcohol and drug abuse both contribute to and result from this pain.

The Royal Commission was able to show how Aboriginal men harm themselves as well as other members of their families and communities in many of these ways:

- 53% of those who died in custody had been convicted of a violent crime;
- 9% of theses convictions were for homicides;
- 12% of them were for serious assault;
- 32% of them were for crimes of sexual violence;
- Alcohol and drug abuse was a contributing factor in most of these cases

(Royal Commission into Aboriginal Deaths in Custody 1990b: 13).

While Aboriginal men comprise 29% of men in custodial care in Australia, Aboriginal women comprise 50% of women in custodial care (Royal Commission into Aboriginal Deaths in Custody 1990a: 3). The Commonwealth government, which is a patriarchal institution which holds power over others who have been made less powerful, has generally ignored the pain of women and children while concentrating on the issue of male deaths in cells. They ignore the fact that more women (and men) have died outside of prison, through violent assault and other related causes, than all of those who died in cells. The Royal Commission has recommended that Aboriginal families, where there has been a cell death, receive grief counselling. This somehow seems to negate or marginalize the grieving needs of those people suffering other forms of trauma. They also need to have access to a counselling and grieving processes. The pain a family feels when one member dies in custody is no more or less than the pain a family feels when a family member commits suicide, dies from domestic violence, or dies from a terminal illness. The grieving needs of women and children who have been betrayed within their families, through rape or criminal assault, must also be recognized.

Colonization impacts differently on women in comparison to men (Atkinson 1993). The essential difference is the sexism integral to racism in colonial conquest. This creates an added layer of oppression for women, for it is historically observable that oppressed males take on the values (and behaviours) of those who have oppressed them (Brownmiller 1975: 31). The pain of their separate experiences is real for both sexes, but the needs arising from their different experiences must be acknowledged and responded to, if Aboriginal women and men are to come together in partnership again. Aboriginal men and women must sit with each other and hear how these separate experiences have shaped their present behaviours. They must share their stories, and in the telling, bridges will be built and healing will begin.

The outcomes of the Royal Commission have largely been to increase the flow of public monies into the very institutions which have functioned abusively on Aborigines and Torres Strait Islanders—improved prison cells, increased expenditure on police and prison supervision. This only increases the power and dominion of these institutions. This is the colonial system's response to indigenous pain. While public servants build careers on a public service system's response to the recommendations of the Royal Commission, unemployed Aboriginal people serving on 'advisory bodies' are growing more and more frustrated and angry, as they feel powerless to change the functions of the bureaucratic systems, economic structures and the psycho-social attitudes which continue to oppress. In our pain we continue to channel our energy into trying to change these systems, while becoming further and further dependent upon and chained to them.

What we now need is an Aboriginal people's centred approach to decolonization. The decolonization process should not just address the systems and structures of oppression and the attitudes and behaviours of the oppressors, but as a priority should include the healing, decolonizing needs of individuals, groups, families and communities. We need to feel the pain, recognize where it comes from, express the anger (in safe and boundaried ways) and grieve our losses. We need to sit for a time with ourselves, to practice Dadirri (deep listening to another), to be reconciled within ourselves and with each other. We need to revitalize our ceremonies, change them if necessary, and through song, dance, art and storytelling recreate and reaffirm our own power for healing the wounds of the past. We can transform the present and the future by reawakening the powerful past with its message that we are both part of the ongoing creation and, perhaps as important, its steward as well.

Impact of Colonization on the Individual

'"Health" to Aboriginal people is a matter of determining all aspects of their life, including control over their physical environment, of dignity, of community self-esteem and of justice' (National Aboriginal Health Strategy Working Party 1989: ix). Aboriginal people understand the interrelationships between dimensions of body, mind, emotions, spirit and environment. They know the connections between the ancestral and historical past and present life experiences which create 'well-health' or 'ill-health'. Similar to the work of Wong and McKeen (1992), they see that we become unwell and behave in destructive and self-destructive ways when our life energy is blocked. It is not insignificant that the leading causes of death for Aboriginal people in Queensland are: circulatory diseases (the heart); neoplasms, in particular cancer of the reproductive organs (life reproduction); injury and poisoning (abuse of others and of self); and respiratory problems (breathing—life force).

The person presenting with symptoms (ill-health, violent behaviours, pain of suppression) is attempting to say something about her or his experience of the world that she or he is unable to express in any other way. There is contained in any person's illness, psychological or physical, a story from that person's life. Oftentimes the person is unaware of the message she or he is trying to convey through the illness. In fact, it is generally this lack of understanding of what needs to be communicated which results in the production of symptoms. Illness exists in the face of failure to communicate in any other way (Wong and McKeen 1992: 125-33).

Within the Aboriginal world view, the dynamism between a person's environment and life experiences are seen as major components in the person's (and group's) well-health or ill-health. The person and group must participate in their own healing path to wellness by accepting responsibility to move away from illness patterns into states of health and openness.   'Dis-ease' is a manifestation of blocks in the natural life energy that underlie our physical reality.   Such blocks are often caused by unexpressed childhood trauma, unexpressed feelings of anger and grief, feelings of helplessness and powerlessness, feelings of lack of control over life circumstances and prolonged feelings of fear from repeated personal boundary violations.   Much of this can be intergenerational.   For example, a violent act perpetrated on a person (a child seeing his or her parent killed, raped, beaten, a removal from land and family) affects all future generations until the abuse is recognized, the pain is fully felt, the grief is expressed and the cycle is broken.

In her analysis of the origins of the behaviours of extremely violent and self-abusive people, Alice Miller's work submits that extremely violent behaviours come from the interrelated experiences of:

- being profoundly hurt and abused as a child;
- being hurt, but in addition being prevented from experiencing or expressing the pain of that hurt;
- having no other single human being in whom one can confide one's true feelings;
- having a lack of education or knowledge and thereby being unable to intellectualize the abuse; and
- having no children on whom one can repeat the cycle of abuse (Miller 1983: xi).

It was from these concepts we felt the need to develop a programme we now call We Al-Li.

A Process Called We Al-Li

Three years ago the authors sat in many long sessions over coffee discussing the best way to help facilitate a recreative whole healing approach to the pain of the Aboriginal and Islander experience.   At that time Coralie Ober was working within the Corrective Services Commission in Queensland, and Judy Atkinson was involved in national programmes on domestic violence.   We saw connections between our separate work fields and we were dissatisfied with both government responses and community reactions.   The more we looked, the more we saw a common factor linking those we were coming into contact with: pain and the emotions and behaviours coming from that pain.   Pain of loss, pain of anger, pain of feeling helpless and powerless, the pain of despair, and the fear of more pain.

We developed a concept for a programme which in retrospect we see as a reflection of our public service and organizational backgrounds.   The programme would be based on an hierarchal structure with a coordinator who would arrange training for workers who would then run community programmes. Fortunately, at that time we intuitively felt we needed to take more time to develop our concepts. Judy Atkinson travelled to Canada under a National Health and Medical Research grant to look at Native Canadian programmes on family violence and alcohol and drug abuse. Her experiences in Canada introduced her to the holistic philosophy for well-health. The greatest power for well-health is within ourselves. Only by understanding ourselves, being within, and looking at our own lives, can we respond responsibly to our own pain. By understanding the trauma of our own life experiences, we are better able to resonate with others in moving together towards well-health. Judy came back from Canada with a strong commitment to acknowledge and work with the causes and symptoms of pain and intergenerational dysfunction within her own family relationships. At the same time, she and Coralie began to review the training packages and programme outlines she brought back with her. Coralie developed a tertiary education (TAFE) course out of some of this material, a core unit they both believed should be fundamental to all learning and educational programmes: 'Health and Self'. This unit, based on the concept of health as a whole body/mind/emotion/spirit/environment interdependency, is now in its second year at the Kangaroo Point TAFE College in Brisbane, and is also the first (compulsory) unit in a Tropical Health Programme course at University of Queensland.

On 25 January 1993, Bob and Ros Muir and family set up a camp on Great Keppel Island. Bob's ancestors are Woppaburra people who were removed from the island by force in 1910. From his own place of pain, anger and need for action, Bob decided to raise the Aboriginal flag on 26 January (Australia Day) to remind the public of the dispossession and oppression suffered by the original Woppaburra people. Bob and Ros also had a vision, unclear and half-formed, but nonetheless, a vision. They wanted to create a place where people who were hurting could come to find sanctuary and reaffirm their Aboriginal spiritual and cultural identity. Judy Atkinson was also on the island at that time, and for most of the two days, she and the Muirs sat in the shade of the pandanus palms and talked of their respective visions.

Some weeks later, Bob suggested we get together to form a group which would work to achieve the visions that had been articulated that day on the beach at Keppel. The group was to be open to anybody who wanted to be involved. The first meeting took place on 14 April 1993. Coralie Ober travelled up to Rockhampton from Brisbane. The meeting comprised a mixed group of sixteen people, Aboriginal and non-Aboriginal. Over the next few months the group found a name, developed its direction by articulating aims and objectives, and worked through group interaction to the stage that members of the group had a clear vision of, and commitment to, what it was trying to do.

The chosen name was We Al-Li, Woppaburra for 'Fire and Water'—two cleansing, life-giving elements essential for life, which balance each other. They are used in conflict management and life renewal ceremonies in different parts of Australia. As someone commented, it also seems appropriate to fight the disaster of 'firewater' (alcohol), with the ceremonial, cleansing, life-giving elements of fire and water.

In the development of We Al-Li, as we became more aware of the multilayered blankets of oppression that are part of the colonial legacy, we were forced to ask ourselves many questions. Is there such a thing as implicit healing? What is it, how does it work and why? First in self-analysis and later, in our interactions with others, we came to understand that there are always significant moments which move us individually and sometimes collectively out of places of victimization and abuse into self-knowledge, empowerment and wholeness. We asked: Is it possible to provide people with experiences which will activate such significant events?

In forming the group, as we started to look at the many layers that were part of our own experiences of abuse and self-abuse, we questioned our expertise and asked, 'Can we be our own healers?'. In group interaction we began not so much to talk about a programme but to participate in an emerging process. We saw that the healing journey, beginning from places of pain and trauma—although very much an individual experience—becomes, by its essential nature, also a shared group experience. In fact, descriptions of the healing journey presented similarities to descriptions of the group healing which takes place during Aboriginal mortuary and conflict management ceremonies. We will attempt to link these concepts as we describe the experiences of the authors in the development of We Al-Li.

CEREMONIES OF HEALING

Expressing Grief, Conflict and Solidarity

The ceremonies that take place at the physical death of an individual recreate the significant events in the individual's unique journey through life. Such ceremonies involve all those who have (ritual) responsibility for the various parts of that journey and confirm individual involvement in the processes of the deceased's past life experiences, while reaffirming kin and group responsibility to the individual for a safe future journey. Howard Morphy, in *Journey to the Crocodile's Nest*, describes the group process that occurs in such ceremonies. The ceremony flows from the Ancestral Past, through the present, into the future, to link the future journeying of the spirit with the past places of its journey (Morphy 1984).

Janice Reid, in 'A Time to Live; A Time to Grieve', claims that such ceremonies are an 'affirmation of the relations and beliefs of the living' (Reid 1979: 342). The owners of the sacred stories, law, songs, dances and paintings contribute their knowledge and power to the body of the ceremony—and as they do so, they give recognition to the sacred aspects of the life experience and affirm human power over life and death.

These points are relevant to this chapter because in describing the conceptual development of We Al-Li, we intend to use physical death as symbolic of other forms of death—of the spirit self and in the 'fatal psychic trauma' which comes from experiencing different forms of power abuse, violence or oppression. The symptoms of trauma are described as 'a numbness of spirit, a susceptibility to anxiety, depression or rage, a sense of helplessness/powerlessness, a heightened apprehension about the physical and social environment, a preoccupation with death, a retreat into dependency and a general loss of ego functions' (Erikson 1976: 255). These are also the symptoms of those whose secure sense of self has been violated in race dominance (as in colonization), gender dominance (as in domestic violence or rape) and in age dominance (as in child abuse or elder abuse). The pain of these oppressions can also be articulated in self-inflicted injuries, suicides, and alcohol and drug abuse, which serve to dull the pain of the trauma.

We feel pain when we are abused or subjected to violence. Generally however, Western culture teaches us it is wrong to show the feelings that result from that pain. These feelings remain blocked in our body, causing illness and 'dis-ease' of body, mind and spirit. Ultimately the painful feelings explode in inappropriate ways, in behaviours that are destructive to self and to others. The pain of anger is often expressed through violence, for in a violent society, we learn to express ourselves with violence. Unexpressed pain, as in a death in a family, unconsenting acts of violence or disaster trauma, pose a threat to the harmony of the group as the emotions of grief of loss, sorrow, fear, anger, despair and helplessness are felt. Bell Hooks, in *Breaking Bread*, says, 'I am moved by the knowledge that we can take our pain, work with it, recycle it and transform it so that it becomes a source of power' (Hooks and West 1992: 8). This is what happens in Aboriginal rituals and ceremonies.

The ceremonies performed at physical death do two important things. They dispel both the collective and the individual feelings of pain of loss, of despair and helplessness. Song, dance, art and ceremony provide a testimony to the power participants hold over life and death, and reaffirm the existence of the Ancestral Past in their lives. In allowing people to work through their feelings of anger and sorrow, in utilizing the interconnecting web of relationships between groups and within kin networks, and in revitalizing the knowledge of responsibility, ceremonies unify the community. In the process, the sacred in both the individual and communal identity is reaffirmed.

In his work among the Mallanpara of the Tully River, Cardwell area in

North Queensland, Roth (1902) describes the structured, ceremonial process of Aboriginal conflict management where anger and discord were settled with activities in which all community members had specified roles. The Prun ground was a large, cleared circular space which was shifted every two or three months. Prun were held every seven to fourteen days. The hosts on whose land the Prun ground happened to be were always the first to arrive. A few days previous to the scheduled event, a messenger was sent to various camps reminding them of the date. As groups came to the Prun ground they camped on the edge of the circle, and came forward into the circle only when they were fully prepared. Those who were decorated—the Ulmba—then chose individuals who were to 'uphold the honour of their particular mob' (Roth 1902). They were accompanied by other men and women. The women carried the Chukaji spears. The group would advance in a half circle, come together and shout, and then move to the edge of the circle to sit and wait for the others. Other groups joined the circle until everybody was assembled.

There were well-recognized laws that no fighting was permitted outside the circle. The fighting which occurred within the circle, however, could not be called violence, because violence can only occur where there is force, and no consent by one to the actions of the other. Roth concludes:

> They go on fighting until dark when more friendly relations are resumed, the waru and other corroborees are performed, and all goes well until the next morning, when just as the sun rises, they have another final bout; and as soon as the fighting is over, they all disperse to their respective homes. Evidently the Prun both helps to settle old scores, and at the same time promotes social intercourse and amusement (Roth 1902).

Within these structured processes conflict was resolved, felt hurts were healed and people retired to their own country refreshed from both the social contact and the resolution of conflict through the release of feelings. This description of group process is similar to the process of an 'Anger, Boundaries and Safety' workshop one of the authors undertook at the 'Haven-by-the-Sea' Centre, Vancouver, Canada (Wong and McKeen 1992). In both cases there were set rules of behaviour, the feelings that contributed to anger were allowed to be expressed, and the underlying pain of hurt or psychic injury was released. Known boundaries provided safety and allowed full feeling of the pain. As the anger in the blocked body found expression, creative human energy was released in song, dance and art. If the soul cannot express and transform its pain, it dies.

The Warlpipi of Central Australia use fire in large communal ceremonies to resolve conflict and to emphasize group solidarity. The Mardudjara of the Western Desert hold large community water fights which are part of the rain-making ceremonies which preserve unity and give a sense of direction and group well-being (Tonkinson 1972).

We Al-Li Objectives

As a group, We Al-Li is still very new, but a nucleus of about 15-20 people are now working together to develop its philosophy and process. We Al-Li established the following set of objectives:

- that the group develop the organization of the project;
- that all members of the group be responsible for and concerned about their own self-care;
- that all members of the group make a commitment to mutual group support;
- that the group work form the basis of cultural maintenance and revival;
- that the group develop training packages and modules;
- that the group put together a resource inventory and network of people with skills we could use in the programme; and
- that the group conduct a needs assessment and document what we are doing as a research process.[1]

We Al-Li plans to coordinate a set of workshops which will eventually be compiled as training packages for community workers. Each workshop will flow from the previous one, beginning with each participant lifting the blankets of oppression that are unique to his or her own experiences of pain and abuse. Participants will be supported in the expression of feelings coming from their pain, while developing a conceptual understanding of the layered context of oppression; to participate in Prun, where safe and boundaried expression of feelings can take place for resolution of conflict and the sharing of stories; in processing the grieving through expressive action and recreation. Workshop themes will come from participant needs, in the processing of the first workshop, and will, for example, provide opportunity for education on issues such as child abuse, rape, domestic violence, suicide, self-inflicted injury, and alcohol and drug abuse. Participants will have opportunities to participate in a process Dudgeon and Mitchell (1991) promote.

Cultural maintenance and revival. We will hold our workshops in places which are culturally and spiritually significant to the past as well as the present. Such places would then become reestablished as significant places for the future.

The regaining of personal and group power. Group process allows us to see and feel that we are not alone. We gain strength from each other for healing when we tell our own stories and listen to those of others in the group. Such a strategy has worked effectively for victims of sexual assault and domestic violence, and seems very similar to the descriptions of dispute management and conflict resolution described by Nancy Williams in her analysis of Aboriginal processes for social organization, social control and group harmony (Williams 1987).

Lifestyle counselling. Such counselling is not a system of blame, but rather places power and responsibility for the process with the individual and group. For example, participants state, 'I am the one who is involved in this process' rather than 'I am [or someone else is] to blame for my pain and they must make me better'. Lifestyle counselling involves having individuals explore the contextual patterns in which they live by looking at their behaviour in relationship to self, family, community and society generally. General counselling skills are seen as important for all workers in Aboriginal service delivery.

Social action and social organization. Individuals commit themselves to continue to be involved in other community-based change processes. These processes have been found to be very powerful in enabling people to look at and work towards changing their own social circumstances. People become their own healers. They become empowered to work towards social change and social justice, beginning at the beginning, from within themselves.

These programmes and workshops will build upon a fundamental base of Aboriginal culture and spirituality, but will also draw upon on Western and Eastern practices and principles for service delivery. They will convey the sociological and structural understanding of institutions and infrastructures within society which reinforce violent and oppressive behaviours and racist and sexist attitudes. They will be based upon the premise that we all in some way contribute to the abusiveness of our situations, that behaviour learnt from childhood experiences within the family and society can be unlearnt. Change, or transformation, begins with the self.

The Group Process

As individual participants, we all came to We Al-Li with a range of backgrounds, pain of experience, and expectations, which continue to determine our basic behaviours within the group. This created tension and influenced interactions. For example, one man quickly stated his priority was to have the group become supportive of his pet project, political action against the family court. He expressed anger at the way the court had treated him. He felt himself a victim of the abusive power of the state. He did not recognize that he had issues that he needed to attend to within himself. We affirmed with him that our energies would be concentrated on ourselves and the programme, that he was welcome to stay in the group so long as he understood that we must be clearly focussed on this goal. A woman came to the original meeting expecting that the group would quickly develop strategies and programmes to help young people who were petrol sniffing. She was frustrated when she realized we were not into 'quick fix' solutions. A few of the people who attended the original meeting dropped out, and others, on hearing what we were doing, asked to be included. Most of us became impatient during the year due to our original expectations that the group would move quickly into running programmes. Many of us found that interaction in the group triggered the issues that brought us into the group in the first place.

Over the months we became skilled in supporting—talking and sharing with each other. In fact, because the healing journey forced us to deal with the issues relevant to our individual lives and our relationships, these issues became accentuated. We began to function like a 'therapeutic community' in our mutual support for each other. We were educating ourselves, listening to other points of view, and yet learning not to speed up the process by imposing our will on others, learning to respect people's right to find their own answers to their needs. We found ourselves redefining our issues; sometimes we did not know what our issues were until they emerged in the group interaction.

Some of the issues we have supported each other through are: relationship tensions, redefining the masculine and feminine, adult children of sexual abuse, abusive behaviours and power dynamics, drug detoxification and rehabilitation, suicide intervention, family breakdown stress, work-related stress, unemployment-related stress and illness-related stress. Over the months, the interaction between each individual and others in the group became one of mutual support and self-supporting growth. We began to find skills and strengths we did not know we had. We found we could work together but that we must be honest with ourselves and each other. We learnt not to judge and to be patient. We came to believe that, yes, we can be our own healers, but it is also okay to look outside the group and use other resources to meet our particular needs. In fact, we started to see a rich range of resources available in the community. Although we did not advertise what we were doing, we found increasing interest and pressure from outside the group to expand our network.

While working together to develop a full concept of what we wanted to do, we made a submission to government for funding to employ full-time staff to develop the programme. This also came from group process, as we individually contributed particular skills to the development of the submission. Those with the least skills in this area learnt the most. When we finally heard we might receive a government grant, however, we were shocked to find that the interactions of the group had essentially done away with the need for a formal hierarchal structure and for someone to coordinate the programme. We had developed the full conceptual structure of the programme through group process, ourselves.

By February 1994 We Al-Li was ready to run two courses: 'Lifting the Blankets of Oppression', an eight-workshop course, and 'Health and Self', also with eight components. By the end of 1994 we hoped to have two full training packages, fifteen trained volunteers, and an evaluated programme which should be flexible enough to presented in any cultural setting.

What Significant Events Started Us on Our Journey?

Working together, we began to more clearly see the significant events that moved us into and along the path of healing. Understanding the process of change or transformation, being able to see the significant steps that take us out of the circles of pain and abuse to healing and wholeness, enables us to empower each other in the change process. No one is totally powerless. Some of us have more power than others, however. In colonized societies, the colonizers have power over the colonized. In patriarchal societies, men hold power over women. In most societies, adults have power over children. Generally, therefore, children are the most powerless within a society and a family.

Alkali Lake is a Shuswap community of approximately 450 people located near Williams Lake in the interior of British Columbia. Over the last twenty years the adult population of this community (and many youth and children) have moved from being 100% alcoholic to 95% sober (Alkali Lake 1986). The lesson of Alkali Lake, as depicted in their video *The Honour of All*, is most important because it emphasizes that even a child has great power for change.

Ivy Chelsea was seven years old when she said to her mother, 'I'm not coming home with you because I don't like your drinking'. Her mother listened. Not just to the words, but to the pain implicit in the words of that small child. *The power of this child was that she felt her feelings and put them into words. She spoke her truth. The next significant step was that somebody listened.* Phylis Chelsea walked to the sink and poured her drink down the sinkhole. Three weeks later, Andy Chelsea, the father of Ivy and husband of Phylis, also stopped drinking. Over the next twenty years they worked to help make their community become sober. The words Ivy Chelsea uttered were significant for many people. Andy and Phylis Chelsea have since taken their story of individual and community healing to many reserves and communities in Canada, the United States, England and Australia.

Another significant event in the healing process of the people at Alkali Lake occurred during a healing circle. A teenage girl turned to one of the community leaders and elders and said, 'You demand I show you respect.

How can I when I know you have sexually abused me'. At Alkali Lake the healing circle has now become a safe place, where people can talk from their place of truth and be supported in the process of doing so.

We have used these stories to illustrate some important points. In the case of Ivy, she was heard and her pain was seen to be real. Her parents moved to change the situation that was the cause of her pain. Sometimes, however, we have to make safe places for people so they can speak to and own their truth. In the case of the alleged sexual abuse, in the safety of the healing circle, the young woman was heard. She was believed. *The community then moved to deal with the truth of what had been disclosed. We need to be prepared to listen, as in Dadirri (deep listening to one another), for unless we listen, we do not know how to act.*

Healing stories are never single-issue stories (e.g., alcohol abuse). They can never be stories complete in themselves. The very nature of the process, the journey, whether it be in the family, in a community, or within society generally, moves us to touch others as we stand in our own place of truth. Those others must then also look to themselves. The story of Alkali Lake winds its way across Canada, and the United States and has even touched us here in Australia. In the process of revealing alcohol abuse, it has also untangled the complex problems of sexual abuse and brutality towards young Indian children in residential schools.

The main issue is that people can move to meet needs when they have a framework for dealing with the 'problem'. In Canada this framework became adopted procedure by the community and other significant organizations, to be followed in the case of sexual abuse disclosure. A paper prepared jointly by the Nechi Institute, the Four Worlds Development Project, the Native Training Institute, and 'New Directions' Training of Alkali Lake was released in 1988. *Healing Is Possible*: *A Joint Statement on the Healing of Sexual Abuse in Native Communities* provides a sound alternate to the Western criminal justice system. These procedures are summarized as follows:

• The victim was to be adequately cared for, helped to process the hurt feelings, helped to realize that what had happened was not his or her fault, given adequate counselling from a trained sexual abuse counsellor, assured safety from future abuse, and was not pressured by the offender or other family members to deny what had happened.

• The focus of community attention would shift to the offender.

• The offender was given the clear choice of being confronted by the victim and the victim's family in a special meeting, guided by a trained sexual abuse counsellor, to admit the full extent of what he or she had done, to take full responsibility for his or her actions, to apologize to the victim (where appropriate as determined by the sexual abuse committee) and to promise never to do it again. Offenders were to listen to the expressions of rage, hurt, anger and contempt that the victim and family members might need to release and agree to follow whatever course of treatment and reparation was decided upon by the sexual abuse committee in consultation with a trained sexual abuse counsellor. Alternatively, the offender could make the choice to be prosecuted by the full extent of the law, with charges pressed not by the victim but by the family and community, who would then assume responsibility to work to restore balance in the situation.

• The offender's spouse or partner would receive personal support through the process (be assigned a counsellor or ally).

• The offender would receive personal support through the process (be assigned a counsellor or ally) (Nechi Institute et al. 1988: 6-7).

This outline has been included to show an indigenous process of conflict resolution, which deals with the issue of abuse in a healing way while allowing family and community to articulate acceptable behaviours. It gives power to the community instead of giving away power to the criminal justice system. It also links the significant event of a young child standing in her truth with a general outcome for healing which has spread itself across communities and countries.

One of the authors traces her significant events, in an interconnecting path, from the first time she acknowledged the pain of her own rape as a child to her present work. In a university tutorial, where an Aboriginal male companion was expressing the Aboriginal male experience as being the only valid colonial pain, she suddenly understood that there was a difference in experience when she asked him, 'Have you ever been raped?'. Ten years later, while working at a community level, she asked a state minister to have his department respond to the needs of Aboriginal children who were being sexually abused, and she felt anger when he replied, 'Oh, don't talk about things like that. People will think self-management isn't working'.

At a Canadian workshop she came to understand that much of her work was driven by her own pain, and she made a decision to use it constructively rather than repressing it. On the beach at Great Keppel Island, she decided to pursue a 'dream'. In a workshop in 1993, she reconnected with 'a deep sense of being, of wholeness, of having roots deep in the ground, of being an Aboriginal woman with links to other old women back through the centuries to the creation times' (J. A. personal journal August 1993). She had the experience of being in connection with other Aboriginal woman and men who have also linked into the 'collective consciousness' of grief and pain of sisters and brothers who have suffered in massacres. Through the layers of abuse, generations of people have lost the essence of their spiritual connections—with the self, with others and with the living land. She now feels a responsibility to act in her stewardship to create safe places for our children of the future. As one of those woman writes: 'We need to acknowledge them [the ancestors] and their need also for healing the deep pain of their experience. I believe our land still feels this pain. It is a collective pain, of the people and of the land' (personal communication, September 1993).

We need to come together, sit with each other in Dadirri, tell our stories and in dance, song, art and ceremony move into the future. We Al-Li is an Aboriginal group process working towards healing. There is no 'implicit' healing, just a series of experiences or processes which connect us, across the boundaries of race, gender, age and class, to others on our various journeys through life. The common connections are with all those who have felt pain and seek a healing. It is how we use our diverse experiences which determines where this journey will take us, individually and collectively.[2]

NOTES

1. By this time Judy Atkinson had begun her Ph.D. with Dr Kayleen Hazlehurst in the Faculty of Arts at Queensland University of Technology. The development and evaluation of the outcomes of We Al-Li will form the major part of her doctoral research. In 1994, Coralie Ober began to work with the group on a Master's programme in the same department and is studying Aboriginal group process through her work with We Al-Li and her other programme development and teaching work at TAFE.

2. The conceptual development of this chapter was made possible by grants from the Public Health Research Grants Committee and the Queensland University of Technology.

REFERENCES

Alkali Lake (1986-1989) (videos) *The Honour of All*, Part 1 and Part 2, *Sharing Innovations that Work, Healing the Hurts*, Alkali Lake, BC: Alkali Lake Reserve.

Atkinson, J. (1990) *Beyond Violence: Finding the Dream,* National Domestic Violence Education Programme, Canberra: Office of the Status of Women.

Atkinson, J. (1993) *The Political and the Personal: Racial Violence against Aboriginal and Torres Strait Islander Women and Women of Non-English Speaking Background,* National Committee on Violence against Women, Canberra: Office of the Status of Women.

Brownmiller, S. (1975) *Against Our Will: Men, Women and Rape*, New York: Bantam.

Dudgeon, P. and Mitchell, R. (1991) *Internalised Racism and Drug Abuse: The Consequences of Racial Oppression in Australia,* Perth: Centre for

Aboriginal Studies, Curtin University.

Erikson, K. (1976) *Everything in Its Path*, New York: Simon and Schuster.

Hooks, B. and West, C. (1992) *Breaking Bread*, Boston: South End.

Langton, M. and Ah Matt, Leslie et al. (1991) 'Too Much Sorry Business', in *Royal Commission into Aboriginal Deaths in Custody, National Report*, Vol. 5, Canberra: Australian Government Printing Services, 275-512.

Miller, A. (1983) *For Your Own Good: Hidden Cruelty in Child-rearing and the Roots of Violence*, New York: NoonDay.

Morphy, H. (1984) *Journey to the Crocodile's Nest*, Canberra: Australian Institute of Aboriginal Studies.

National Aboriginal Health Strategy Working Party (1989) *A National Aboriginal Health Strategy*, Canberra: Department of Aboriginal Affairs.

Nechi Institute, Four Worlds Development Project, Native Training Institute, and 'New Directions' Training—Alkali Lake (1988) *Healing Is Possible: A Joint Statement on the Healing of Sexual Abuse in Native Communities*, Edmonton: Nechi Institute on Alcohol and Drug Education and Research Centre.

Nordstrum, C. (1993) 'Creativity and Chaos: War on the Frontlines', in C. Nordstrum and A. Robbin (eds.) *Cultures in Crisis: Fieldwork under Fire*, California: University of California Press.

Reid, J. (1979) 'A Time to Live; a Time to Grieve: Patterns and Processes of Mourning among the Yolnger in Australia', *Culture, Medicine and Psychiatry*, 3: 319-46.

Roth, W. E. (1902) North Queensland Ethnography: Bulletin No 4, Games, Sports and Amusements. Republished in: W. E. Roth *The Queensland Aborigines*, Vol. II, editor K. F. MacIntyre, Facsimile edition, Carlisle, W. A.: Hesperian Press.

Royal Commission into Aboriginal Deaths in Custody (1990a) *Research Paper No 8*, RCIADC, Canberra: Australian Government Publishing Services.

Royal Commission into Aboriginal Deaths in Custody (1990b) *Research Paper No 11*, RCIADC, Canberra: Australian Government Publishing Services.

Royal Commission into Aboriginal Deaths in Custody (1991) *National Reports 1-5*, Canberra: Australian Government Printing Services.

Tonkinson, R. (1972) 'Nagawajil: A Western Desert Aboriginal Rainmaking Ritual', Ph.D Thesis in Anthropology, Vancouver: University of British Columbia.

Williams, N. (1987) *Two Laws: Managing Disputes in a Contemporary Aboriginal Community,* Canberra: Australian Institute of Aboriginal Studies.

Wong, B. and McKeen, J. (1992) *A Manual for Life*, Gabriola Island, British Columbia: PD Seminars.

INDEX

About the Editor and Contributors

KAYLEEN M. HAZLEHURST is a Senior Lecturer in Cross-Cultural Studies at the Queensland University of Technology and was previously a Senior Criminologist at the Australian Institute of Criminology. Since 1972 she has worked as a researcher and consultant in Australia, Canada, and New Zealand. Her most recent books are *Political Expression and Ethnicity: Statecraft and Mobilisation in the Maori World* (Praeger, 1993) and *A Healing Place: Indigenous Visions for Personal Empowerment and Community Recovery* (1994).

AMANDA NIELSEN ADKINS, following six years of employment with the Native Counselling Services of Alberta, moved into independent research consulting. She is a freelance writer and is responsible for the development of the Research Department and Library at NCSA. Her works encompass various studies, submissions, and evaluations on Alberta's aboriginal people. Her latest publication is *Vision for Our Future: A Crime Prevention Guide for Native Communities* (1991).

A. H. ANGELO is a Professor and Dean of Law at the Victoria University of Wellington, New Zealand and Legal Advisor to the Elders of Tokerlau. His special academic interests are in contributing to South Pacific Legal systems, comparative law, conflict of laws, Pacific legal studies, and legislative drafting. He is also editor of the current texts of the laws of Mauritius, Tokelau, Niue, and Cook Islands.

JUDY ATKINSON has worked as a researcher and consultant with various organizations, such as the Aboriginal Co-ordinating Council, the Department of Aboriginal Affairs, and the Office of the Status of Women. She is a founding member of We Al-Li, which explores programmes for Aboriginal community recovery and personal healing. She is presently pursuing doctoral studies with the Faculty of Arts, Queensland University of Technology, Brisbane.

CHARLENE BELLEAU is the Family Violence Co-ordinator for the Canim Lake Indian Band, British Columbia. She has worked actively in the field of community healing and has previously held the position of Chief of the Alkali Lake Indian Band.

CURT TAYLOR GRIFFITHS is a Professor in the School of Criminology, Simon Fraser University, and is the principal investigator for the Crime, Law and Justice Among Inuit in the Baffin Region, N.W.T. study. He is currently the Director of the Northern Justice Society Resource Centre, Simon Fraser University.

MAGGIE HODGSON is the Executive Director of Nechi Institute on Alcohol and Drug Education. She has had twenty years of experience in the addictions field. Her other areas of expertise include suicide prevention, sexual abuse, family violence, communications, mental health, and community development. Hodgson co-authored a book with Brenda Daily on child sexual abuse entitled *The Spirit Weeps* (1988). She is Chairperson of the Special Section on Indigenous Peoples for the International Council on Alcohol and Drug Abuse Programmes from Lausanne, Switzerland.

MARCIA L. HOYLE is a Ph.D. candidate in Anthropology at McMaster University, Hamilton, Canada. In an Ojibway reserve community in the province of Ontario, she is presently conducting a year-long participatory research project that aims to document historical and contemporary socio-legal process and dispute resolution. Her primary interests are the relationship between indigenous peoples and the nation-state, and extrajudicial conflict resolution and legal processes.

JOHN H. HYLTON is Executive Director of the Canadian Mental Health Association in Saskatchewan, Canada. Prior to joining CMHA he held senior positions with the Saskatchewan government and taught at the University of Regina. He has published extensively on public policy issues and aboriginal people in Canada, and has been an adviser to a number of federal and provincial commissions of inquiry.

GABRIELLE M. MAXWELL is a psychologist. She is Senior Researcher, Office of the Commissioner for Children, Wellington, New Zealand and Honorary Fellow, Institute of Criminology, Victoria University of Wellington, Wellington, New Zealand. She was one of the principal researchers on the youth justice study, conducted by the Institute between 1990-1992 and since published as *Families, Victims and Culture: Youth Justice in New Zealand* (1993). Her current research interests are care and protection and family violence with particular emphasis on violence against children.

ALLISON MORRIS is a criminologist. She is currently Director and Reader in Criminology at the Institute of Criminology, Victoria University of Wellington, Wellington, New Zealand. She was one of the principal researchers on the youth justice study carried out by the Institute between 1990-1992 and since published as *Families, Victims and Culture: Youth Justice in New Zealand* (1993). Her current research interests are women's imprisonment, cultural justice and family violence.

CORALIE OBER has, over the past twenty years, been employed by the Queensland government in the areas of health, corrections, education, guidance and counselling, and social services. She teaches several certificate, associate diploma, and degree courses for Aboriginal and Islander students at Kangaroo Point TAFE. Her present interests are in examining indigenous group process for the treatment of trauma and personal crisis, and in developing related educational and workshop packages. Coralie is a founding member of We Al-Li.

MARG O'DONNELL is the founding Director of the Alternative Dispute Resolution Division in the Queensland Department of Justice and Attorney-General and the Arts. Prior to joining the department she was Director of the Women's Information Service of Queensland, an outposting of the Office of the Status of Women, Department of Prime Minister and Cabinet. She was also a senior conciliator for three years with the office of the Human Rights Commission when it opened in Brisbane in 1985. Her major areas of interest include social justice issues for indigenous people, sex and race discrimination, alternatives to the criminal and civil justice systems and environmental issues.

TERESEA OLSEN, Ngati Porou is a *marae* worker, currently running a Maori Women's Health Centre. She also coordinates and is a trainer for a Maori Women's Refuge and is a counsellor for the Family Court and New Zealand Children and Young Persons Service. She was a researcher on the youth justice study carried out by the Institute of Criminology, Victoria University of Wellington, Wellington, New Zealand between 1990-1992 and since published as *Families, Victims and Culture: Youth Justice in New Zealand* (1993).

ELSIE B. REDBIRD is an instructor in the Women's Studies Department and Native American Studies Programme of the University of New Mexico and manages a consulting firm, Native Rights Advocates in Albuquerque, New Mexico. She is concerned about the recording and recognition of Indian women's knowledge as a unique epistemological and life experience.

ROBERT YAZZIE was appointed as the Chief Justice of the Navajo Nation on January 20, 1992. His appointment followed seven years as the presiding judge of the District Court, Window Rock, Navajo Nation (Arizona). His legal experience includes work as an advocate with D.N.A. - People's Legal Services, Inc. from 1974 through 1979. He compiled the first glossary of legal terms in an Indian language with his wife, Esther Dennison Yazzie, published by the United States District Court for the District of New Mexico. His goals for the Courts of the Navajo Nation include continued development of Navajo common law as the law of preference of the Navajo Nation, greater use of the Navajo Peacemaker Court, professional education programmes for judges and practitioners, and making justice more accessible to the consumers of law.

JAMES W. ZION B.A. University of Saint Thomas, 1966. J.D., Columbus School of Law, Catholic University of America, 1969. Mr Zion is the solicitor to the Courts of the Navajo Nation. He has published extensively on traditional Indian law, Navajo common law and the human rights of native peoples under international law. His planning work with the Courts of the Navajo Nation focuses upon the integration of traditional justice in modern Native justice systems to avoid imposed authoritarian models.

ISBN 0-275-95131-6

90000>

EAN

9 780275 951313

HARDCOVER BAR CODE

D0214643